The Law of Global Custody

The Law of Global Custody

Joanna Benjamin

Director, Financial Services Research, Clifford Chance,
Senior Research Fellow, Kings College, London

Butterworths
London, Charlottesville, Dublin, Durban, Edinburgh,
Kuala Lumpur, Singapore, Sydney, Toronto, Wellington
1996

United Kingdom	Butterworths, a Division of Reed Elsevier (UK) Ltd, Halsbury House, 35 Chancery Lane, LONDON WC2A 1EL and 4 Hill Street, EDINBURGH EH2 3JZ
Australia	Butterworths, SYDNEY, MELBOURNE, BRISBANE, ADELAIDE, PERTH, CANBERRA and HOBART
Canada	Butterworths Canada Ltd, TORONTO and VANCOUVER
Ireland	Butterworth (Ireland) Ltd, DUBLIN
Malaysia	Malayan Law Journal Sdn Bhd, KUALA LUMPUR
New Zealand	Butterworths of New Zealand Ltd, WELLINGTON and AUCKLAND
Singapore	Reed Elsevier (Singapore) Pte Ltd, SINGAPORE
South Africa	Butterworths Publishers (Pty) Ltd, DURBAN
USA	Michie, CHARLOTTESVILLE, Virginia

Any Crown copyright material is reproduced with the permission of the Controller of Her Majesty's Stationery Office.

A CIP Catalogue record for this book is available from the British Library.

ISBN 0 406 04836 3

Typeset by Kerrypress Ltd, Luton
Printed and bound in Great Britain by Antony Rowe Ltd, Chippenham, Wilts

To Nina Farhi

With recognition and love,

Joanna.

Preface

I wrote this book because my practice in advising London-based global custodians convinced me that an adequate legal account of global custody was missing.

Global custody is a service whereby a single custodian holds its client's international portfolio through a network of local sub-custodians, clearing systems and depositaries. Modern custodial practice is electronic and cross-border. The lack of a tangible and allocated subject matter cuts across the traditional characterisation of custody as bailment. Ambiguities as to the location of custody assets raise novel questions of conflict of laws.

The basic legal principles that underlie proprietary and other rights in custody assets under English law are considered.

It is argued that computerised debt securities are not negotiable instruments, but that the benefits of negotiability are available by other means, in particular the rules of equity and of private international law. It is argued that the impact of computerisation of registered securities is more limited, due to the historically intangible and unallocated nature of company shares.

Traditionally, the custodian is a bailee in respect of securities, and a bank debtor in respect of cash. It is argued that because computerised custody securities are intangible and fungible, the custodian is not a bailee but a trustee.

Where the securities of different clients are commingled, the difficulty in showing certainty of subject matter for a valid trust is discussed. It is suggested that commingled clients should be treated as equitable tenants in common.

Principles of private international law are discussed in relation to: global custody generally, negotiability, taking security and custodian insolvency.

The fiduciary duties of the custodian are considered in the light of recent case law.

Legal and regulatory aspects of depositary receipts are discussed.

Following a chapter on the general principles of legal risk in settlement, separate chapters consider the CGO, the CMO and CREST.

It is concluded that the uncertainties raised by the electronic and cross-border nature of global custody may largely be addressed by greater use of the principles of the law of trusts, and careful drafting in customer documentation.

Regulation and withholding tax will be dealt with in a separate supplement to be published in 1997.

Joanna Benjamin
September 1996

Acknowledgments

I am indebted to many people for their help in preparing this book. In particular, I wish to thank the following: David Hayton of King's College, London, Roy Goode of St John's College, Oxford and Ross Cranston of the London School of Economics for their comments. (Unfortunately, the publisher's timetable did not permit all their helpful comments to be incorporated at this stage and some will have to be reflected in later editions.) Tim Herrington of Clifford Chance, Mark Harding of UBS Limited (formerly of Clifford Chance) together with the other Clifford Chance partners for their support in enabling me to combine research and practice; Madeleine Timms of Clifford Chance for ably keeping all the plates in the air while I have been in the law library; Verity Pride of Clifford Chance for reviewing the taxation aspects of the book; Dermot Turing of Clifford Chance for reviewing the section on cross-border insolvency; Paul Giordano of Clifford Chance for reviewing the chapter on depositary receipts; Ian Jackson of Clifford Chance for guidance on the intricacies of the eurobond markets; Mark Kirby of CRESTCo for reviewing the chapter on CREST; my custody clients and, in particular, Jan Mentha of the Chase Manhattan Bank, N.A. for practical guidance; Barbara Macmillan of Clifford Chance for word processing this book and for keeping calm; my sister Lesley and other family members for moral support; and above all my partner, Robert Reiner, for help which is impossible to specify.

The views expressed in this book are my own as, of course, are any errors.

Contents

Table of statutes

References in this Table of *Statutes* are to Halsbury's Statutes of England (Fourth Edition) showing the volume and page at which the annotated text of the Act will be found.

Table of cases

Y

Chapter 1

Introduction

'Knowledge of these things would be much easier learnt in the City than in the courts.'[1]

1 The global network[2]

Global custody is a service whereby a single custodian assumes responsibility for the safekeeping of its client's portfolio of international securities and cash. In respect of overseas assets, it may perform its obligations either directly through overseas branches, or through sub-custodians.[3] The global custodian, its overseas branches and sub-custodians may in turn use nominees, clearing and settlement systems and common depositaries. The client's contractual relationship and dealings are only with the custodian, who keeps the global network behind the scenes.

2 The service

The traditional custody product comprises the core services of safekeeping and settlement.[4] Customarily associated with this core product are basic

---

[1] Blackstone, quoted in Fifoot, *The Development of the Law of Negotiable Instruments and the Law of Trusts*, Journal of the Institute of Bankers, lix, 433–456.

[2] 'A global custodian provides its customers with access to settlement and custody services in multiple markets through a single gateway by integrating services performed by a network of sub-custodians, including the global custodian's own local branches and other local agents. The primary advantage to institutional investors of using a global custodian rather than a network of local custodians appears to be lower costs made possible by the global custodian's realisation of economies of scale and scope. The provision of custody and settlement services requires significant investments in information technology, communications systems and local agent networks. A global custodian, through economies of scale and scope, is able to spread its fixed costs over more transactions and to offer a variety of reporting, information, accounting and credit services to the investor at lower cost than if these services were purchased separately from a variety of service providers and local agents. By using a global custodian, an investor also avoids the burdens imposed by the need to maintain multiple communications links, conform to multiple formats for inputting settlement instructions, and receive and interpret reports from local agents in each local market in which it trades.' Bank for International Settlements, *Cross-Border Securities Settlements*, March 1995, p 15.

[3] 'Sub-custodians play a large role in cross-border settlements. Participation in domestic settlement systems is typically restricted to local entities. In other cases, the custodian may be unwilling to take on the risks or obligations of direct participation.' Bank for International Settlements, *Cross-Border Securities Settlements*, March 1995, p 15.

[4] Ie the receipt and delivery of securities and cash to settle client trades.

portfolio administration[1] together with foreign exchange services.[2] These core and associated functions are supplemented by value-added services, whereby the custodian cross-sells front office financial products to its clients.[3] However, 1996 saw a dearth of new value-added services.

3 The participants

Global custody was first developed in the United States, in response to the regulatory needs of pension funds, including the obligation to have independent custodians. The service was developed in London in the 1980s, and today many of the leading global custodians operating in London are the UK branches of US banks. Custodians have traditionally been banks. Certainly, non-bank entities play a role. For example some fund managers and brokers provide custody 'in-house' for their clients, and clearing systems with international depository networks are upgrading their services to approach the role of the global custodian. Global custody requires an enormous investment in electronic and other systems. It is in some respects a distressed industry, with the over-provision of custody services pushing fees downward,[4] while the measure of systemic risk associated with cross-border safekeeping and settlement is a source of increasing concern. Recent years have seen some significant withdrawals from the industry, while a number of mergers and business transfers has further reduced the number of global custodians.[5]

The major clients of global custody have always been private pension funds. For demographic reasons, private pension funds will continue to grow in the decades ahead. With an increasing trend towards cross-border investment,[6] driven by many factors including EC harmonisation (together with continuing settlement inefficiencies in local markets) the need for global custody will remain. This is emphasised by the huge increase in recent decades towards investment in the emerging markets. Non-pension managed funds also constitute a growth industry requiring custodial services.[7] In addition, clients of the global custodian include other entities having large international securities portfolios, such as insurance companies, building societies, banks and corporate treasury operations.

---

[1] Ie income and dividend collection and withholding tax reclamation, proxy voting, handling corporate actions and trade portfolio reporting.

[2] Eg converting sale proceeds from one currency into another in order to finance a purchase.

[3] These include cash management, cash lending, stocklending, repos (repurchase agreements) and derivatives. With the master trust product, custodians offer enhanced administrative services such as consolidated and multi-currency reporting, valuation and portfolio analysis including performance measurement. A large majority of custodians offer 'contractual income', ie crediting the client with dividend and/or proceeds of sale on the date they should have been paid to the custodian, whether or not they are paid on time. Some custodians offer index tracking and even investment recommendations.

The profits derived by custodians from fees and other income from value-added services are so great that certain custodians provide the core functions for free; it has even been predicted that (in view of this profitability and in response to commercial pressures from fund managers) custodians will pay their clients to place their assets with them.

[4] Clients often require 'unbundled' pricing.

[5] There were fewer providers in 1996 than in 1995, and the trend is likely to continue.

[6] Particularly among US and German pension funds.

[7] 'Last year, the European Federation for Retirement Provision predicted a near-doubling in the percentage of the population aged 65 and over in each OECD country by 2040' Dr Anthony Kirby, *One Nation No More*, ICB Magazine, Jan/Feb 1996, p 15.

4 Uncertainty

At the date of writing, there is a lack of consensus as to the correct legal analysis of global custody under English law. The principal reason for this is that English law has failed to keep pace with modern global custodial practice. Many of the relevant cases date from an era when banker's custody meant promissory notes in strong boxes. The ideas judicially developed in those cases (relating to the ownership and safekeeping of securities) rested on the assumption that documentation, and therefore physical possession, were involved. With trends towards dematerialisation in the securities markets, securities are increasingly intangible in the hands of the global custodian.[1] In the absence of legislative clarification, therefore, the position has become uncertain. The traditional characterisations of bearer debt securities as negotiable,[2] and of the custodian as a bailee,[3] are no longer appropriate where there is no paper. If the legal status of the portfolio and of the custodian is unclear, the rights and liabilities of the custodian and its client cannot be established with certainty. Risk analysis and risk management are frustrated.

Another source of legal uncertainty is the international aspect of global custody. This raises complex issues of private international law, on which there is a dearth of directly relevant case law.[4] The following analysis of global custody under English domestic and private international law is an attempt to reduce this uncertainty.[5]

5 Analytic context

This work was written in the context of a body of analysis relating directly and indirectly to custody. The SIB custody review has now been completed. International settlement risk has been addressed in a number of reports[6] while the role of the clearing systems has been analysed in recent articles.[7]

6 Scope

It is assumed throughout that the global custodian operates in London and that English law governs the global custody contract.

General legal principles relating to global custody under English domestic

---

[1] See chapter 3 for a full discussion of the computerisation of securities.
[2] See chapter 3, section B, below.
[3] See chapter 4.
[4] See chapters 6 and 7.
[5] The context of this is a wider uncertainty affecting many aspects of financial practice. Colin Bamford of the Financial Law Panel comments, 'At the end of the 1980s, and into the beginning of the 1990s, there was a growing feeling in the financial markets that the pace of development of concepts and products was much greater than that of development in the legal system.' Editorial, (1995) 9 JBFL.
[6] These include: Group of Thirty, *Clearance and Settlement Systems in the World's Securities Markets*, (1989); Group of Ten, *Delivery v Payment in Securities Systems*, (1992); and Morgan Guaranty, *Cross-Border Clearance, Settlement and Custody: Beyond the G30 Recommendations*, (1993).
[7] CW Mooney, *Beyond Negotiability*, (1990); Randall Guynn, IBA, *Modernising Securities Ownership Transfer and Pledging Laws*, (1996); and RM Goode, *The Nature and Transfer of Rights in Dematerialised and Immobilised Securities*, (1996) 11 JIBFL 162–167.

law are considered in chapters 2 to 5. Chapters 6 and 7 discuss cross-border issues under English private international law.

At a more practical level, the custodian's duties and liabilities are considered in chapter 8. Chapter 9 is devoted to depositors' receipts, including relevant US securities regulation. Risk in cross-border settlement is discussed in chapter 10; the chief English settlement systems (the CGO, the CMO and CREST) are reviewed in chapters 11, 12 and 13 respectively.

At the time of writing, the Treasury proposals for the direct regulation of custody under the Financial Services Act 1986 have been published, together with the SIB standards for custody. However, the true shape of the proposed regulatory regime will not be clear until the SFA and IMRO publish their detailed rules on the subject. Because the regulation of custody is in a state of important transition, the publication of a chapter on regulation has been deferred. It is proposed to be issued as a supplement to this book.

In order to keep to a manageable size, tax and derivatives are dealt with only incidentally. Each topic deserves a book in itself. At the time of writing, the withholding tax regime in relation to custody procedures has not been finalised. A brief discussion of withholding tax will appear in the regulatory supplement.

Chapter 2

English domestic law principles

In this chapter the legal principles will be discussed that have historically determined proprietary and other rights in custody assets under English domestic law. The following chapters will consider the impact on these traditional principles of the computerisation of securities.

1 Assets, possession and property

Firstly it is necessary to distinguish between assets, possession and property.

(a) The terms

A person's assets are those of its resources which are legally available for the payment of its debts (for example its money but not its body). Possession is the control of an asset. When physical control is combined with awareness of the situation by the controller, possession arises. The author possesses the pen with which she writes this. Property is ownership of an asset. It is a bundle of rights, including the right to possession. The pen in the author's possession is the property of her employers. She has it, but it is not hers.

We speak loosely of a person's possessions and property as if they were assets. More accurately, the words 'possession' and 'property' refer to legal relationships between persons and things, or persons in respect of assets. If an asset is a thing (such as the pen) and possession is a relationship between a person and a thing (such as the author's control of the pen), property is a legal relationship between persons in respect of things (the right of the employer to say to the author, 'Give it back'). However, it is often in practice convenient to think of property in the same terms as possession, as a relationship between persons and things.

Where ownership and possession of an asset are with two different persons, the legal relationship between those persons is usually described as a bailment.

In practice, property and possession usually coincide in the same person. However, there are important differences between the two terms. While possession is, finally, based on questions of fact, ownership is a question of law. As a corollary of this, possession is absolute but property is relative. Different persons may have property in the same asset. Proprietary rights may be future, conditional and partial. They may subsist as against some persons but not others. Any right of property may be relative to competing proprietary rights in the same asset.

5

(b)   Property and possession originally remedies

The concept of possession evolved from court procedures for disputes concerning tangible property.

Without the concept of property, one could not assert rights to assets in the hands of others (and 'custody' would be a meaningless term). Property is the courts' recognition of the rights of the owner out of possession. It is (in origin) a remedy which evolved from judicial decisions, and it is inseparable from the old court procedures through which they were reached. Property does not exist in any abstract sense. It arises only in order to resolve disputes.

Two consequences flow from this. Firstly, these legal concepts cannot develop ahead of case law. They consist of case law and, where events run ahead, the legal ideas are left behind. As an example of this conservatism, it will be argued (in section 2, below, and in chapters 3 and 4) that the computerisation of the securities markets have taken them beyond the scope of the concept of possession. Secondly, the value of seeking to extrapolate abstract principles from case law is limited. The historic function of property is as procedure for resolving situations in which competing claims to assets have arisen. It is only possible and only necessary to understand property in the context of those situations. The need for a concrete and pragmatic approach is most clear in the cross-border proprietary aspects of global custody, as discussed in chapter 7.

(c)   Categories of property

English law distinguishes between real and personal property. Real property relates to freehold land and personal property relates to other assets.

There are two types of personal property, choses in possession and choses in action. A chose in possession is a right of property in a tangible asset, which can be enforced by taking physical possession of the asset. Choses in action are property rights in intangibles such as debts. Documentary intangibles form an intermediate class comprising negotiable securities such as bearer bonds where the debt is considered to be locked up in the paper instrument that constitutes it.

Another necessary distinction is that between legal and equitable property. Legal or technical ownership has been compared to the shell of a nut and equitable or beneficial ownership to its kernel. The legal owner of an asset must be involved in any dealing with third parties. Thus, the legal owner of shares receives the dividends from the issuing company and must be involved in any transfer of the shares. The beneficial owner of assets is entitled to enjoy them. Thus, the legal owner of shares must account for dividends and proceeds of sale to the beneficial owner. Where the legal and beneficial ownership of an asset are held by different persons, the relationship between the legal and beneficial owner is generally described as a trust.

(d)   Summary: personal assets

Assets (or at least tangible assets) can be the subject of possession as well as of property. Where physical possession and property are with two different persons, with the consent of the owner, a bailment generally arises. A right of property in a tangible asset is called a chose in possession and a right of property in an intangible asset is called a chose in action. Property may be legal or equitable. Where legal and equitable ownership are with two different persons, a trust generally arises.

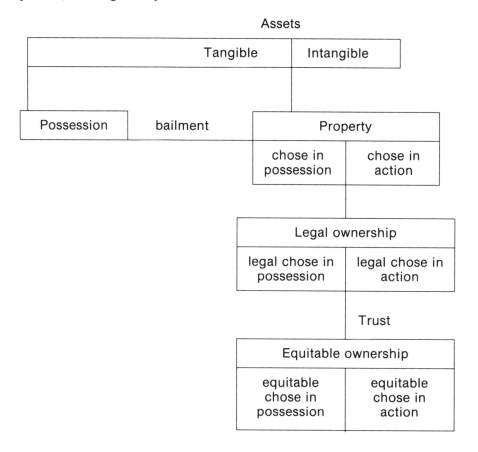

In the modern securities markets, as a result of the widespread use of nominees and of trends towards dematerialisation and the pooling of securities (as chapter 3 below will argue) the rights of most investors in securities are (as a matter of English law) equitable choses in action.

2   Possession of intangibles

Equitable choses in action are intangible. Intangible property is incapable of *physical* possession. Might it be argued that intangibles are otherwise capable of possession?

(a)   Legal possession

It is true that the law recognises both physical (or actual) and legal (or civil) possession. Legal possession has been described as the right to possess.

However, the ultimate basis of possession is always fact rather than law because 'the existence of the *de facto* relation of control or apparent dominion [is] required as the foundation of the alleged right.'[1]

(b)   Constructive possession

The concept of legal possession, then, does not help in showing that intangibles are capable of possession. The concept of constructive possession seems more promising at first sight. Possession in fact need not involve direct physical possession, for the law recognises constructive (or symbolic), as opposed to actual (or physical) possession. Relevant case law is mainly concerned with keys to rooms and boxes in which physical property is contained. However, as with legal possession, the concept of constructive possession is derived from the concept of actual possession (ie physical possession)[2] and therefore cannot apply to intangibles.

(c)   Intangibles

Nowhere is there authority that, in English common law, intangible personal property is capable of possession in the context of safekeeping.[3]

A major part of the difficulty in extending the doctrine of possession to intangibles is the lack of procedural precedent. The modern common law of possession evolved from the legal procedures developed from the disputes relating to land and goods. There was no procedure for, and hence there is no clear concept of, possessory remedies in relation to personal intangibles such as securities.

(d)   Common law and equity

In the context of custody, the prudent approach is therefore to assume that intangibles are incapable of possession at common law. The courts of equity have always been more comfortable with intangibles than the common law courts, because an interest under a trust is intangible. If the handing over to a third party of control of intangible personal property for the purposes of safekeeping or security cannot give rise to the common law possessory concepts of bailment or pledge, it can give rise to their equitable equivalents, trust and charge. Therefore where control of assets (such as securities) are handed over to third parties, by way of safekeeping or security, the dematerialisation of such assets has the effect of diverting the custodial or security relationship from common law to equity: no longer bailment, but trust; no longer pledge, but charge. This is legally significant because the

---

[1] Pollock, *An Essay on Possession in the Common Law*, (1888) Clarendon Press, Oxford, p 10.

[2] 'A person has actual possession (*de facto* possession, possession in fact) of a thing when he exercises physical control over it ... A person has constructive possession ... when someone representing him has actual possession of the thing.' *Jowitt's Dictionary of English Law*, under 'Possession'.

[3] The term possession is used in different ways in different contexts. As indicated above, a concrete and context-specific approach is necessary. While other branches of law offer examples of the possession of intangibles (such as, in land law, the feudal concept of seisen) they do not assist here.

shift from bailment to trust raises questions of higher fiduciary duty,[1] and the shift from bailment to charge raises questions of registration.[2]

3 Proprietary and personal rights

(a) Generally

The preceding section discussed proprietary rights in assets. There is another class of rights in respect of assets: that of personal rights. Since medieval times, English law has treated the difference between the two classes as fundamental.

If A buys 10 cases of claret from B, who has more than 10 cases and who earmarks 10 specific cases for A in his cellar, A acquires 10 cases of claret (a proprietary right). If, however, B does not identify the 10 cases, then, provided A has not yet paid for the wine,[3] A may merely acquire a contractual right against B for delivery of 10 cases of claret (a personal right).

The difference for A is clear on B's insolvency. A proprietary right attaches to the asset and is unaffected by B's insolvency.[4] However, a personal right does not make A the owner of 10 cases but merely the unsecured creditor of an insolvent, and therefore A's claim will be subject to delay and abatement depending on the outcome of the liquidation.[5]

A personal right is only as good as one's ability successfully to sue the obligor; this may be defeated by the obligor's insolvency.[6] For this reason, legal commentators draw a fundamental distinction between personal and proprietary rights (or between obligations and ownership).[7]

The distinction is fundamental in the context of custody. If the custody client's rights are merely personal against the custodian, it takes the custodian's credit risk. If its rights are proprietary, it does not. However, one must tread with light feet in making the distinction here, because (at first sight) the custody assets themselves are personal (and not proprietary) in nature.

The concepts of property and obligation are both dynamic, and have changed from time to time. Both concern the remedies made available by the courts in the context of disputes, and throughout legal history both have evolved as the approach of the courts, and the remedies made available by them,

---

[1] Chapter 8 will examine these issues in detail.

[2] While a pledge is not registrable, a charge may be. It is therefore important to ensure that a purported pledge over intangible securities is not void as an unregistered charge under section 395 of the Companies Act 1985.

[3] Sale of Goods Act 1979, section 20A.

[4] Provided the transaction is not at an undervalue or otherwise voidable under the Insolvency Act 1986.

[5] See chapter 5, below.

[6] And by other matters such as the lapsing of statutory limitation periods, set-off and estoppel.

[7] 'The distinction between real and personal rights may be expressed as the distinction between property and obligation, between what I *own* and what I *am owed*. The common law observed this distinction strictly.' RM Goode, *Commercial Law*, (2 edn, 1995), Penguin, London, p 31. (Before the Victorian advent of corporate insolvency law, the importance of the distinction was, primarily, transferability: see section b, below.)

have changed. Indeed, the development of certain branches of the law might be summarily described as the evolution of remedies (and therefore of rights) from the personal into the proprietary. Two leading examples of this are the law of equity, and the law of choses in action. As already indicated, chapter 3 below will argue that rights of investors in securities are often, as a matter of English domestic law, equitable choses in action. Each of the categories of choses in action, and equitable property, has a personal (and not proprietary) flavour.

(b)   Nature of choses in action

It has been noted that a chose in action is property in an intangible. To understand the nature of choses in action it is helpful briefly to look at their history. Choses in action, or claims (for example those arising under a debt or other contract), became increasingly identified, during the modern period, with the documents that evidenced them. Over the course of the last three centuries choses in action, in the financial world, began their long journey from intangibility to paper (before, with computerisation in the mid-20th century, starting the journey back again).

Choses in action were originally treated as *personal* rights of action, and for that reason were not assignable. Maintenance (or the abusive trafficking in rights of action) was a serious concern in medieval England. The general restriction on assignment of choses in action persisted long into the modern era, until it was eroded by the development of exceptions to accommodate the needs of commerce, permitting the capital markets to arise. Before the beginning of corporate insolvency law in the 19th century, a key characteristic distinguishing personal rights from proprietary rights was their non-assignability. Therefore, when the benefit[1] of choses in action became in some cases assignable they also became, in those cases, proprietary.

Where assets are held in custody, the difference between personal and proprietary rights is important in the event of insolvency. A chose in action such as a bond, which is held in custody, is personal as against the issuer, and will clearly be affected by the insolvency of the issuer. However, as against the custodian, it can (if it is held on trust or bailment) be proprietary and can therefore be unaffected by the custodian's insolvency. In other words, securities (being choses in action) can be proprietary only where there is intermediation, or custody. It is only in the context of custody that the proprietary nature of securities arises. The proprietary nature of securities is their enforceability through the hands of a custodian (or, more precisely, in its insolvency). Broadly speaking, the law of property in the securities markets is the law of insolvency as it relates to custodians.

(c)   Nature of equitable property

Like choses in action, equitable proprietary rights began their legal history as personal rights, and then evolved into hybrid rights that are capable, upon a custodian's insolvency, of being proprietary.

---

[1] Although the benefit of a contract may be assignable, its burden generally is not: see *Chitty on Contracts*, (26 edn, 1989), Sweet & Maxwell, London, Vol 1, para 1431.

Historically and conceptually, equitable property begins with the personal fiduciary obligation (which the law of equity implies) of a trustee to hold trust property for the benefit of the beneficiary. This personal obligation gives the beneficiary a matching personal right against the trustee, to require that the obligation be observed. The gap between a personal right against the trustee *in respect of* trust property, and a proprietary right *in* the trust property that will survive the trustee's insolvency, is bridged by the convenient equitable doctrine of conversion: equity regards that as done which ought to be done. The law regards the trust property as belonging to the beneficiary, in equity, because the trustee should account to the beneficiary for the trust property.

(d) Conclusions

The question of whether custody assets are personal or proprietary is important in determining whether they will be at risk on the insolvency of the custodian. Much of the custody portfolio consists, under English law, of equitable choses in action. Equitable property and choses in action, considered in abstract terms, share the characteristic of being partly personal and partly proprietary.[1] In the late 19th century and early 20th century, there was uncertainty as to the correct treatment of choses in action in insolvency. Today, the position is clear. Not all the assets held by an insolvent are available for distribution among its creditors, but only those which belong to it.[2] Distributable assets do not include assets held by the insolvent but owned by third parties, whether or not that third party ownership is equitable, and whether or not the assets are choses in action.

However, in seeking to benefit from this rule in the era of electronic custody, clients face certain legal risks. Computerisation affects both the legal nature of the custody securities, and that of the custody relationship, as discussed in chapters 3 and 4.

---

[1] 'The ambivalent quality, for example, of the contractual chose in action provides a constant reminder of the fluid nature of [the] classifications ["contractual" and "proprietary"].' '[N]o quantum leap differentiates contract from "property", for "property" has no clear threshold.' Kevin Gray, *Property in Thin Air*, pp 302, 303.

[2] In the case of the bankruptcy of an individual, assets held by the individual on trust are excluded from his estate by section 283(3)(a) of the Insolvency Act 1986. In the case of corporate insolvency, the authority for the exclusion of trust assets lies in the general principle that only assets owned by the company form part of its estate, as reflected in case law. See for example, *Barclays Bank Ltd v Quistclose Investments Ltd* [1968] 3 All ER 651 and *Re Kayford Ltd* [1975] 1 All ER 604.

Chapter 3

Computerisation and securities[1]

In the late 20th century, the securities markets have seen a growing trend towards computerisation. Paper instruments and certificates are replaced by electronic records. Because these databases are in general maintained by intermediaries and not issuers, increased computerisation means increased intermediation.

The reason for computerisation is the efficiency of electronic technology. However, it has far-reaching legal consequences. In the absence of clarifying legislation and case law, these consequences have not been fully analysed.[2] Computerisation has brought both a new order of operational efficiency and a new order of legal uncertainty to the securities markets.

The consequences of computerisation fall into two categories: changes to the legal nature of securities, and changes to the legal nature of the custodial relationship between investors and the intermediaries with whom they have a direct relationship. This chapter will discuss the effect of computerisation on securities. Its effect on the custodial relationship will be discussed in the next chapter.

Commercial arrangements relating to computerised securities are often cross-border, and a legal analysis of them necessarily involves a consideration of private international law. However, the starting point of this analysis is the position under English domestic law, and the following discussion is made on the basis that English domestic law governs the commercial arrangements relating to computerised securities. While somewhat artificial, it is a necessary preliminary to a consideration of the position under English private international law, which will follow in chapters 6 and 7 below.

A Computerised securities

The shift away from paper and towards electronic or book-entry records is called dematerialisation. Securities may take a variety of forms in wholly or partially dematerialised environments. These will be referred to as computerised securities. They include the following:

---

[1] See J Benjamin, *Negotiability and Computerisation*, (1995) 10 JIBFL 253 to 357.
[2] See RM Goode, *The Nature and Transfer of Rights in Dematerialised and Immobilised Securities,* (1996) 10 JIBFL 167.

1 Immobilised securities

Immobilisation has been defined as 'The storage of securities certificates in a vault in order to eliminate physical movement of certificates/documents in transfers of ownership.'[1] The two major European immobilisation systems are Euroclear and Cedel:

> 'The first on the scene was Euroclear, founded in Brussels in late 1968 by Morgan Guaranty Trust. Cedel was organised and established in Luxembourg within 12 months, commencing operations in 1971 … The clearing systems were founded because they were necessary for the construction of the international bond market. Before the foundation of the automated systems both issue and trading depended on a system of physical delivery and transfer. The system could not keep up with the increasing number of trades and issues with the result that by 1967 the position was unsatisfactory and the system in difficulties … The underlying purposes of the two systems are ease of transfer of bonds and security. So long as most investors within the international bond market do not wish to have actual physical possession of their bonds, a physical delivery on initial issue or subsequent transfer would constitute a time-consuming, expensive, potentially insecure, and unnecessary function. Far better that the bonds should physically always remain in a safe and authorised depositary, and transfers merely be effected on the records of the two clearing systems. Risks are further reduced by the use of the systems because, when settlements are effected within them, they can be carried out by simultaneous transfers of cash and securities within the systems.'[2]

Euroclear and Cedel in turn maintain accounts with local depositaries, and other local clearing systems and depositaries.

2 Global securities[3]

On the closing of an issue of eurobonds,[4] the paper customarily issued by the issuer is not made up of definitive bonds, but takes the form of a global bond in substitution for the entire issue of definitives. The global bond is held by a common depositary. The common depositary agrees, in a letter of acknowledgment to the issuer, to hold the global for Euroclear and Cedel, who (in accordance with their general terms and conditions) in turn hold their interests in the global bond for those of their participants to whose accounts interests under the global are credited. The issuer promises to pay principal and interest to the holder of the global.

The primary reason for issuing globals instead of definitives is the desire to avoid adverse US taxation consequences. In the case of *temporary* global bonds, at the end of a 40-day 'lock up' period, definitives are issued to the common depositary, upon the certification by Cedel or Euroclear that the participants to whom definitives are to be issued have in turn certified that the investments are not beneficially owned by US persons. Further, while definitives are security printed, globals are not. Because of the expense of security printing, bonds are sometimes issued in *permanent* global form and

---

[1] Group of Thirty, *Clearance and Settlement in the World's Securities Markets*, (1989).
[2] Terence Prime, *International Bonds and Certificates of Deposit*, (1990) Butterworths, London, pp 233, 234.
[3] '… 60% of issues are now represented in global form' F Christie and H Dosanjh, *The Practical Aspects of Settlement and Custody*, F Oditah, *The Future for the Global Securities Market*, (1996) Clarendon, Oxford, p 133.
[4] Ie bonds issued in a currency other than that of the jurisdiction of the issuer.

definitives are never issued. It is also customary for euronotes[1] and eurocommercial paper[2] to be issued in permanent global form. The temporary global is exchangeable wholly or in part at the request of the holder for definitives, and is reduced in value pro rata the value of definitives issued in exchange. Partial exchanges are endorsed on the global, which is cancelled when it is exchanged in full. In contrast, a permanent global is generally only exchangeable for definitives upon the default of the issuer or the closure of the clearing system. (In the case of temporary globals, the holder is however only entitled to payment if the issuer defaults in its obligations to issue definitives on request.)[3]

3   Repackaged securities

The chief example of a repackaged security is a depositary receipt. Underlying securities are legally acquired by a depositary (with certificates held on its behalf by a custodian). The depositary holds its interest in the underlying securities on trust for holders of depositary receipts. The identity of depositary receipt holders from time to time is determined by reference to a register maintained by the depositary. Securities are repackaged primarily to change their jurisdiction. Originally developed in the United States, an American depositary receipt (ADR) programme permitted US investors to invest indirectly in non-US securities, where direct investment in such securities was not possible or not attractive for currency, administrative, settlement, taxation, or regulatory reasons.

4   Dematerialised securities

Dematerialisation is defined as follows in the *G30 Report*: 'The elimination of physical certificates or documents of title which represent ownership of securities so that securities exist only as computer records.' In the UK, examples of dematerialised registered securities (see below) are gilts held within the Central Gilts Office, and equities and other registered corporate securities within CREST. Some bearer securities are dematerialised in the Central Moneymarkets Office.

The above categories are not exclusive; for example, global securities are always also immobilised, ie held through Euroclear and Cedel; depositary

---

[1] Ie short-term promissory notes denominated in a currency other than that of the jurisdiction of the issuer.

[2] Ie short-term debt instruments denominated in a currency other than that of the jurisdiction of the issuer.

[3] If the issuer fails to issue definitives on default, the following enforcement problem arises. Investors have no *locus standi* against the issuer, as they are not the holders of notes. Their rights under the global may be enforced through a trustee (in cases where a trustee is appointed). However, where no trustee is appointed, their rights under the global can only be enforced through the common depositary; in practice common depositories are unwilling to enforce on behalf of investors as they have a customer relationship with the issuer.

To overcome this problem, it is usually provided that, if the issuer fails to issue definitives within 30 days of default, the obligations of the issuer under the global will become void; in their place, new obligations on the issuer arise under a deed poll executed directly in favour of investors (ie participants in Euroclear and Cedel having entitlements under the global credited to their accounts). Such provision will be referred to as 'the disappearing global'.

receipts are usually issued in global as well as definitive form, and global depositary receipts are immobilised through Euroclear, Cedel and/or the Depository Trust Company of New York ('DTC').

Securities may be held through chains of intermediaries with a large number of links. For the sake of simplicity, the term 'Investor' will be taken here to mean an investor whose interest is as direct as possible, ie (in the case of immobilised and global securities) the participant in the clearing system; (in the case of repackaged securities) the holder of the depositary receipt; and (in the case of dematerialised securities) the registered holder of registered securities or the participant in the clearing system in the case of dematerialised bearer securities. The term 'computerised securities' will be used to mean the interest of the investor in each of the above, and the term 'physical securities' to mean securities which are not computerised securities.

This work will seek to establish the effect of the computerisation on the legal nature of securities. The issue falls naturally into two parts, as securities fall broadly into two categories: bearer securities and registered securities. The precise difference between them is a matter of extensive debate, but (in broad terms) may be summarised as relating to the procedure for their legal transfer. A bearer security promises on its face to pay the bearer, and the chose in action against the issuer is considered at law to be locked up in the instrument issued in respect of it. Because they consist of tangible instruments, bearer securities are choses in possession. In general, whoever possesses the instrument legally owns the bearer security, which is transferable by delivery of the instrument. In this sense, bearer instruments are like cash. Examples of bearer securities are bearer bonds and certificates of deposits. In contrast, legal ownership of registered securities is determined prima facie by the register of members of the issuer.[1] In order legally to transfer a registered security, it is necessary for the register to be amended in favour of the transferee. Examples of registered securities are equities[2] and gilts.[3] Bearer securities will be considered in section B, below and registered securities in section C.

B   Computerised bearer securities

The most important example of the computerisation of bearer securities is the eurobond markets, where most securities are both immobilised and issued (initially at least) in global form.[4]

Because eurobonds are characteristically immobilised and/or issued in global form, these forms of computerisation will be considered in this section.

---

[1] *Société Générale de Paris v Walker* (1885) 11 App Cas 20. While certificates may be issued, they are not documents of title, but merely documents evidencing title.
[2] Ie shares of companies.
[3] Ie registered debt securities issued by the government of the United Kingdom through the Bank of England.
[4] '...definitive Eurobonds are usually warehoused with a "common depository" for the two clearance systems Euroclear and Cedel. Euroclear and Cedel hold the bonds for the account of their respective securities account holders in each clearance system; where a transfer takes place it always takes place between one account holder of the clearance system and another; consequently, all transfers are effected by an electronic book entry system without any movement of the physical definitive Eurobonds.' Ravi C Tennekoon, *The Law and Regulation of International Finance*, (1991) Butterworths, London, p 167.

The other forms of computerisation, repackaging and dematerialisation, will be discussed in the section on registered securities below.[1]

The major impact of computerisation on bearer securities appears to be the loss of negotiable status.

In this discussion the term 'computerised bearer securities' will mean computerised securities which are derived from bearer securities.[2]

1   Negotiability

The secondary markets in bearer securities have traditionally benefited from the doctrine of negotiability. A negotiable instrument has two attractive features. Firstly, it is transferable without formalities.[3] Secondly, honest acquisition confers good title (even if the transferor did not have good title[4]). Thus, market transfers are rapid and reliable. The holder in due course takes the instrument free from prior equities or defects in the title of the transferor. The general view is that these benefits are not available to securities which are not negotiable instruments.

An instrument may acquire negotiable status either by statute or by commercial usage, as reflected in the law merchant.

It is generally[5] established that physical bearer securities in the secondary

---

[1] In practice, the underlying securities in depository receipt programmes are generally limited to registered equities. In this jurisdiction, the major initiative for dematerialisation is CREST, which relates to registered corporate equities and debt. However, certain bearer securities may be dematerialised in the UK through the Central Moneymarkets Office ('CMO'). It is also true that, although generally global securities are only issued in respect of bearer securities, registered securities may be issued in global form and immobilised in a clearing system. Of course, a global form of registered security is not the exact equivalent of the global form of bearer securities. It is not a global note but a global certificate, for it does not constitute but merely represents the underlying securities, which are not and cannot be constituted by paper. While the underlying securities of a bearer global may be unissued, those of a registered global are unissuable. The exact status under English law of a bearer global is somewhat uncertain, but English law treats a registered global in the same way as a registered definitive, as evidencing the title of the person entered on the register as the owner of the securities. Indeed, the terms 'global' and 'definitive' in the context of registered securities owes more to practice borrowed from the bearer markets than to legal analysis. Another difference between bearer and registered globals is that the disappearing global problem discussed above does not arise with registered globals, for (as there is no need for any definitive paper to be issued on the issuer's default, but merely for reregistration from the name of the global holder into the name of the investors) the enforcement difficulties driving the disappearing global should not be present. The author is grateful to Ian Jackson, partner in Clifford Chance, for this analysis.

[2] Derived because (in the case of immobilised) the underlying securities are in bearer form or (in the case of global securities) the definitive securities are, or would if issued be, in bearer form.

[3] By physical delivery, or by endorsement and delivery in the case of certain instruments requiring endorsement, such as cheques.

[4] Provided the instrument is negotiated prior to maturity: see *Brown v Davies* (1789) 100 ER 466.

[5] Certain provisions that have been incorporated in commercial paper have been considered to affect their status as promissory notes negotiable under section 83 of the Bills of Exchange Act 1882. Such provisions include withholding tax grossing up provisions (having the result that the note is not a promise to pay a sum certain) and restrictions (driven by US regulatory requirements) on negotiation of the instrument to nationals of certain countries (so that the note is not an unconditional promise to pay) and the enfacement of guarantees on the instrument. These provisions must be considered on a case by case basis.

markets are negotiable instruments.[1] It might therefore seem desirable to argue that the movement of bearer instruments into computerised form has not been at the expense of their negotiable status.[2]

2 A new class of negotiable instrument?

There is no statutory confirmation of the negotiable status of bearer computerised securities. Therefore, to show that computerised securities are negotiable, it would be necessary to argue that they have been recognised under the law merchant as a new class of negotiable instrument.

There is ample authority that the law merchant is a dynamic branch of law, evolving to reflect changing commercial practice from time to time. Thus, in principle, the law merchant is capable of recognising bearer computerised securities as negotiable. The question is whether it has in fact done so.

3 Arguments against negotiability

It will be argued here that the law merchant has not recognised bearer computerised securities as a new class of negotiable instrument, primarily because they are intangible.

(a) Indirect

One obstacle to treating bearer computerised securities as negotiable is their indirect nature. The ability of the holder from time to time of an instrument to enforce it against its issuer in his own name has generally been taken

---

[1] Domestic corporate bonds: *Re General Estates* (1868) 3 Ch App 758; *Higgs v Assam Tea Co Ltd* (1869) LR 4 Ex Ch 387; *Re Imperial Land Co* (1870) LR 11 Eq 478; *Bechuanaland Exploration Co v London Trading Bank* [1898] 2 QB 658.

Foreign government and corporate bonds: *Gorgier v Mieville* (1824) 3 B & C 45; *Simmons v London Joint Stock Bank* [1891] 1 Ch 270; *Bentinck v London Joint Stock Bank* [1893] 2 Ch 120; *Venables v Baring* [1892] 3 Ch 527.

Scrip for bonds (ie certificates acknowledging the holder's entitlement to be issued with bonds): *Goodwin v Robarts* (1875) LR 10 Ex Ch 337.

Scrip for shares (ie certificates acknowledging the holder's entitlement to be issued with shares): *Rumball v Metropolitan* (1877) 2 QBD 194.

Secured bearer bonds: *Webb v Herne Bay* (1870) LR 5 QB 642.

Letters of credit: *Re Agra and Masterman's Bank* (1867) 2 Ch App 391; *Johnnessen v Munroe* 185 NY 641 (1899).

The above references are quoted in Ewart, *Negotiability and Estoppel*, (1900), 14 LQR 135, p 156. See also the following:

Bearer bonds whether foreign or domestic, corporate or government: *Edelstein v Schuler* [1902] All ER Rep 884.

Certificates of deposit: *Customs and Excise Comrs v Guy Butler (International) Ltd* [1977] QB 377 at 382; *Libyan Arab Foreign Bank v Bankers Trust Co* [1988] 1 Lloyd's Rep 259 at 276 (quoted in *Encyclopedia of Banking Law*, (1994) Butterworths, London, F(116) n1).

The more recent introduction of Euro-notes and Euro-commercial paper to the London secondary markets raised the question of whether these new forms of bearer security were negotiable in the absence of clear statutory or judicial authority. The general consensus in the legal community is that these physical instruments have become negotiable on the basis of commercial custom in London.

[2] Under the US Uniform Commercial Code, computerised securities are not negotiable except in respect of transfers across the books of clearing corporations.

to be an essential criterion of negotiability.[1] It was noted above that, in general, an investor in computerised securities does not have directly enforceable rights against the issuer.[2]

However, an alternative view has been expressed. In the past the London legal community considered this question in relation to physical Eurodollar bonds constituted under a trust deed which imposed limitations on bondholders' rights to sue the issuer so that generally only the trustee had rights of enforcement, and bondholders were able to sue the issuer only if the trustee failed in its duties on their behalf. One leading counsel argued that the instruments were not negotiable because on the face of the bonds the person holding them for the time being was prevented from suing on them in his own name. Another leading counsel argued that the instruments were negotiable, and that the requirement of negotiability was not that the holder should have an unrestricted right to sue, but that in circumstances where he is given such a right, he should not need to sue in the names of prior holders. For this reason, the indirect nature of computerised securities may not necessarily be incompatible with negotiable status.

(b)   Intangible

The clearer argument against computerised securities being negotiable is their intangibility. The early negotiable instruments (bills of exchange and promissory notes) were recognised as negotiable because they were like money, and used by merchants as an alternative method of payment for goods.[3] Indeed, the test of negotiability has been held to be that the instrument should pass from hand to hand like money.[4] 'Money passes with good title because it is money; and notes because they are like money.'[5]

The rule with money is that property passes with possession. Equally, 'For the purpose of rendering bills of exchange negotiable, the rights of property in them passes with the bills ... The property and the possession are inseparable.'[6]

Property is always with the holder, or the person having possession. For this reason, a negotiable instrument must be capable of possession. If it were incapable of possession, it could not confer upon its possessor (a holder) the status of holder in due course.

Computerised securities, being the interest of the investor, are intangible.[7]

---

[1] See *London and County Banking Co Ltd v London and River Plate Bank Ltd* (1887) 20 QBD 232, at 226. See also *Crouch v Crédit Foncier of England* (1873) LR 8 QB 374 per Blackburn J.

[2] Even in the case of dematerialised securities in the CMO, the right of the investor to sue the issuer does not arise under an instrument, but is merely contractual, arising under the Master Dematerialisation Agreement.

[3] The term 'money' is said in its strict sense, as current coin and bank notes, rather than credit, or the balance of a bank account. See Mann, *The Legal Aspects of Money*, p 5: 'Bank accounts, for instance, are debts, not money...'.

'A Bill of exchange is a security, originally invented among merchants in different countries, for the more easy remittance of money from the one to the other, which since spread itself into almost all pecuniary transactions.' Blackstone, *Commentaries*, Book II, at 466.

[4] See *Lang v Smyth* (1831) 7 Bing 284; *Miller v Race* (1758) 1 Burr 452 and *Friedlander v Texas* 130 US 416 (1889).

[5] Ewart, op cit, p 152.

[6] Per Eyre CJ *Collins v Martin* (1797) 1 Bos & P 648 at 651.

[7] Investors have the right to call for underlying physical securities; however, if they do so, they convert their investment from a computerised security to a physical security.

It has been argued, in chapter 2, above, that intangibles are not capable of possession at common law, but only in equity. Equitable possession does not assist in the context of negotiability, which is part of the law merchant. As intangibles are incapable of possession outside the realms of equity, computerised securities cannot confer upon anyone the status of holder for the purposes of the law merchant, and it is only through such a person that the benefits of negotiability can be enjoyed.

Intangibility poses another problem: an intangible cannot be an instrument. 'An "Instrument" is a Writing, and generally imports a document of a formal legal kind.'[1] The Bills of Exchange Act 1882 defines both bills of exchange[2] and promissory notes[3] as being 'in writing' and provides that ' "writing" includes print'.[4] The author could find no authority for extending the meaning of the term 'instrument' to intangibles such as computerised securities.[5]

If the basis of negotiability is possession, and if the nature of an instrument is tangible, it is not clear that computerised bearer securities can be either negotiable or instruments. There is no clear authority for treating an intangible as a negotiable instrument, and it may be legally impossible to do so. The way forward may be to extend the concept of negotiability to intangibles. However, this would be a quantum leap from the existing law merchant, and perhaps only achievable by statute.

It is true that in the case of immobilised and global securities, there will be tangible instruments (and directly enforceable rights) in the hands of an intermediary depository or custodian.[6] This does not, however, render the interest of the Investor a negotiable instrument, because all negotiable instruments 'are intended to be ambulatory'.[7] The physical securities

---

[1] John S James, *Stroud's Judicial Dictionary of Words and Phrases*, (5 edn, 1986), Sweet & Maxwell, London.

[2] In section 3(1).

[3] In section 83(1).

[4] In section 2.

[5] Although an instrument cannot be intangible, there is authority that information stored on the hard disc of a computer may be a document for the purposes of orders for discovery under RSC Ord 24: see *Alliance and Leicester Building Society v Ghahremani* [1992] NLJR 313 and *Derby & Co Ltd v Weldon* (No 9) [1991] 2 All ER 901, per Vinelott J. However this principle is confined to the context of discovery. In *Derby*, Vinelott J bases his judgment on the principle in the earlier case of *Grant v Southwestern and County Properties Ltd* [1974] 2 All ER 465. In the passage he quotes from that judgment, the policy basis for that decision, which ties it to its litigation context, is clear: 'A litigant who keeps all his documents in microdot form could not avoid discovery because in order to read the information extremely powerful microscopes or other sophisticated instruments would be required.' (quoted at 906). Vinelott J goes on to comment, at 906: 'The question in this case is not, I think, whether the database is a document but as to the circumstances in which and the means by which a party seeking discovery is entitled to inspect and take copies of that document.' It would therefore be unsafe to seek to extrapolate a general principle from these cases.

On a slightly different point, section 10 of the Civil Evidence Act 1968 defines 'document' to include '... any disc, tape, sound track or other device in which sounds or other data ... are embodied so as to be capable ... of being reproduced therefrom ...'. See sections 127(1) and 127(2) of the Finance Act 1988.

[6] Ie the underlying physical securities in the case of immobilised securities, and the global note itself in the case of globals.

These underlying physical securities will also be expressed on their face to be negotiable; this is also a necessary criterion of negotiability: *London and County Banking Co v London and River Plate Bank Ltd* (1880) 20 QBD 232; *Jones & Co v Coventry* [1909] 2 KB 1029, quoted in Prime, op cit, p 242.

[7] Ewart, op cit, p 155.

underlying the immobilised securities are (as the term suggests) immobilised in Euroclear or Cedel. Moreover, computerised securities are not expressed to be negotiable on their face because, being intangible, they have no face. Thus the indicia of negotiability are distributed between the intermediary and the investor. The physical instrument (expressed to be negotiable) and directly enforceable rights are held by the intermediary, and the 'ambulatory' security (ie one that passes from hand to hand like money) is held by the investors.

(c)   Conclusion

In the absence of authority to the contrary, the test of negotiability appears to remain firstly, that the instrument should be transferable, like cash, by delivery and secondly (subject to the comments at (a), above) that the instrument should be capable of being sued upon by the holder from time to time.[1]

Delivery is the transfer of possession. As an intangible a computerised security is incapable of possession and therefore of delivery in the technical legal sense of that term.[2] It would therefore seem that computerised securities are neither instruments, nor capable of delivery (nor yet of being sued upon by the holder from time to time) and cannot be negotiable instruments.

This analysis is made under English domestic law. As stated above, arrangements for the issue and transfer of bearer computerised securities are characteristically cross-border and therefore involve issues of private international law. These are considered in chapter 6.

In crossing into the electronic era, the secondary markets in bearer securities crossed an important legal boundary, and left the law merchant. The later part of this chapter suggest a solution to this problem.

4   Intermediate securities

If computerised bearer securities are not negotiable instruments, what are they?

(a)   Functional status

The continuing computerisation of securities is inevitable. As an interim stage in the journey towards pure dematerialisation G30 recommends immobilis-

---

[1] 'It may therefore be laid down as a safe rule that where an instrument is by the custom of trade transferable, like cash, by delivery, and is also capable of being sued upon by the person holding it pro tempore, then it is entitled to the name of a *negotiable instrument*, and the property in it passes to a bona fide transferee for value, though the transfer may not have taken place in market overt. But that if either of the above requisites be wanting, ie, if it be either not accustomably transferable, or, though it be accustomably transferable, yet, if its nature be such as to render it incapable of being put in suit by the party holding it pro tempore, it is not a *negotiable instrument*, nor will delivery of it pass the property of it to a vendee, however bona fide, if the transferor himself have not a good title to it, and the transfer be made out of market overt.' Blackburn J, *Crouch v Crédit Foncier* (1873) LR 8 QB 374 at 381, quoting from the notes to *Miller v Race* (1758) 1 Burr 452.

[2] The discussion that follows will continue to use 'delivery' in relation to computerised securities in its market sense, ie the crediting of the purchaser's account with the computerised securities in fulfilment of a bargain.

ation.[1] Immobilisation is a form of custody, and the interest of the investor in the immobilised securities may be described as the interest of a custody client. Immobilisation involves intermediation, and in this way immobilised securities (and global securities and repackaged securities) are akin to the interests of all custody clients. Thus, if one wishes to classify securities according to the manner in which the investor's interest is held, it is possible to identify three broad types:

(1) *physical securities*, consisting of or represented by paper issued by the issuer and held directly by the investor;

(2) *dematerialised securities*, where the investor holds, and there is, in fact, no underlying paper; and

(3) *intermediate securities*, where an underlying security is issued (or agreed to be issued) in paper form to an intermediary depository, trustee or custodian ('intermediary') who holds the underlying paper (directly or indirectly) for the investor, so that the investor's interest is intangible and enforceable, not directly against the issuer, but only indirectly, through the intermediary.[2]

It might be said that physical securities belong to the past, dematerialised securities to the future and intermediate securities to the transitional present.[3] With intermediate securities, the interposition of the intermediary serves to bridge old (paper-based) and new (electronic) practice.

(b)   Legal nature

The legal nature of international securities is discussed in detail in Appendix 1. Briefly, the interest of the investor is indirect and enforceable against the issuer only through the intermediary. Therefore, under English law, the investor's interest will be recognised as if it were an interest under a trust. Moreover, the interest of the investor is unallocated. It is therefore a form of co-ownership interest, namely an interest under an equitable tenancy in common.

5   The benefits of negotiability

To recap, it has been argued that intermediate securities are not negotiable instruments, and are interests under equitable tenancies in common. The

---

[1] Having commented that in jurisdictions where dematerialisation is not possible, consideration should be given to changing local laws to permit dematerialisation, it goes on to comment: 'However, the major goals of the depository can be accomplished by immobilising certificates, provided a system is in place that permits settlement without transfer and re-registration. This is typically accomplished through the use of a system in which the CSD [central securities depository] acts as a nominee for the beneficial owner.' Group of Thirty, *Securities Clearance and Settlement*, p 8. '... the key development in the modern securities settlement system in the United States has been "immobilization" ...' SJ Rogers, *Policy Perspectives on Revised UCC Article 8*, UCLA Law Rev, June 96, p 1413 at p 1443.

[2] An important example of intermediate securities are the rights of clients holding securities through intermediaries under the Revised Article 8 of the US Uniform Commercial Code, defined as a "security entitlement". 'One of the principal advantages of the security entitlement structure is that it makes clear a basic feature of the indirect holding system – that an entitlement holder's property interest is a bundle of rights that can be asserted directly only against the entitlement holder's own intermediary.' SJ Rogers, *Policy Perspectives on the Revised UCC Article 8* UCLA Law Rev, June 1996, p 1431, at 1455.

[3] Some might argue that, for this reason, custody (in the sense of safekeeping) is not a long-term industry.

benefits of negotiability are ease[1] and integrity[1] of secondary market trans-actions. It is argued (in sections 6 and 7, below) that such benefits may also be enjoyed by intermediate securities, if not under the law merchant, then under other branches of law including the law of equity.

6   Ease of secondary market transactions

The old common law rule was that choses in action were not assignable, because of a policy against maintenance. An exception was evolved by the law merchant from the medieval period onwards in favour of negotiable instruments.[3] Then, in 1873[4] a statutory exception was created, which was later replaced by section 136 of the Law of Property Act 1925.[5] This permits the legal assignment of choses in action provided certain formalities and restrictions are observed. These are (broadly) that:

- the assignment is absolute;
- the assignment is in writing; and
- written notice of the assignment is given to the obligor.

Compliance with the last two items would be inconvenient in the secondary markets,[6] and hence part of the concern to preserve negotiable status.[7]

It was argued above (in chapter 3, section B.4) that intermediate securities[8] are not legal but equitable. Equitable property cannot be legally transferred.[9] Any assignment of an intermediate security must therefore be an equitable assignment.

The law of equity has long recognised assignments of choses in action. Because equity and the common law are separate branches of law it is not necessary to identify an exception to the old common law rule to permit a chose in action to be assigned in equity, and accordingly neither negotiable status nor compliance with section 136 are necessary for equitable assignments.

However, writing is required for dispositions of equitable interests under section 53(1)(c) of the Law of Property Act 1925.[10]

---

[1] Ie no need for written transfers.

[2] Ie the general inability of the trade to be reversed.

[3] Indeed, the original meaning of negotiable was transferable.

[4] Under the Supreme Court of Judicature Act 1873, s 25(6) (repealed).

[5] The statutory regimes for the transfer of registered securities are currently provided by and under the Stock Transfer Act 1963 in the case of physical equities and gilts, the Stock Transfer Act 1982 in the case of dematerialised gilts and the Companies Act 1989 in the case of dematerialised corporate securities.

[6] In particular, the need for the assignment to be in writing would be problematic. Secondary market transactions in computerised bearer securities, like the securities themselves, are characteristically electronic, with no written instrument of transfer. Written contract notes or other confirmations may be issued, but these are merely in the nature of records.

[7] In theory, the Uncertificated Securities Regulations 1996 which form the basis for CREST may also be used to permit electronic transfers in the eurobond markets, as the regulations are not limited to the CREST system.

[8] The term 'intermediate securities' is defined in chapter 3, section 4, to include immobilised securities.

[9] Because the common law cannot recognise the transfer of property which it does not in turn recognise. However, legal property can be the subject of an equitable assignment.

[10] The section replaced section 9 of the Statute of Frauds (1677) (repealed).

The effect of a purported equitable assignment that does not comply with this section will be to confer on the assignee merely contractual rights, leaving it vulnerable to the vendor's insolvency or double dealing.[1]

As indicated above, in an electronic environment, it would be impracticable to obtain the signature of the assignor. Contract notes and other confirmations may be issued in writing, but these are in the nature of records and not dispositions. It would therefore be desirable to show that section 53(1)(c) does not apply.

(a) No disposition

A good argument can be made that section 53(1)(c) does not apply because it relates to dispositions, and no disposition is involved in a secondary market transaction in intermediate securities. The interest of the investor[2] in intermediate securities arises under a statutory quasi-trust which is not expressed to be in favour of individually identified investors, but in favour of investors as a class. Property is thus an incident of class membership, and remains at all times with the class. Secondary market transactions are settled by changes in the composition of the class.

A disposition involves the movement of property in an asset from one person, or class of persons, to another.[3]

No such movement is involved here. The position is akin to changes in the membership of unincorporated associations; although new members

---

[1] Upon the purported assignor's insolvency, the purported assignee would be merely an unsecured creditor. If the purported assignor went on fraudulently to dispose of the securities to a third party under an assignment complying with section 53(1)(c), then provided the third party had no notice of the fraud, it would take the securities free of any interest of the purported assignee.

Legal commentators customarily identify the following disadvantages of equitable (as opposed to legal) assignment, in addition to section 53(1)(c):

(i) the risk that the assignor may subsequently dispose of the assigned asset under a legal assignment to a bona fide third party without notice of the prior equitable assignment, the legal assignee taking priority over the equitable assignee ('the priority disadvantage');

(ii) the risk that the assignee may owe moneys to the issuer, which may be set off by the issuer against the payment obligation under the assigned instrument ('the set-off disadvantage'); and

(iii) the disadvantage that an equitable assignee cannot sue the issuer in its own name, but must join the assignor ('the enforcement disadvantage').

However, these are relative disadvantages of equitable as opposed to legal assignment, and arise in respect of equitable assignments of property which is capable of both legal and equitable transfer. We saw that intermediate securities are equitable and therefore incapable of legal transfer. The analysis is therefore different. The priority disadvantage cannot arise if there can be no such thing as a legal transferee. The set-off disadvantage cannot arise because the only legal owner of the intermediate securities is the first intermediary, and the issuer is on notice that the first intermediary does not own the intermediate securities beneficially, and would therefore not be entitled to set-off. The enforcement disadvantage does not apply to immobilised securities. The assignee need not join any assignor if it wishes to sue the issuer. It may need to join an intermediary, but this is not an incident of equitable transfer, but due to intermediation. (It was also shown that, in the case of global securities where no trust deed is executed, the investor will be able to sue the issuer directly in its own name, under the deed of covenant.) Further, under the rules of private international law, the enforcement disadvantage may not apply where the proper law of the assigned property is not English law: see Mark Moshinsky, *The Assignment of Debts in the Conflict of Laws*, (1992) 109 LQR 591.

[2] Ie an account holder at Euroclear or Cedel.

[3] See *Grey v IRC* [1959] 3 All ER 603.

become entitled to equitable interests in association property, writing has never been required for changes in association membership.[1]

An alternative but somewhat similar argument can be based in the rule in *R v Preddy*.[2] This establishes the principle that the movement of moneys from one bank account into another does not involve the transfer of property, but rather the extinguishment of one claim and the creation of another. The same principle can be applied to intermediate securities; the debt obligation of a bank and the quasi-trust obligation of a clearer are both choses in action.

(b)   Private international law

A simpler and more pragmatic argument can be based on private international law. As chapter 6, section E below will argue in detail, the approach of the Rome Convention to formality of transfer is generous. A transfer will be formally valid if (broadly) it satisfies the requirements *either* of the law governing the transfer *or* the law of the jurisdiction in which either of the parties (or any agent acting on their behalf) is situated. Thus, the restrictions of section 53(1)(c) can be avoided by routing a transaction through an agent situated in a jurisdiction with no equivalent to that section.

(c)   Conclusions

Taken together, the above arguments may provide a reasonable basis for the view that section 53(1)(c) is not relevant to the secondary markets in intermediate securities,[3] and therefore that the absence of negotiable status is not a disadvantage for intermediate securities for the purpose of ease of secondary market transactions. However, in the absence of statutory clarification, a small measure of uncertainty must remain.

7   Integrity of secondary market transactions

It was stated above that the first benefit of negotiability is ease of secondary market transactions, and that the second benefit is the integrity of those transactions (ie the general inability of trades to be reversed).[4] Section 6 argued that the first benefit is probably available to non-negotiable securities. The same may be true of the second. On the basis that intermediate securities are not negotiable, this section will examine the position of a purchaser where the vendor does not have a good and unencumbered title.

---

[1] The association from this purpose to be 'quasi-corporate', so that changes in membership do not involve dispositions of property. See for example *Carne v Long* (1860) 2 De GF & J 75, 49 ER 550, *Neville Estates v Madden* [1961] 3 All ER 769; *Grant's Will Trust* [1979] 3 All ER 359, at 366. (The treatment of trusts as quasi-corporate is well precedented in English law, as equity played a major role in the development of company law.)

[2] [1996] 3 All ER 481.

[3] Even if the 'no disposition' argument fails, the courts may take a robust approach to the matter. The case of *Re AEG Unit Trust (Managers) Ltd's Deed, Midland Bank Executor and Trustee Co Ltd v AEG Unit Trust Managers Ltd* [1957] Ch 415 is cited by Terence Prime (in *International Bonds and Certificates of Deposit*, (1990), Butterworths, London, p 244, note 3), with the comment, 'It may well be that in any case the Law of Property Act 1925 has no application to situations which are primarily commercial and where application would lead to absurdity.'

[4] This same concept is also called 'security of receipt'. See Peter Birks, *Overview: Tracing, Claiming and Defences, Laundering and Tracing*, (1995) ed P Birks, Clarendon, Oxford.

(a) Adverse claims

Two kinds of adverse claims must be considered; claims by the issuer and claims by earlier holders of the security.

Equity addresses competing claims to assets by considering the priorities between them. The rule is that a bona fide purchaser of the legal estate for value without notice of the prior equitable interest takes free of it.[1] Of course, this rule cannot assist in relation to intermediate securities for they are equitable and their purchaser therefore does not acquire a legal estate.[2]

It will therefore be necessary to find a basis for the integrity of the secondary markets in intermediate securities other than the law merchant and the principles of equitable priority.

(b) Estoppel[3]

Adverse issuer claims can be addressed by estoppel. When choses in action are issued on terms that they will circulate freely in the secondary market, the issuer is estopped by the provision to pay the bearer from setting up claims against an innocent transferee.[4]

This argument can be applied to intermediate securities, as follows. The issuer is estopped from setting up equities against the first intermediary (the common depositary or depositary of the clearer) by its representation to pay the bearer. No such estoppel operates against the first intermediary in favour of the second intermediary (the clearer) or the second intermediary in favour of the investor. However, no estoppels are necessary. The first and second intermediaries cannot set up adverse claims because, in their hands, the securities are not debts or similar choses in action owed by them, but property which is beneficially owned by another.

(c) Contractual provision

However, the problem of third party adverse claims still remains. Contractual provision in the terms and conditions of issue of the securities may exclude adverse claims between the investors who are bound by them, but cannot exclude adverse claims from third parties who are not contractually bound (such as beneficiaries under a trust).

---

[1] *Pilcher v Rawlins* (1872) 7 Ch App 259.
[2] This point is drawn out in the case of *Macmillan Inc v Bishopsgate Investment Trust plc (No 3)* [1995] 3 All ER 747 at 770 in relation to transfers of shares in the DTC. A transfer of shares into the DTC as indirect nominee for a beneficial owner may permit the rule to be invoked; however, an intra-DTC transfer cannot, for in such a transfer the legal title does not move.
[3] 'There is said to be an estoppel where a party is not allowed to say that a certain statement of fact is untrue, whether in reality it is true or not. [Note: See Co Litt 352a "Estoppel is when one is concluded and forbidden in law to speak against his own act or deed, yea though it be to say the truth" ...] Estoppel may therefore be defined as a disability whereby a party is precluded from alleging or proving in legal proceedings that a fact is otherwise than it has been made to appear by the matter giving rise to that disability. Estoppel is often described as a rule of evidence, but the whole concept is more correctly viewed as a substantive rule of law.' 16 *Halsbury's Laws of England*, (4 edn), para 951. See *Simm v Anglo-American Telegraph Co* (1879) 5 QBD 188, per Brett LJ at 206, 207: 'The estoppel assumes that the reality is contrary to that which the person is estopped from denying, and the estoppel has no effect at all upon the reality of the circumstances. ... In my view estoppel has no effect upon the real nature of the transaction: it only creates a cause of action between the person in whose favour the estoppel exists and the person who is estopped.'
[4] See Ewart, *Negotiability and Estoppel*, (1900) 14 LQR 135.

(d)   Tracing

A pragmatic partial solution may be offered by the equitable rules of tracing. In legal theory, third party claims may attach to intermediate securities in the hands of a purchaser. In practice, however, they may not be able to attach to them, because of the impossibility of actual allocation through fungible accounts. It was shown above that intermediate securities are held through accounts at Euroclear and Cedel which are, in general, fungible.

The earlier tracing cases proceeded on the basis of notional allocation where actual allocation was not possible, attributing particular debits in an account to particular credits in accordance with rules that varied with the circumstances.

In the late 20th century, financial arrangements and financial fraud have become more complex, and these rules would often be impracticable today. For this reason, the rules have been modified with a view to obviating the need for even notional allocation.[1]

In *Barlow Clowes v Vaughan*,[2] fund investors suffered loss due to the fraud of a fiduciary. It was held that to have sought to allocate particular losses to particular investors[3] would have been impracticable and arbitrary and the losses were therefore borne ratably.[4]

In circumstances where the fraud is not discovered until holdings of the stock have been transferred across the accounts of many participants, the rule in *Barlow Clowes* may operate to allocate the shortfall ratably among all participants holding such stock within the clearing system, so that no one investor must bear all the loss.[5]

(e)   Private international law

Again a simpler argument can be based in private international law. Under the principles discussed in chapter 6, section D, below, the question of whether true owner's equities will bind a purchaser will be governed by *lex situs*. Chapter 7, section C.6, below, argues that *lex situs* of intermediate securities is the jurisdiction of the clearer. In view of the dominant role of the continental clearers, integrity of English transfer may routinely fall to be determined by Belgian and Luxembourg law.

In Luxembourg, article 7 of the Grand Ducal Regulation of 17 February 1971 Modifying the Circulation of Securities has the effect of transferring the risk of true owner's equities from the purchaser to the clearing system. The Belgian Royal Decree of 1962 has the effect of defeating unpublished adverse claims once securities have entered the clearing system.

As in the context of section 53(1)(c), a problem with relying on this argument is that it prejudices English clearing systems in favour of their overseas rivals.

---

[1] See P Birks, *Overview: Tracing, Claiming and Defences, Laundering and Tracing*, (1995) ed P Birks, Clarendon, Oxford, p 304 for a discussion of the absurdity of notional allocation in tracing money, through the banking system. See also *Agip (Africa) Ltd v Jackson* [1990] Ch 265, Ch D; affd [1991] Ch 547, CA and *Bank Tejarat v HSBC* [1995] 1 Lloyd's Rep 239.

[2] *Barlow Clowes International Ltd (in liquidation) v Vaughan* [1992] 4 All ER 22. See also *Re Eastern Capital Futures (in liquidation)* [1989] BCLC 371.

[3] Following the 'rolling charge' method developed in the US and Canadian courts, taking account of the times at which investors acquired their interests.

[4] In support of pro ration in complex cases, see also *Equity's Identification Rules* DJ Hayton, *Laundering and Tracing*, op cit, pp 14, 16 and *Overview: Tracing, Claiming and Defences*, P Birks, *Laundering and Tracing*, op cit, p 297.

[5] Article 9 for the Luxembourg Grand Ducal Decree of 17 February 1991 provides in effect for the pro ration of shortfalls or the insolvency of Cedel.

(f)   Conclusions

Although not negotiable instruments, intermediate securities are protected from the adverse claims of issuers by the doctrine of estoppel. The risk of third party claims may in practice be so reduced by contractual provision, the rules of tracing and private international law, as to be more theoretical than real.

8   Conclusions

Because they are computerised, intermediate securities are not negotiable instruments. In view of this, English domestic law cannot, finally, provide a completely certain and legally robust basis for the secondary markets in intermediate securities. However, English private international law has the probable result that the possible disadvantages under English domestic law of loss of negotiable status (section 53(1)(c) of the Law of Property Act 1925 and third party claims) are inapplicable, because in questions of transfer formalities and competing proprietary claims, it will apply the local law of the clearer. The position under Belgian and Luxembourg law is comparable to that under English domestic law for negotiable instruments.

It is ironic that English law should in effect require participants in the bond markets to go abroad to overcome the difficulties it raises, and a legislative solution to these problems would be welcome.

9   Taxation consequences

This section will consider the taxation consequences of the computerisation of the markets in bearer securities.

(a)   Withholding tax

A concern among the issuers of eurobonds is to retain the benefit of the 'Eurobond exemption'. This concerns withholding tax payable on UK-source interest. There are clear commercial advantages for issuers and investors if interest is to be paid gross. Under section 349(2) of the Income and Corporation Taxes Act 1988 ('ICTA'), interest paid to a person in the UK must in general be paid net of withholding tax, subject to certain exceptions. One exception is created by section 124, broadly and inter alia in favour of interest paid on any quoted Eurobond held in a recognised clearing system and beneficially owned by a non-UK resident. Cedel, Euroclear, the Depositary Trust Company of New York, the European Settlements Office and the First Chicago Clearing Centre are currently recognised clearing systems for this purpose. A 'quoted Eurobond' is defined as a security which, inter alia, is in bearer form.[1] This raises the following concern. The benefit of the Eurobond exemption may be lost in respect of computerised bearer securities, because the interest of the investor in such securities is unallocated and intangible (ie not in bearer form).

---

[1] Section 124(6)(c).

The concern is more apparent than real, in the case of immobilised and global securities. Although the interest of the investor may not be in bearer form, the global or definitive paper issued by the issuer is expressed on its face to be in bearer form, and it is on this paper that interest is payable by the issuer.

(b)   Stamp duty

For the purposes of stamp duty, the London legal community has considered whether issues of global securities may fall for taxation purposes within the definition of a unit trust (on the basis that the second Intermediary or clearer was the trustee). It did so because adverse tax consequences would flow from an issue of globals being a unit trust. Firstly, prior to 1988, unit trust instrument duty was payable upon the creation of a unit trust; however, unit trust instrument duty was abolished in 1988. Secondly, transfers of units generally attract stamp duty.[1] Of course, stamp duty is a tax on instruments of transfer, and will not affect dematerialised transfers. However these may attract stamp duty reserve tax ('SDRT') which is payable on agreements to transfer chargeable securities.

Chargeable securities are defined in section 99 of the Finance Act 1986 to include units under unit trust schemes. While depositary receipts are exempted from the definition, there is no exemption for other interests held through clearing systems. Accordingly, if global securities and immobilised securities are units in unit trusts, secondary market transactions in them may attract SDRT. This would be particularly hard because the Revenue imposes a triple charge on transfers of securities into clearing systems under sections 70 to 72 and 96 to 97 of the Finance Act 1986 (equating to a triple charge for depositary receipt arrangements in sections 67 to 69 and 93 to 95 of the same Act) on the basis that transfers thereafter will not attract stamp duty.

The taxation definition of unit trust that applied before 1987 might arguably have been wide enough to catch arrangements for immobilised and global securities.[2] However, the definition in section 57 was amended by the Finance Act 1987 generally to follow the definition of unit trust in the Financial Services Act 1986.[3]

---

[1] In the case of unit trusts expressly established as such, stamp duty is avoided by structuring secondary market transactions as issues and redemptions; while transfers to the manager of the unit trust do take place, these are subject to special provisions.

[2] Section 57(1) of the Finance Act 1946 used to provide:
'"unit trust scheme" means any arrangements made for the purpose, or having the effect, of providing, for persons having funds available for investment, facilities for the participation by them, as beneficiaries under a trust, in any profits or income arising from the acquisition, holding, management or disposal of any property whatsoever.'

[3] Section 75(8) of the Financial Services Act provides as follows:
'In this Act–
  "a unit trust scheme" means a collective investment scheme under which the property in question is held on trust for the participants; . . .'
Section 75(1) provides:
'In this Act "a collective investment scheme" means, subject to the provisions of this section, any arrangements with respect to property of any description, including money, the purpose or effect of which is to enable persons taking part in the arrangements (whether by becoming owners of the property or any part of it or otherwise) to participate in or receive profits or income arising from the acquisition, holding, management or disposal of the property of sums paid out of such profits or income.'

Immobilised and global securities do not fall within the new definition.[1] For this reason, they are not unit trusts for taxation purposes or subject to SDRT.

10   Regulatory consequences

(a)   Collective investment schemes

For the reasons outlined above, arrangements for immobilised and global securities are not collective investment schemes for the purposes of the Financial Services Act 1986. However, it is arguable that if investors delegated management decisions to the first intermediary, the arrangement might fall within the definition of a collective investment scheme. The regulatory consequences of this would be that promotion restrictions would apply under section 76, and that the business of operating the arrangement would amount to investment business requiring authorisation under the Financial Services Act 1986. In addition, SDRT might be payable.

(b)   Balance sheet

The intermediation of computerised securities should not affect their risk weighting for the purposes of regulatory capital. Although, it has been argued, the interest of the investor is equitable, unallocated and generally enforceable only through the intermediary, the investor does not take the credit risk of the intermediary, because its interest is protected in the intermediary's insolvency by a trust. Risk weighting follows credit risk, which remains that of the underlying issuer.

11   General conclusions

The operational result of the computerisation of debt securities has been intermediation and intangibility. The legal consequence under English law is that computerised debt securities are not negotiable instruments but are interests under equitable tenancies in common. The loss of negotiability does not necessarily entail the loss of the benefits of negotiability. A number of alternative arguments are available under English domestic and private international law to demonstrate that written transfers are unnecessary for secondary market transactions, and it can be shown that the purchaser takes the securities free of any issuer's equities on the basis of estoppel. In theory, it is not entirely clear that, under English domestic law, the purchaser takes free of the true owner's equities. However, modern tracing rules lessen the

[1] It may be argued that arrangements for immobilised securities and global securities do not satisfy this primary definition as the purpose and effect of such arrangements are not participation in or receipt of profits or income. Although that may be the purpose and effect of investment in the underlying issue, the purpose and effect of interposing an intermediary to create immobilised or global securities are the achievement of settlement efficiencies and compliance with US securities restrictions. In any case, immobilised and global securities are taken out of the definition by virtue of section 75(2), which provides that:
  'The arrangements must be such that the persons who are to participate as mentioned in sub-section (1) above ... [ie Investors] do not have day to day control over the management of the property in question...'.

impact of true owner's equities by spreading the burden of any shortfall ratably among all participants in the relevant clearing system. In any case, English private international law will probably refer questions of adverse proprietary rights to the law of the place of the clearing system in which intermediate securities are held, and the local law of the major clearers addresses these problems. In general, computerisation has no adverse taxation or balance sheet consequences. While the old bases for a legally robust secondary market have been lost, new ones are available. The fundamental legal nature of the securities has changed, but the legal operation of the secondary markets should be unaffected.

C   Registered computerised securities[1]

This section will assess the impact of computerisation on the legal nature of registered securities.

1   Computerisation[2]

Examples of English computerised registered securities are securities held in the CGO and CREST.[3] All computerised registered securities are intangible. In addition, repackaged securities are unallocated, and indirect (because of the interposition of the depositary).

It was argued above that computerisation has had a profound effect on the legal nature of bearer securities[4] by giving them these characteristics. However, it will be argued that (in the case of registered securities) these characteristics do not represent significant changes, because of the nature of traditional registered securities.

2   Intangible nature of traditional registered securities

The paradigm registered security is the share. Shares are intangible. A share is not the same as a share certificate, which is not a document of title but a document evidencing title.[5]

This chapter will argue that shares are also unallocated and indirect. These

---

[1] Registered securities in computerised form will be referred to as computerised registered securities, and registered securities not in computerised form as traditional registered securities.

[2] Transfers of stock through the CGO ('exempt transfers') are removed from the scope of section 53(1)(c) by the provisions of section 1(2) of the Stock Transfer Act 1982.

There is no need for CGO transfers to comply with the restrictions in section 136, for the following reasons. Section 136 provides an exception to the general common law restriction on the assignment of choses in action. A more appropriate exemption is provided under a special statutory regime for stock. Section 47(1)(a) of the Finance Act 1942 (as amended by the Stock Transfer Act 1982) permits the Treasury to make regulations providing 'for the transfer in law by instruments in writing or otherwise' of government stock. Under this section, the following provision was made in paragraph 4 of the Government Stock Regulations 1965 (SI 1965/1420 as amended by SI 1981/1004 and SI 1985/1146), which permits stock to be transferred through the CGO without written instruments.

Outside the CGO, instruments of transfer are currently required by paragraph 4 of the Government Stock Regulations 1965 (SI 1965/1420).

[3] See the separate chapters on these topics.

[4] Although this legal change does not necessarily have adverse commercial consequences.

[5] A share is a chose in action (*Colonial Bank v Whinney* (1886) 11 App Cas 426).

features are only clear when one examines the history of company law, and in particular its debts to the laws of partnership and equity.

3 Unallocated nature of traditional registered securities

(a) Partnership[1]

The unallocated nature of traditional registered securities owes much to the law of partnership. When, after the South Sea Bubble, the Bubble Act of 1720 rendered incorporation impracticable, business ventures were conducted through unregistered associations. These associations were, at law, partnerships[2] with transferable stock. Thus, the commercial and financial activity of the industrial revolution was supported largely by the company in the form of a partnership.

(b) Undivided share

Partnership property is undivided, for it is held by the partners under a joint tenancy.

This accords with the historical function of the registered security, which developed as a means of permitting interests in joint stock to be transferable.[3] While the terminology used to describe this interest has varied, the characteristic that distinguished the joint stock companies from the older forms of association that preceded them was the fact that the interest of each investor was undivided. This is of course reflected today in the balance sheet treatment of registered securities.[4]

(c) Registered debt securities

Registered securities may be issued in the form of debentures, or as debt as well as in the form of equity. However, registered debt securities as well as shares are unallocated: while shares represent the undivided interest of members of a company in its capital, registered debt represents the undivided interest of co-debtors to an entity in the common debt.[5]

(d) No identity

A registered security represents the undivided and indistinguishable interest of the investor in assets which are jointly co-owned by it with all other investors

---

[1] Today the term company is generally used to mean a company incorporated under the Companies Acts, and a distinction is made between corporations (having legal personality and limited liability) and partnerships, having neither. (The registered limited partnership is a hybrid.) However, historically, this distinction was not so clear. There is no necessary link between limited liability and separate legal personality: see RR Formoy, *The Historical Foundations of Modern Company Law*, (1923), London, Sweet & Maxwell, p 58. Moreover there is some old authority for treating partnerships as having separate legal personality: Holdsworth, Vol III, pp 197, 198.
[2] 'Legally speaking these bodies were partnerships...' PS Atiyah, *The Rise and Fall of Freedom of Contract*, (1979), Clarendon Press, Oxford, p 562.
[3] See *Re Bahia and San Francisco Rly Co* (1868) LR 3 QB 584 per Blackburn J at 595, 596.
[4] With, in general, no allocation between the two sides of the balance sheet.
[5] See Holdsworth, *History of English Law*, Vol III, p 207.

in securities of the same issue. Because they are not legally divided one from the other, registered securities are legally indistinguishable one from the other.

The law in this area is somewhat unclear, but the better view is that there is no inherent identity in registered securities.[1] It is impossible to distinguish A's securities from B's securities (except of course by reference to their current ownership), not merely because they are the same as each other, but because they are not divided from each other.[2]

(e)   Numbering of shares

Case law relating to the numbering of shares is somewhat contradictory. The better authority seems to be *Ind's Case*,[3] which held that shares having different numbers do not differ one from the other.[4]

(f)   Fraudulent transfer cases

Case law relating to fraudulent transfers of registered securities also indicate that traditional registered securities are unallocated.

The point is well illustrated in *Bank of England v Cutler*.[5] Following the fraudulent transfer, the name of the original stockholder was removed from the register, and later restored to the register. During this period, her property and title were unaffected.[6] The case indicates that her interest was quantitative and not qualitative, in the sense that her property and title did not attach to particular units of stock.[7]

'There is no identity in stock'.[8] Issues of traditional registered securities are divided into units for the purpose of quantification, but not for the purpose of individual identification, for they are undivided.

---

[1] In the discussion that follows it is assumed that the securities in question belong to a class, all the securities in which are pari passu and fully paid.

[2] This is the position as between the issuer and the investors. The position differs if the interests of third parties are taken into account. For example: Company A issues to both B and C shares in a class all of which are fully paid and pari passu. As between A, B and C, all the shares are the same. If B charges its shares to D, as far as D is concerned, A's shares and B's shares differ in that A's shares (and not B's shares) are subject to its charge. This is a further example of the relative nature of property discussed in chapter 3, above. In this discussion the interests of third parties will not be considered further.

[3] (1872) 7 Ch App 485.

[4] 'I think that the numbering of the shares is simply directory for the purposes of enabling the title of particular persons to be traced, but that one share, being merely an incorporeal right to a certain portion of the profits of the company, is the same as another, and that share No 1 is not distinguishable for that purpose from share No 2, in the same way that a grey horse is distinguishable from a black horse.' Per Mellish LJ at 487.

[5] [1907] 1 KB 889.

[6] Per Lawrence J at 908.

[7] Indeed the judgment prevents one from considering her interest in qualitative terms. If her interest had consisted of a particular parcel of stock, it must have ceased to attach to the original stock when that was transferred from her, and can only have attached to the new stock when that was in turn transferred to her. However the judgment indicates that her title to stock was continuous. Although the bank was under a duty to buy in stock in order to eliminate any dilution of the total stock in issue, this buying in was not a precondition of the stockholder's proprietary interest, for she never lost it. '... [W]hen this had been done her property in law and her apparent title upon the books would once more accord' per Lawrence LJ at 908.

[8] Per Lawrence J at 909.

(g) Contrast bearer securities

In their unallocated nature, traditional registered securities differ from physical bearer securities, which are historically derived, not from joint stock enterprises, but from commercial trading debt. Although today both registered and bearer securities are launched in the primary market in large issues, physical bearer securities were issued singly long before they were issued in large numbers together. Traditional registered securities were never issued singly. A traditional registered security represents an unallocated share of a larger fund, whereas a physical bearer security constitutes a distinct debt: it is constituted by a separate covenant to pay, or chose in action in favour of the holder, whereas a registered security is a fractional share in the obligation of the issuer.

4 The historically indirect nature of traditional registered securities

(a) Repackaged securities

The repackaging of securities into depositary receipts involves the intermediation of a depositary, who holds its interest in the underlying securities on trust for investors. Their interest is indirect and equitable. This does not represent a radical departure from the position of traditional registered securities, which historically owes much to the law of trusts.

(b) Equity

Unincorporated companies sought to address the legal difficulties associated with the lack of separate legal personality, by appointing trustees under deeds of settlement. The trustees could hold and convey the company's assets, and bring any actions in the name of the company. While the common law would govern the relations between the trustees and the outside world, the internal affairs of the company (including its winding up) were governed by equity. Another reason for avoiding the common law courts was the irregular status of these associations during the currency of the Bubble Act. Equitable jurisdiction over unincorporated commercial associations was well established by the late 17th century.

Registered shares were brought out of equity and into the common law by the Joint Stock Companies Act of 1856, which replaced the deed of settlement with a memorandum of association, thereby ending the central role of the trust in the constitution of companies. However, it is still customary for issues of registered debentures to be made under a trust deed, so that registered corporate debt remains in most cases equitable and not legal.

5 Summary

The computerisation of registered securities has not changed their fundamental legal nature, as both traditional and computerised registered securities are intangible and unallocated.

D   Conclusions – bearer and registered securities

This chapter has considered the consequences of computerisation for the legal nature of securities. It has been shown that, for bearer securities, computerisation has cost negotiability. However, in practice the secondary markets should not be affected, as the benefits of negotiability are available by other means. In the case of registered securities, computerisation has no profound effect on the legal nature of the security.

It was shown above that the effect of computerisation was (broadly speaking) to turn bearer securities from negotiable instruments into intermediate securities. It was noted that intermediate securities are unallocated, intangible and equitable. The difference between bearer and registered securities might be summarised as follows:

(i) Unallocated and allocated   While the interest of the holder of a registered security is unallocated, the interest of the holder of a bearer security is allocated; a bearer security is not an undivided share of a larger fund co-owned with other investors, but a distinct debt owed by the issuer to the bearer alone and constituted by the instrument.

(ii) Intangible and tangible   While registered securities are intangible and certificates in respect of them are merely evidence of title, in the case of bearer securities the chose in action against the issuer is locked up in the bearer document, which is a tangible document of title.

(iii) Equity and the law merchant   While the law relating to registered securities owes much to equity, bearer securities are the creation of the law merchant.

On this basis, it is submitted that the effect of computerisation has been to turn bearer securities into registered securities.

Chapter 4

Computerisation and the custody relationship[1]

The effect of computerisation on the legal nature of securities has been considered. Its effect on the legal nature of the custody relationship will now be assessed.

1 The traditional view

The global custodian usually maintains two types of account in the name of the client: securities accounts and cash accounts. The cash from time to time credited to the cash accounts may represent the proceeds of sale of custody assets, dividends and other income received in respect of custody securities.

Both the cash and the securities accounts represent choses in action owned by the client. The cash accounts represent debts owed by the custodian. The traditional view is that the securities accounts represent choses in action owed directly by the underlying issuer, and held for the client by the custodian as bailee.

2 Cash

(a) The debtor/creditor principle

Custodians have traditionally been banks. It is a clearly established principle that the deposit of cash with a bank establishes the relationship of debtor and creditor between the bank and the depositor.[2] Customers' money is not held by the bank by way of trust.[3] The bank is free to use the deposited money as it pleases[4] and the depositor's rights of repayment are contractual and not proprietary.[5] On the bank's insolvency, therefore, the depositor must prove as an unsecured creditor.[6]

It has generally been assumed that the debtor/creditor principle applies

---

[1] See J Benjamin, *Custody; an English Law Analysis*, (1994) 9 JIBFL 121.
[2] *Carr v Carr* (1811) 1 Mer 541n.
[3] *Foley v Hill* (1848) 2 HL Cas 28.
[4] *South Australian Insurance Co v Randell* (1869) 16 ER 775 at 759.
[5] 'True it is that in the case of money paid into the banker's account it is converted into a debt, while in the case of money placed in a special repository it remains in specie.' *Re Halletts Estate, Knatchbull v Hallett* [1874–80] All ER Rep 793 per Thesiger LJ at 746.
[6] *Space Investments Ltd v Canadian Imperial Bank of Commerce Trust Co (Bahamas) Ltd* [1986] 3 All ER 75.

to custodians in respect of clients' cash accounts.[1] Custodians generally conduct their business on the basis that it does, using the money credited to the custody cash accounts for their own purposes, and not segregating it as trust money. While this approach is probably correct, two points arise. The debtor/creditor principle applies to money deposited with banks. Custodians may not be banks, and the credit balance of the custody cash accounts may not represent deposits.

(b)   Trust over cash

The credit balances of the cash accounts may represent not deposits, but rather the proceeds of sale of custody assets or income derived from custody assets. Section 3, below, will argue that (notwithstanding the traditional view), in a computerised environment, custody assets may in most cases be held by the custodian not as bailee but as trustee for the client. The proceeds of sale of trust property,[2] and income derived from trust property,[3] are generally subject to the same trusts as the property to which they relate. This raises the risk for custodians of a duty to segregate cash.

The answer to this problem for the bank custodian is provided by the case of *Space Investments*.[4] In this case it was held that, where a bank trustee lawfully deposits trust money with itself *as banker*, it becomes beneficially entitled to that money, and owes only a contractual duty of repayment. In order to be certain of benefiting from this rule, bank custodians should consider including express wording in their custody agreements, authorising them to deposit any trust money credited to the cash accounts with themselves *as banker*.

Under the Client Money Regulations,[5] client money held by persons authorised under the Financial Services Act 1986 in connection with investment business must in general be held on a statutory trust in accordance with those regulations. However, the regulations do not apply to an approved bank, insofar as it holds money on behalf of its clients in an account with itself.[6] 'Approved bank' is defined to include (in respect of accounts opened in the UK) an institution authorised under the Banking Act 1987. Moreover, a pure custodial service (ie one involving only safekeeping, settlement and administration) does not currently involve investment business for the purposes of the Financial Services Act, so that the Client Money Regulations will not apply. However, this will change when the Financial Services Act 1986 is extended to cover custody in the near future.

(c)   Deposit-taking business

Section 3 of the Banking Act 1987 provides that no person shall in the United Kingdom accept a deposit in the course of carrying on a deposit-taking

---

[1] Barings Brothers & Co Limited is a global custodian. In March 1995, after the company went into administration and before the announcement of the agreement of ING Bank to buy the Barings group and take over its debts, it was generally assumed that the balance of the cash accounts held by the company for the pension funds which were its custody clients was at risk. This money amounted to some £100 million.
[2] See *Re Hallett's Estate, Knatchbull v Hallett* [1874–80] All ER Rep 793.
[3] *Swain v Law Society* [1981] 3 All ER 797, 813, CA per Lord Justice Oliver.
[4] *Space Investments Ltd v Canadian Imperial Bank of Commerce Trust Co (Bahamas) Ltd* [1986] 3 All ER 75.
[5] The Financial Services (Client Money) Regulations 1995.
[6] Paragraph 4 of regulation 1.02.

business other than an authorised institution.[1] Breach of section 3 is a criminal offence.

While the point is arguable, it would be prudent to assume that the maintenance of a custody cash account may amount to deposit-taking business for this purpose. Regulation 14 of the Banking Act 1987 (Exempt Transactions) Regulations 1988[2] creates an exemption in favour of the acceptance of deposits (broadly) by a person who is authorised under the Financial Services Act 1986, if accepted in the course of or for the purpose of engaging in dealing, arranging deals, managing investments or operating collective investment schemes with or on behalf of the depositor. Custodians are generally (but not universally) so authorised. However, it would be prudent to assume that the provision of the core custodial services does not amount to an 'investment business' activity for the purposes of the exemption.

Therefore any global custodian which is not a bank should maintain a custody cash account as client money in the name of the client with a third party bank and operate the account as trustee on the client's behalf.

3 Securities

The traditional characterisation of the custodian in respect of securities[3] (and other non-cash assets such as bullion[4]) is as the bailee of the client.

> 'A bailment arises whenever specific goods are delivered into the possession of someone other than the person immediately entitled to them, on condition that those identical goods are returned to the deliveror or disposed of in accordance with his instructions when the purpose of the bailment is fulfilled'.[5, 6]

The essence of bailment is the delivery of possession (as opposed to the delivery of title) by the bailor to the bailee. Thus, the custodian has possession of the custody securities, but they are owned by the client and are unavailable to the creditors of the custodian upon its insolvency.

This traditional view of the custody relationship is challenged by computerisation for a number of reasons. The chief of these is dematerialisation. As discussed in chapter 3, securities are increasingly intangible, they are therefore incapable of possession and bailment.[7] This section will argue that the natural characterisation of the modern custody relationship under English

---

[1] 'Deposit' is defined in section 5 broadly as a sum of money paid on terms under which it will be repaid with or without interest on demand or at an agreed time, and which is not referrable to the provision of property or services or the giving of security. Section 6 provides broadly that the term 'deposit-taking' applies to a business if in its course money received by way of deposit is lent to others, or any other activity of the business is financed wholly or to any material extent out of the capital or the interest on money received by way of deposit.

[2] SI 1988/646 (as amended).

[3] 'These bonds are her bonds deposited with Mr Hallett according to the receipt, for safe custody, which would make him, no doubt, an ordinary bailee.' *Re Hallett's Estates, Knatchbull v Hallett* [1874–80] All ER Rep 793, per Jessell MR at 708. See also *Kahler v Midland Bank* [1950] AC 24, HL.

[4] See *Dollfus Mieg v Bank of England* [1949] Ch 369.

[5] NE Palmer, *Liability of Bankers as Custodians of Client Property*, p 1.

[6] See also the classification of bailments in the judgment of Holt CJ in *Coggs v Bernard* (1703) 2 Ld Raym 909.

[7] For a discussion of whether an intangible is capable of possession, see chapter 2, section 2, above.

domestic law is therefore not bailment, but trust (with the consequent commercial need for the custodian carefully to limit the level of its duties by contract).[1]

(a) Possession

A similarity between trustees and bailees is that both may (if so authorised) delegate the safekeeping of the asset entrusted to their care to another person.[2] A trustee may appoint a sub-custodian; a bailee may appoint a sub-bailee. Thus, neither is obliged to retain possession of the property.

A difference between trusts and bailments is that while trust property may be incapable of possession (ie it may be intangible for '... any property may be held in trust'[3]), 'the essence of bailment is possession ... without possession there can be no relationship of bailor and bailee.'[4]

The traditional analysis of the custodian as bailee is based on the deposit with the custodian of physical documents such as bearer bonds. '"Custody" here clearly relates to the possession or control of the certificates as physical objects.'[5] As discussed in chapter 3, the securities held in modern global custody are dematerialised (or immobilised, in global form or repackaged), and represented, not by physical certificates, but by entries in the books of the relevant intermediary. In the hands of the global custodian, such securities are intangible.

Chapter 2, above, argued that intangible property is incapable of possession. Accordingly, it is '... improbable that the courts will develop the ... supposition that there may be a bailment of an intangible thing.'[6] 'It is almost universally agreed that no one can become a bailee without possession of a tangible chattel.'[7] The apparent incompatibility of intangibles with bailment, and their compatibility with trust, suggests that the global custodian is a trustee.

(b) Fungible custody and equivalent redelivery

Global custodial arrangements in respect of securities are often fungible, in the following sense. The global custodian aggregates client holdings in a particular security into one commingled holding ('client holding'). In the case of securities held through a sub-custodian, the client holding will be represented in the books of the sub-custodian by an account in the name of the global custodian. In cases where a sub-custodian is not employed, the client holding in registrable securities will be registered in the name of the global custodian or its nominee, and the client holding in bearer securities (held through a clearing system in which the global custodian is a participant) will be held in an account in the name of the global custodian. While the global custodian's house position in any security will be segregated from the client holding, there will in general be no record of any allocation between clients in the

---

[1] For a discussion of contractual limitation of implied fiduciary duty, see chapter 8, below.
[2] Subject to the general principle, *delegatus non potest delegare*, or a delegate may not delegate.
[3] *Snell's Principles of Equity*, (28 edn, 1982), Sweet & Maxwell, London, p 92.
[4] *Palmer*, p 192.
[5] *Swiss Bank Corpn v Lloyds Bank Ltd* [1980] 2 All ER 419, CA, per Buckley LJ 431.
[6] Palmer, *Bailment*, p 13.
[7] Ibid, p 99. See also Dias, *Jurisprudence*, at 281: 'A bailee is a person who gets possession of a chattel from another with his consent.'

books of the sub-custodian, in the relevant register of registrable securities or the books of the global depositary, as the case may be. The only note of the respective entitlements of the individual clients to the client holding will be in the books of the global custodian. This arrangement will be referred to as 'fungible custody'.[1]

Thus, while it is possible at any time to determine how many of the individual securities comprised in the client holding are attributable to a particular client, it is not possible to determine which ones.

A corollary of fungible custody is that the redelivery obligation owed by the global custodian to clients is not an obligation to return the securities originally deposited in specie, but merely an obligation to return securities equivalent to those originally deposited. The shares that a client receives (or delivers) out of global custody will almost certainly not be the same ones that it put in. The pooling of different clients' custody securities is not incompatible with trust. Provided that the custodian segregates the deposited assets from its own, a trust may be identified over the whole of the custody assets, of which the custody clients are equitable tenants in common. This idea will be developed in chapter 5, below.

However, case law indicates that the deposit of fungibles without a duty of segregation and without in specie redelivery rights may not be compatible with bailment. In *South Australian Insurance Co Ltd v Randell*[2] it was held that an arrangement having these features was not a bailment. The case of *United States of America v Dollfus Mieg et Compagnie, SA*[3] provides further evidence for the view that fungible custody and equivalent redelivery are incompatible with bailment. This case indicates that where there is no segregation, there is no bailment and a creditor/debtor relationship arises. These cases indicate that fungible custody is incompatible with bailment. However, conflicting authority is available in *Harding v Inland Revenue Comr*[4] that, while traditionally bailment requires the in specie return of the goods originally deposited, 'equivalent' redelivery obligations are compatible with bailment. See also *Mercer v Craven*.[5] In this case, the plaintiff's property was commingled with other property in the hands of the defendant, while there was clear contractual provision that the plaintiffs should retain title. The defendant was held to be a bailee, and the plaintiffs were owners in common of the bulk. Thus, provided it can be shown that the parties intended that the client should retain a proprietary interest in the custody securities, the mere fact that the bank's redelivery obligations are 'equivalent' and not in specie may not itself defeat such intention.

(c) Summary

While fungible custody is not necessarily incompatible with bailment, dematerialisation probably is.

The role of the custodian has evolved far beyond its traditional role as a bailee. The question arises, has it taken the law relating to bailment with

---

[1] Reasons for fungible custody include economies of scale, administrative convenience and accounting facility.
[2] (1869) 6 Moo PCCNS 341.
[3] [1952] AC 582 HL.
[4] [1976] 1 NZLR 337.
[5] (12 February 1993, unreported), CA; affd (17 March 1994, unreported), HL.

it, so that bailment may now relate to intangibles? Or has it left bailment behind so that now the global custodian is a trustee?

In the absence of direct judicial authority, it would be prudent to assume that the law is today what it was yesterday, and that the global custodian, by moving into the late 20th century, has moved into a new legal category, and is a trustee.[1] This accords with the approach in the US with the revised article 8 of the Uniform Commercial Code:

'Relatively early in the drafting process, the decision was reached to eschew the approach of trying to squeeze the analysis of the property interest of a person who holds securities through an intermediary into old legal concepts, such as bailment.'[2]

(d)   Custodian trustees

Global custodians who are trustees should not be confused with custodian trustees for the purposes of section 4(3) of the Public Trustee Act 1907. Statutory custodian trustees hold trust property while leaving the administration and management of the trust to managing trustees. Custodian trustees may be appointed in connection with a debenture issue.

---

[1] For a contrary view, see A Beaves *Global Custody – A Tentative Analysis of Property and Contract Interests in Goods*, (1993) ed N Palmer and E McEndrick, Lloyds of London Press, London. The bailment analysis will still, of course, be available where physical instruments are held.

[2] JS Rogers, *Policy Perspectives on Revised UCC Article 8*, UCLA Law Rev, June 1996, p 1431, at p 1496.

Chapter 5

The allocation problem[1]

A Identity in securities

Recent case law has caused some concern in London among custodians and their clients, and prompted a debate in the legal community about what will be referred to in this work as 'the allocation problem'. This arises where there is fungible custody.[2] The allocation problem is the possible legal difficulty in asserting proprietary rights over assets forming part of the commingled pool, when one cannot identify which particular assets within the pool are subject to such proprietary rights.

B The allocation problem

1 Loss of property risk

The allocation problem concerns '... the law's insistence that proprietary rights cannot be acquired in fungibles forming an unidentified part of a bulk until they have been separated by some suitable act of appropriation'.[3] This arises both at law and in equity. The common law rule is well established in case law concerning the sale of goods,[4] and is given statutory force in section 16 of the Sale of Goods Act 1979.[5] The rule in equity is based on the principle

---

[1] See J Benjamin, *Custody; an English Law Analysis*, (1994) 9 JIBFL 188.

[2] This term was defined in chapter 4 to mean, broadly, the commingling of the assets of different clients in a pool.

[3] RM Goode, *Ownership and Obligation in Commercial Transactions*, LQR 103, July 1987, 433 at 436.

[4] See *Healy v Howlett & Sons* [1917] 1 KB 337; *Re Wait* [1927] 1 Ch 606; *Carlos Federspiel & Co SA v Charles Twigg & Co Ltd* [1957] 1 Lloyd's Rep 240; *Re London Wine Co (Shippers) Ltd* [1986] PCC 121; *Re Stapylton Fletcher Ltd* [1994] 1 WLR 1181, and other cases referred to in the last cited case.

[5] This provides as follows: 'Subject to section 20A below, where there is a contract for the sale of unascertained goods no property in the goods is transferred to the buyer unless and until the goods are ascertained.'

Section 20A (inserted by the Sale of Goods (Amendment) Act 1994, section 1(1) in response to Law Commission paper No 215) provides for title in ex-bulk goods to pass under a tenancy in common, where the purchase price has been paid.

The rule relates to goods, and securities are not goods but (generally) choses in action. Goods are defined in Section 61(1) of the Sale of Goods Act to exclude things in action.

that a trust cannot be validly established without certainty of subject matter.[1] Accordingly, a trust cannot be created by the legal owner of a commingled pool of assets who purports to transfer to a beneficiary equitable title of an unallocated portion of that pool.[2]

Because, in fungible custody, the custody securities of respective clients are not individually identifiable, some commentators have argued that the rights of clients may be confined (broadly) to a contractual right against the custodian, arising under the custody agreement, to call for redelivery of securities equivalent to those deposited.[3] The risk that clients' rights in this respect may be merely contractual will be called 'loss of property risk'.

The implications are serious, both for the clients and for the custodian. With loss of property risk, the client's assets would be available to general creditors in the custodian's insolvency. Clear tax problems would arise.[4] Further, the value of the portfolio as collateral would be reduced.[5] It is therefore important to address the allocation problem (and therefore loss of property risk) in the context of custody.

2   The cases

Debate about the allocation problem has focused on the following line of cases.

(a)   Re London Wine (Shippers) Ltd[6]

This case concerned a wine importing company to which a receiver had been appointed pursuant to a floating charge in favour of a bank. The company held wine in various warehouses. Most of the wine had been sold to individuals who left the wine in the possession of the company's warehouse agent. There was no segregation of any wine crates or cases in favour of any particular individual. The individuals claimed that they had a proprietary interest in

---

[1] *Knight v Knight* (1840) 3 Beav 148.
[2] See *Re Wait* [1927] 1 Ch 606.
[3] See RM Goode, *Ownership and Obligation in Commercial Transactions*, (1987) 103 LQR, 433 and Robert Ryan, *Taking Security Over Investment Portfolios held in Global Custody*, [1990] 10 JIBL 404.
[4] If the delivery of securities by the client to the custodian involves transferring property in those securities to the custodian, and if the redelivery of securities to the client at the end of the custody arrangement involves transferring property in those securities to the client (or to its order) both steps may be treated as a disposal for taxation purposes giving rise to a potential liability for capital gains tax (or corporation tax on chargeable gains). Furthermore, if the entire property interest passes to the custodian, so too will the entitlement to underlying tax credits, leaving the custodian potentially in the position of a dividend manufacturer and potentially prejudicing the availability of treaty reliefs. The stamp duty implications of such transfers would also need to be reviewed if they involved a change in the beneficial ownership of the securities concerned. (Clearly, this is not the way that custody is viewed by the Inland Revenue. If it were, the extensive collecting agent rules would be redundant, and the manufactured dividend legislation would have been introduced and achieved greater prominence far earlier.)
[5] If the client has no proprietary rights in the custody securities, he cannot charge those securities (whether in favour of the custodian or a third party). It has been suggested, however, that a charge may be given over the client's contractual rights against the custodian under the custody agreement. The value of such security to any third party will depend upon the credit risk of the custodian. Thus, the value of portfolios of securities held in custody as collateral for borrowing will be reduced, as it will be subject to the credit risk of the custodian as well as that of the issuer.
[6] [1986] PCC 121.

the relevant crates or cases of wine. The receiver argued that they had merely unsecured claims for delivery of wine against the company.

Judgment was given in favour of the receiver, on the basis that the individuals did not have any proprietary interests in the wine because there had been no allocation; proprietary rights could not pass at law for want of allocation or in equity for want of certainty of subject matter.

(b)   Re Stapylton Fletcher Ltd[1]

The facts of this case were similar to those of *Re London Wine*, except that the wine intended for customers was segregated from the trading stock of the company. This difference was held to be crucial[2] and judgment was given in favour of the claimants from the liquidators. 'They will take as tenants in common.'[3]

As custodians segregate their house positions from client holdings, it might be thought that fungible custody can benefit from the rule in *Stapylton Fletcher*. However, the allocation problem concerns want of certainty of subject matter for an equitable interest to arise, and the case (unlike *Re London Wine*) related only to legal interests arising in the sale of goods.[4] A later case, *Re Goldcorp*, considered both equity and law.

(c)   Hunter v Moss

Hunter v Moss[5] may be of assistance in the search for authority that a trust can be created over an unallocated part of a holding of registered securities. The facts of this case were as follows. Moss was the registered holder of 950 shares in a company with 1,000 shares in issue. Moss made a declaration of trust over 5% of the company's issued share capital in favour of Hunter. A valid trust was held to have been created over 50 of Moss's shares. Moss applied by motion for the judgment to be recalled, arguing that the trust failed for want of certainty of subject matter.

The motion was dismissed by Rimer QC, on the basis that, in a trust over intangibles, the requirement for certainty of subject matter does not necessarily entail segregation or appropriation.

> 'The defendant did not identify any particular 50 shares for the plaintiff because to do so was unnecessary and irrelevant. All 950 of his shares carried identical rights ... Any suggested uncertainty as to subject matter appears to me to be theoretical and conceptual rather than real and practical.'[6]

---

[1] *Re Stapylton Fletcher Ltd, Re Ellis, Son & Vidler Ltd* [1944] 1 WLR 1181.

[2] 'I do not regard that decision [in *Re London Wine*] as inevitably governing the case before me. One obvious difference in the present case is the segregation of the wine purchased by the customers in a separate part of the warehouse and the careful maintenance of records within the company. Further as the London Wine Company was free to sell its stock and satisfy the customers from any other available source, there was no ascertainable bulk in that case.' per Judge Paul Baker QC at 1194.

[3] At 1200.

[4] 'As I have found for the first four claimants in the case relating to ESV on the basis of the passing of property at law, I do not have to consider the alternative lines of argument based on trusts, fiduciary relationships or other equitable principles in relation to these claims.' (at 1201).

[5] [1993] 1 WLR 934; affd [1994] 1 WLR 452, CA.

[6] Per Colin Rimer QC (sitting as deputy High Court Judge) at 946. The reasoning in the Court of Appeal does not clearly advance new arguments in support of the decision, other than analogy with probate which may be misguided.

This decision should be treated with some caution.[1] On the particular facts of the case, it was clearly in the interests of justice that a valid trust should be found. The judgment, which was pragmatic, focused more on the merits of the dispute before the court than the wider principles of equity discussed earlier in this chapter. There is plenty of authority that certainty of subject matter is essential to a trust over intangibles, which is not adequately dealt with in this case.[2] Furthermore, the shares in question were in a private company, and the implications for the custody and settlement in the markets in publicly traded securities were not considered.

(d)   Re Goldcorp Exchange Ltd (in receivership)[3]

Goldcorp, a dealer in precious metals, agreed with certain customers to sell gold to them and hold it for them on an unallocated basis. It represented that it would set aside and hold a pool of gold sufficient to meet the claims of unallocated customers, but did not do so. It became insolvent and its stock of gold was insufficient to meet unallocated customers' claims. In a dispute between receivers appointed pursuant to a floating charge and unallocated customers, judgment was given (reversing the decision of the New Zealand Court of Appeal reported in *Liggett v Kensington*) in favour of the receivers. The claims of the unallocated customers were merely contractual.

The case distinguishes 'generic' goods (the source of which is not specified) from 'ex-bulk' goods (which must come from a specified source).[4] The case for the claimants failed (both at law and in equity) because on the facts *Goldcorp* was an example of generic goods.[5] If it had been a question of ex-bulk goods, the position might have been different.[6] Thus, it could be argued that, because custodians segregate house position from client holdings, the allocation problem does not arise.

However, the position remains unclear. Nowhere is it clearly stated that if client and house assets had been segregated, the interest of unallocated clients would have been proprietary. As Cooke P understated in the court below, '... it is a difficult area of law'.[7]

Because of the seriousness of loss of property risk, the prudent view would be to assume that it may be present.

C   Equitable tenancy in common

The allocation problem can be partly addressed on the basis of timing, as follows.

---

[1] See David Hayton, *Uncertainty of Subject-Matter of Trusts*, (1994) 110 LQR 335. In particular, in the Court of Appeal, inter vivos transfers are not distinguished from testamentary transfers.

[2] See, for example, *Mac-Jordan Construction Ltd v Brookmount Erostin Ltd* [1992] BCLC 350. See also *Re Jartray Development Ltd* (1982) 22 BLR 134; *Rayack Construction v Lampeter Meat Co Ltd* (1979) 12 BLR 30; *Neste Oy v Lloyds Bank plc* [1983] 2 Lloyd's Rep 658; and *Concorde Constructions Co Ltd v Colgan Ltd* (1984) 29 BLR 120. A purported trust over an unallocated part of a pool of intangibles may create a mere charge: *Swiss Bank v Lloyds Bank* [1979] 2 All ER 853; revsd [1980] 2 All ER 419; affd [1981] 2 All ER 449.

[3] [1994] 2 All ER 806.

[4] At 814.

[5] At 814.

[6] At 820.

[7] *Liggett v Kensington* [1993] 1 NZLR 257 at 268.

1 Timing

(a) Two lines of cases

The issue under consideration in *Re London Wine* was the acquisition, by the purchasers, of proprietary interests in assets forming part of a fungible pool. The key cases discussed in the judgment relate to the sale of goods transactions in which the same issue arose, ie whether property can be effectively transferred in respect of an unallocated portion of a pool. The important point is that in all these cases the mixing of the whole *antedates* the possible ownership of part.

In one case that was discussed, the mixing of the whole *predates* the ownership of part, and this case is clearly distinguished by Oliver J.[1] This case concerned the preservation of existing proprietary rights, as opposed to the creation of new ones.

English case law makes a clear distinction between two situations. The first is where there is a purported transfer of an unidentified part of a fungible bulk without appropriation. The second is where property belonging to several persons is commingled into a fungible bulk without segregation (commingling). In the former, *Re London Wine* and *Goldcorp* indicate that new proprietary rights do not arise, whether in law or equity, and this is the Allocation Problem. In the latter, the position is different.

(b) Commingling

There is a long line of authority establishing the principle, based on Roman law, that where the goods of different owners are mixed together so that they cannot be separated, the owners will hold the commingled goods as tenants in common.[2] These cases concern accidental or wrongful commingling; the parties have not intended it or agreed upon its outcome.

(c) Old and new custody securities

This principle applies to fungible custody as follows. Those custody securities that were transferred to the custodian at the initiation of the custody relationship will be referred to as 'the old custody securities'. In the case of old custody securities, the client's proprietary interest is not extinguished, but continues as an interest in an equitable tenancy in common.

However, this may not be true of securities purchased by the client and transferred to the custodian during the currency of the custody service ('new custody securities'). Where the custodian is instructed by a client (client 1)

---

[1] 'The cases principally relied on in support of [the submission (1868) LR 3 CP 427 that the buyers own the wine as tenants in common] were *Spence v Union Marine Insurance* (1868) LR 3 CP 427, and *Inglis v Stock* (1885) 10 App Cas 263. The former is of little help because it was concerned with *a wholly different question* [the author's italics], namely, what is the result when specific goods which undoubtedly were in separate individual ownership to start with became so mixed as to be indistinguishable' at 136.

[2] See *Buckley v Gross* (1863) 3 B & S 566, 122 ER 213; *Spence v Union Marine Insurance Co Ltd* (1868) LR 3 CP 427; and *Indian Oil Corpn Ltd v Greenstone Shipping SA, The Ypatianna* [1987] 3 All ER 893.

to settle a purchase transaction of 50 bonds on its behalf, the manner in which the custodian delivers those bonds into the client's custody account may be as follows. If the counterparty employs a broker (acting as principal) who also acts for another client of the global custodian (client 2), and if client 2 purchases bonds on the same day through the same broker, the broker may aggregate the orders, or the global custodian may aggregate the settlement of the bonds of clients 1 and 2, so that one transfer of bonds into the client holding may satisfy both of them.[1]

In such a case it is not possible to identify the particular bonds to which the transaction relates. Such identification would only be possible if the delivery obligation was satisfied by a transfer into the client holding of 50 bonds (and perhaps only if no other such transfer took place on the same business day). This may be unlikely in practice. Because it may not, in practice, be possible to identify such securities before they enter the pool of the client holding, it may not be possible to argue that the holding of them is an example of commingling. Therefore it would be prudent to assume that the allocation problem may be relevant to the fungible custody of physical bearer securities.

2   Tenancy in common

However, it is possible to address loss of property risk by appropriate wording in the custody documentation expressly creating a tenancy in common.

The natural answer to the allocation problem is co-ownership. Rather than seek to identify a trust in favour of each client over their unallocated portion of the client securities, one may identify one global trust over all the client securities of a particular type in favour of all relevant clients as tenants in common.

It was shown (in section 1(b), above) that such equitable tenancies in common probably arise by operation of law in cases of confusio or commingling, in relation to old securities, so that pre-existing proprietary rights are not extinguished by fungible custody. However, it was also noted that such co-ownership arrangements may not arise by operation of law where it is sought to create new proprietary rights over part of a pool.[2] (The position differs

---

[1] Another possibility is 'internal settlement', where one client of the global custodian sells securities to another such client. 'Internal settlement. A settlement that is effected through transfers of securities and funds on the books of a single intermediary. An internal settlement requires both counterparties to maintain their securities and funds accounts with the same intermediary' Bank for International Settlements, *Cross-Border Securities Settlements*, May 1995, Basle, Glossary.

[2] See the comments of Mustill J in *Karlshamns Oljefabriker v Eastport Navigation Corpn* [1982] 1 All ER 208 at 214, quoted by Judge Paul Baker QC in *Re Stapylton Fletcher* at 1197 in the following passage: 'The passing of property is concerned with the creation of rights in rem, which the purchaser can assert, not only against the vendor but against the world at large, and which he can alienate in such a way as to create similar rights in a transferee. Where there are multiple contracts of sale in the hands of different buyers, in relation to undivided bulk, there are only two possible solutions. First, to hold that the buyers take as joint owners in undivided shares. English law has rejected this solution. The only alternative is to hold that the property does not pass until the goods are not only physically separated but separated in a way which enables an individual buyer to say that a particular portion has become his property under the contract of sale ...'. And see also *Re Goldcorp Exchange Ltd* [1994] 2 All ER 806 at 820.

in New York where, under the Uniform Commercial Code, co-ownership is implied in such circumstances.[1])

The judgment in *Re London Wine* indicates that, in these circumstances, while a tenancy in common will not arise by operation of law, it may be established by clear express provision.[2]

The prudent course would therefore be to include very clear express wording in the custody documentation to create such equitable tenancies in common among the custody clients over the commingled client holdings.

The structure of these equitable tenancies in common is comparable to the structure of a unit trust. Each client will have an interest in an undivided portion of the securities comprised in the tenancy in common equal to that which the number of such securities credited to their account in the global custodian's books bears to the total number of such securities in the client position.

A separate tenancy in common exists in relation to each type of security from time to time comprised in clients' portfolios. This is because, in practice, it will not be the case that each client's portfolio includes the same range of securities in the same proportions. A necessary feature of a tenancy in common is unity of possession.[3] 'Unity of possession is common to all forms of co-ownership. Each co-owner is as much entitled to possession of any part of the [property] as the others.'[4]

This multiplication of tenancies in common should not create any administrative difficulty, because their existence is notional and automatic, and does not require any practical step to be taken.

In conclusion, the natural solution to the allocation problem is the equitable co-ownership of the client securities by the clients under tenancies in common. The case law indicates that such arrangements may not arise by operation of law, at least in respect of New Securities. It is possible that (because the historical role of the custodian, the current market perception of that role and the taxation and regulatory treatment of global custody all indicate an intention that client property in custody assets should be preserved) the courts would hold that tenancies in common do so arise. The likelihood that the courts would not so hold may be considered remote. However, the impact of such an event would be serious. Therefore, in the absence of direct authority for tenancies in common arising over new securities by operation of law, it would be prudent to establish such equitable co-ownership arrangements

---

[1] Article 8–313. See Judge Paul Baker QC in *Re Stapylton Fletcher* at 1197: 'The reference to English law as rejecting the solution of undivided shares is a reminder that in the United States of America that solution has been adopted.'

[2] 'I cannot see how, for instance, a farmer who declares himself to be a trustee of two sheep (without identifying them) can be said to have created a perfect and complete trust whatever right he may confer by such declaration as a matter of contract. And it would seem to me to be immaterial that at the time he had a flock of sheep out of which he could satisfy the interest. Of course, he could by appropriate words, declare himself to be a trustee of a specified proportion of his whole flock and thus create an equitable tenancy in common between himself and the named beneficiary, so that a proprietary interest would arise in the beneficiary in an undivided share of the flock and its produce. But the *mere* declaration that a given number of animals would be held upon trust could not, I should have thought, without very clear words pointing to such an intention, result in the creation of an interest in common in the proportion which that number bears to the number of the whole at the time of the declaration.' Oliver J at 137.

[3] See 35 *Halsbury's Laws of England*, (4 edn), para 636.

[4] Megarry and Wade, *The Law of Real Property*, (5 edn), p 419.

by clear express wording.[1] This wording could be included in the custody contract, or even behind the scenes in a deed poll executed by the custodian.

D   Conclusions

Where the securities of more than one client are commingled in fungible custody, there is some doubt that such clients have adequate proprietary rights in such securities. Such doubt could readily be removed by legislation.[2] An alternative approach is contractual, establishing co-ownership rights in equity.[3] Such wording should be included in the custody agreement as a matter of prudence.

[1] This is the approach taken by London Settlement Systems in addressing the same legal problem arising when securities are pooled in the course of settlement. See the Talisman Clearing House Regulations, regulation E.5.13.a and the Central Gilts Office Reference Manual, section 8.2.8.

[2] See, for example, the Belgian Royal Decree No 62 of November 1967, the Luxembourg Grand-Ducal Decree of February 1971, the German Depotgesetz of 1937 and article 8–302 of the New York Uniform Commercial Code.

[3] See, for example, CGO Reference Manual, section 8.2.8 and Talisman Clearing House Regulations, regulation E.5.1.3.a.

Chapter 6

English private international law[1]

'It has not been easy for the conflict of laws to adapt itself to the changes in social and commercial life which the twentieth century has witnessed.'[2]

A General

1 Legal uncertainty

Two great changes have affected the securities markets in the late 20th century: internationalisation and computerisation. The rise of cross-border investment made global custody necessary; computers made it possible. But although securities business is international and electronic, settled law does not yet reflect this. Chapters 3 and 4 considered how traditional concepts of personal property fail adequately to account for assets in the securities markets which are intangible and unallocated.

The legal aspects of cross-border arrangements are inherently unpredictable.

While much admirable work has recently been done in advocating[3] and implementing[4] reform of private international law on a local and multi-lateral basis in developed jurisdictions, such reform will not introduce certainty into the securities markets as long as courts of unreformed countries may assume jurisdiction. The problem is particularly acute in the emerging markets, where local courts may be unlikely to decline jurisdiction in matters concerning locally issued securities, and where the legal understanding of cross-border securities arrangements may differ from that in the developed markets. For this reason, in practice, the forum of a dispute is the key issue.[5] Further, enforcement of judgments is of central importance. Even where judgment is obtained in England concerning assets held abroad, local recognition and enforcement

---

[1] This is a complex area of law, and discussed in highly summary form in this section. The following is not a systematic treatment of the subject, and merely considers those aspects of conflicts of law that are of particular interest in the context of the proprietary aspects of global custody.

[2] Dicey and Morris, *The Conflict of Laws*, (12 edn, 1993), Sweet & Maxwell, London, p 7.

[3] See Randall Guynn, *Modernising Securities Ownership, Transfer and Pledging Laws*, (1996) IBA, London.

[4] See the revised article 8 of the US Uniform Commercial Code, section 8–110.

[5] Once an action concerning foreign securities has been commenced in the jurisdiction of the issuer, the English courts would be most unlikely to entertain an action on the same issue. This underlines the importance of jurisdiction clauses in global custody documentation.

of that judgment remains a further obstacle to be surmounted, while the enforcement of competing local or foreign judgments against the assets cannot be excluded.

This chapter will consider English private international law as it relates to global custody, and the following chapter will consider general issues of private international law as they relate to taking security over, and the intermediation of, custody assets.

2   Cash and securities

Cases concerning the securities held in global custody may involve private international law, as such securities may constitute property situated in a foreign country. It might be thought that the same will be true of the cash element of a custody portfolio, but this is not the case.

A portfolio of international securities is likely to generate multi-currency cash balances. This is because income and proceeds of sale of securities are likely to be denominated in the currencies that are legal tender in the jurisdictions from which they are paid. Because of the structure of the international banking settlement system, currency is generally held in the jurisdiction in which it is legal tender.[1] Thus, where a London global custodian[2] maintains a credit balance of US $1 million for a custody client, it will not of course keep a huge pile of dollar bills in its vaults in London to match that credit balance. The asset of the global custodian corresponding to that credit balance will be a further credit balance of $1 million (or, more likely, part of a larger balance) in favour of the global custodian in the books of its correspondent bank in New York.[3] The dollar account of the global custodian at the New York correspondent may be said to constitute dollars, while that of the custody client at the London global custodian may be said to constitute Eurodollars. Where US dollar income or proceeds of sale of custody securities are paid to the global custodian on behalf of custody clients, they are likely to be paid directly to its New York correspondent bank.

Because of the use of correspondent banks, it might be thought that the global custodian is holding the client's non-sterling money overseas. However, this is not the case. The asset of the client is not the dollars in New York, but the Eurodollars in London. Chapter 4 considered the legal relationship between the custodian and its client. It was seen that, in the case of that part of the custody portfolio consisting of cash, this relationship is generally that of debtor and creditor. In other words, where a custody portfolio includes a positive balance of $1 million, the asset of the custody client is a debt owed to it by the global custodian to pay the client $1 million. The Eurodollar deposit of the global custodian with the New York correspondent is the asset, not of custody clients, but of the global custodian. The cash asset of the custody client is not located in a foreign country. For this reason, the discussion

---

[1] See the discussion of Eurodollars by Terence Prime, in *International Bonds and Certificates of Deposit*, (1990) Butterworths, London, pp 4, 5.

[2] It is assumed here that the global custodian in London is a bank.

[3] The correspondent bank is also most unlikely to keep a pile of dollar bills; instead, its asset corresponding to its dollar liability to the global custodian, is likely to be a credit balance in its favour with the Federal Reserve Bank, or a settlement bank if it does not have an account at the Fed.

of private international law in this and the following chapter will be confined to securities.

3   Approach of the courts

'The questions that arise in conflict of laws cases are of two main types: first, has the English court jurisdiction to determine this case? And secondly, if so, what law should it apply?'[1] As the first issue before the courts will always be the question of jurisdiction, it will be considered first in section B, below. Section C, below, will consider the approach of the courts to choice of law in general terms.

B   Jurisdiction

The rules that determine whether the English courts will have jurisdiction in any particular case concerning global custody, differ according to whether or not the matter is related to insolvency. Insolvency jurisdiction is considered in chapter 7. Non-insolvency jurisdiction is considered in this section.

Every action in the English High Court must be started by writ. Two different regimes apply depending on whether or not the defendant is domiciled in the EC (including England) or the EFTA. If it is so domiciled, the Civil Jurisdiction and Judgments Act 1982 (as amended by the Civil Jurisdiction and Judgments Act 1991) ('the Act') applies, harmonising English jurisdiction rules with European rules. Broadly speaking, if the defendant is domiciled elsewhere, the general law jurisdiction rules apply. These two regimes will be considered in sections 1 and 2, below; section 3, below, will go on briefly to consider the circumstances in which the court may lose or decline to exercise jurisdiction which it *prima facie* has.

1   The Act

The Act gives effect in English law to the Brussels and Lugano Conventions on Jurisdiction and the Enforcement of Judgments ('the Conventions'[2]).[3] The Brussels Convention was made between EC member states, and the Lugano Convention was made between EC and EFTA member states. The two Conventions are in like form. Title II of each of the Conventions relates to jurisdiction. Austria, Belgium, Denmark, Germany, Greece, Finland, France, Iceland, Ireland, Italy, Luxembourg, The Netherlands, Norway, Portugal, Sweden, Switzerland and the United Kingdom have signed one or both of the Conventions, and they will be referred to as contracting states.

---

[1] *Dicey and Morris*, vol 1, p 4. The passage continues, 'There may be sometimes a third question, namely, will the English court recognise or enforce a foreign judgment purporting to determine the issue between the parties?' Recognition of foreign judgments will not be considered in detail in this work.

[2] For the full titles of the Conventions, see section 1(1) of the Act.

[3] In sections 2(1) and 3A(1) of the Act respectively.

(a) Scope

Broadly speaking, the Conventions cover civil and commercial matters (but not insolvency-related matters or arbitration).

(b) Domicile

The rules determining jurisdiction under the Conventions are primarily based on the domicile of the defendant. The general rule is that a defendant may be sued in the contracting state where he is domiciled, and may be sued by another contracting state only in accordance with special rules of jurisdiction.

To determine the meaning of domicile, the Conventions and the Act must be read together. Under the Conventions, the seat of a company or other legal person is treated as its domicile.[1] In order to determine that seat, the courts must apply its rules of private international law.[2] These rules are provided in section 42 of the Act.

Under section 42, companies having a seat in England would generally include both companies incorporated in England, and foreign companies having a registered branch in England, having (in each case) a place of business (ie carrying on any activity[3]) in England (whether or not amounting to central management and control). Thus, foreign sub-custodians may be domiciled in England if they have a London branch. A company has its seat in a contracting state other than the United Kingdom if (broadly) that state is *either* its place of incorporation and registered office (or official place of service) *or* its place of central management and control[4] *and* it has its seat in that state under local law.[5]

(c) Non-exclusive jurisdiction

Defendant domiciled in England   If the defendant is domiciled in England, the English courts generally have jurisdiction.[6] They will not, however, have jurisdiction if another contracting state has exclusive jurisdiction (see section (d), below) or if proceedings have already begun in another contracting state.

This might confer jurisdiction on the English court where a suit is brought against an English global custodian or sub-custodian, or a foreign sub-custodian with a branch in London.

English trust   The English courts generally have jurisdiction in claims against a trustee or a beneficiary under a trust if the trust is domiciled in England[7] or in connection with a trust governed by English law.[8]

It was seen (in chapter 4) that the relationship between the custodian and its client under English law is likely to be characterised as that of trustee

---

[1] This provision is duplicated in section 42(1) of the Act.
[2] Article 53, first paragraph.
[3] 'Business' includes any activity carried on by a corporation or association, and 'place of business' shall be construed accordingly' (section 42(8)).
[4] Section 42(6).
[5] Section 42(7).
[6] Article 2.
[7] Article 5(6) of the Conventions.
[8] Article 17, paragraph 2 of the Conventions.

and beneficiary. A trust is domiciled in England for this purpose[1] if English law is the system of law with which the trust has its closest and most real connection. This should be the case if a global custody agreement is in place and the global custody relationship (and therefore the trust) is governed by that document. Therefore, assuming the global custody agreement is governed by English law, the English court should have jurisdiction in all litigation against the global custodian or its client concerning the proprietary and fiduciary aspects of the relationship between them.

Movable property in England While the situs of property is important in cases outside the scope of the Act and the Conventions, in general, under the Act and the Conventions, jurisdiction follows the domicile of the defendant, and not the situs of property. However, an exception is made under the Act where the defendant is domiciled in Scotland or Northern Ireland and the case concerns proprietary rights in movable property.[2]

(d) Exclusive jurisdiction

Public register Regardless of domicile, the Conventions confer exclusive jurisdiction on the courts of the relevant contracting states in certain circumstances. These include proceedings which have as their object the validity of entries in public registers,[3] and in this case jurisdiction is conferred on the courts of the contracting state in which the register is kept.[4] Dicey comments, 'In England it is not likely to be of practical significance except in connection with problems relating to registered land ...'.[5] However, it might be argued that public registers for this purpose include the registers of public companies. Thus, if a custody client sought an order that a French register be amended in its favour, the French courts might have exclusive jurisdiction in the matter.

Submission Very broadly, where two parties, one of whom is domiciled in a contracting state,[6] agree (in customary written form) that the court of a contracting state is to have jurisdiction in connection with their relationship, that court will have exclusive jurisdiction.[7]

Submission to the jurisdiction of a contracting state in a trust instrument confers exclusive jurisdiction in any proceedings brought against (inter alia) trustee or beneficiary involving the trust relationship.[8] On the basis that the

---

[1] In accordance with article 53 of the Conventions and section 45 of the Act. 'Of course it is artificial and novel to speak of the domicile of a trust at all. But it is a convenient form of shorthand.' Dicey and Morris, *The Conflict of Laws*, p 81.
[2] Including security interests, and the right to dispose of the property: Schedule 4, article 5(8).
[3] Other cases are (broadly) proceedings concerning immovable property, the constitution of companies, patents and trade marks and the enforcement of judgments.
[4] Article 16(3) of the Conventions.
[5] *Dicey and Morris*, vol 1, p 385.
[6] A different rule applies for such agreements where neither party is so domiciled: article 17, paragraph 2.
[7] Article 17 of each of the Conventions, which are in different form. For the position before the Conventions were implemented, see *Trendtex Trading v Crédit Suisse* [1980] QB 629, per Denning MR at 658: 'At once we come upon the clause which gives exclusive jurisdiction to the Court of Geneva. That clause must be given full effect unless its enforcement would be unreasonable and unjust or that the clause was invoked for such reasons as fraud...'.
[8] For exceptions to this rule, see Article 17, paragraph 4.

global custodian is a trustee, this would include jurisdiction clauses in the global custody agreement.

(e) Summary

As a broad rule, in non-insolvency related proprietary matters, it should be possible to sue the following persons in England:

- the *London global custodian* (probably under every head discussed above other than public register and movable property);
- the *client* if it is incorporated in England or has an English branch, and carries on some activity in England (English domicile);
- or if the client is domiciled in another contracting state and the global custody agreement is governed by English law (English trust) or again if there is a submission to the English courts in the global custody agreement; and
- *the foreign sub-custodian* which is domiciled in another contracting state if the sub-custody agreement is governed by English law (English trust) or contains a submission to the English court.[1]

2 General law

In cases outside the Act (broadly, where the defendant is not domiciled in the EC or EFTA)[2] the jurisdiction rules under the general law will apply, as follows. Whereas the 'European' regime discussed above is based on *domicile*, the 'old English' regime discussed below is based on *presence*.

The English court has jurisdiction if the defendant is present (at the time of service of the writ, even fleetingly) in England, or submits to the jurisdiction of the court. Otherwise, the court has discretionary power to assume jurisdiction (by giving leave for service out of the jurisdiction) in the cases mentioned in Order 11 of the Rules of the Supreme Court.

(a) Present in England

Service of a writ is permissible on a defendant who is present in England, provided it is not domiciled in another contracting state and provided also the matter is not one in which another contracting state has exclusive jurisdiction.[3] In addition to companies incorporated in England and those

---

[1] It should also be noted that under article 24 of the Conventions, the English courts have jurisdiction 'for such provisional, including protective, measures as may be available under the law of [England], even if, under this Convention, the courts of another Contracting State have jurisdiction as to the substance of the matter.' Thus, even where the substance of a dispute is to be brought in France, the English courts would be able to grant a Mareva injunction (restraining a defendant from removing his assets out of the jurisdiction pending trial) or an Anton Piller order (for the inspection of premises to discover documents or chattels to which the plaintiff may be entitled). Both of these may affect an English custodian holding documents or securities for its clients in London.

[2] And in cases otherwise outside the scope of the Conventions, but not in cases in which article 16 of the Conventions confers exclusive jurisdiction on a contracting state, regardless of domicile (eg proceedings concerning public registers, and also not in cases where the parties have submitted to the jurisdiction of a Contracting State in accordance with article 17).

[3] *Dicey and Morris*, rule 24, vol 1, p 298.

having registered branches in England, any foreign company carrying on business in England (whether or not registered here) is present for these purposes.[1]

Thus, it should be possible to sue a foreign sub-custodian which carries on business in London (whether or not through a registered branch) provided (broadly) that its head office is not located in the EC or EFTA. This is true whether or not the sub-custody agreement is governed by English law or contains a submission to the jurisdiction of the English court (although an exclusive submission to another court might displace English jurisdiction: see section 3, below).

(b) Submission

The court has jurisdiction where the defendant submits to it. Submission can be inferred from conduct[2] or from contractual terms. Such a jurisdiction clause will be effective, provided there is proper provision for the service of process on the defendant (or its agent).[3]

Thus a well drafted English jurisdiction clause (appointing an English process agent) will bring a foreign sub-custodian within the jurisdiction of the English court. It would seem that this is the case even where the action relates to movable property which is situated in another jurisdiction. Therefore, in the absence of insolvency, the English court could make an order concerning the ownership of foreign securities. The willingness of foreign courts to recognise such an order may be another matter.

(c) Leave to serve writ outside the jurisdiction

In addition, the English court has a discretionary power to assume jurisdiction by granting leave to serve a writ outside the jurisdiction in certain circumstances under RSC Order 11, rule 1(1).[4] The plaintiff must make out a strong case before leave will be granted.[5] The grounds listed in Order 11, rule 1(1) include the following.[6]

English contract Service of a writ out of the jurisdiction is permissible with the leave of the court if the claim is brought to enforce, rescind, dissolve,

---

[1] Service may be effected under the Companies Act 1985, section 725(1) (in the case of English incorporated companies) and section 695(1) in the case of English registered branches of foreign companies, and otherwise under RSC Order 65, rule 3 (in the case of companies carrying on business in England at common law but unregistered at the companies registry).

[2] Eg acknowledging service of the writ.

[3] Where (broadly) a process agent is appointed in England, service may be effected without leave of the court for service abroad: RSC Order 10, rule 3.

[4] Provided, of course, the defendant is not domiciled in a contracting state, or the matter is one over which a contracting state has exclusive jurisdiction.

[5] Under Order 11, rule 4(2), no leave will be granted 'unless it shall be made sufficiently to appear to the Court that the case is a proper one for service out of the jurisdiction under this Order.'

[6] Service of a writ out of the jurisdiction is also permissible with the leave of the court if relief is sought against a person domiciled within the jurisdiction (Order 11, rule 1(1)(a)). (Domicile for this purpose is determined in accordance with the Act: Order 11, rule 1(4)).) However, this is unlikely to be important for present purposes, as any company domiciled in England is likely also to be present in England.

annul or otherwise affect a contract which (inter alia) was made within the jurisdiction.[1]

Accordingly, an action against a foreign sub-custodian which has no presence in England, under a sub-custody contract which is not governed by English law and which does not contain a submission to English jurisdiction, may be within this provision if it was accepted by fax received in England.

Property situated in England   Service of a writ out of the jurisdiction is permissible with the leave of the court if (inter alia) the claim is made to assert, declare or determine proprietary or possessory rights, or rights of security, in or over movable property, or to obtain authority to dispose of movable property, situate within the jurisdiction.[2] 'This jurisdiction, it will be observed, is essentially directed *in rem*, and does not extend to personal jurisdiction over persons outside England beyond dealing with property in England.'[3]

Chapter 4 argued that the proprietary interest of the client in the custody assets will in most cases be an interest under a trust of which the global custodian is the trustee. The location of this interest will be considered in section C.6 of chapter 7, below, where it will be argued that such trust interest is situated in the jurisdiction of the custodian, ie in England. This has the possible result that, irrespective of the location of the underlying securities, the English courts have jurisdiction to hear cases concerning all aspects of the client's proprietary rights in the custody assets, and the claims of others to whom the client has given a security interest (or other proprietary interest) in the portfolio (eg the global custodian under 'flawed asset' or security arrangements, third party secured lenders or tracing claimants). The interposition of the custody trust, it is argued, confers jurisdiction on the English courts in such matters. This is particularly important in connection with the use of the portfolio as collateral.

English law trust   Service of a writ out of the jurisdiction is permissible with the leave of the court (broadly) in an action against a trustee to execute a written trust governed by English law.[4] This applies whether or not the trust property is situate in England.[5] On the basis that the global custodian is a trustee, this may apply to actions to enforce the terms of the global custody agreement.

---

[1] 'If the parties enter into negotiations by correspondence from different countries, the contract is made where the letter of acceptance is posted. The same is the case if the acceptance is by telegram. But in commercial transactions today communication by telephone, telex and telefax is much more common than by post or telegram. It is now well established, following the decision of the Court of Appeal in *Entores v Miles Far East Corpn* [1955] 2 QB 327 (which has been approved by the House of Lords) that is the parties use 'instantaneous' means of communication such as telephone, telex or telefax, the contract is made where the acceptance is communicated to the offeror.' *Dicey and Morris*, vol 1, p 329.

[2] Order 11, rule 1(1)(i).

[3] This provision is modelled on article 5(8) of Schedule 4 to the Act, which confers jurisdiction under the Act where movable property is situated in England and the defendant is domiciled in Scotland or Northern Ireland.

[4] RSC, Ord 11, rule 1(1)(j).

[5] See *Dicey and Morris*, vol 1, p 354.

3 Loss of jurisdiction

The English court may lose or decline jurisdiction which it *prima facie* has in accordance with certain rules, including the following.

The rule of sovereign immunity[1] provides that a foreign state is generally immune from the jurisdiction of the English courts, subject to important exceptions.[2]

In accordance with the doctrine of *forum non conveniens* the English courts may inter alia stay or strike out an action when this is necessary to prevent injustice. The doctrine is based on the view that some other forum is more appropriate, and may be invoked to prevent jurisdiction shopping.[3] However, this discretion does not seem to extend to cases in which jurisdiction is conferred by the Convention.[4]

The related doctrine of *lis alibi pendens* applies when simultaneous actions are pending in different contracting states involving the same parties and the same or related matters. In the case of simultaneous actions in England and (broadly) EC or EFTA countries, the Conventions require proceedings in the second jurisdiction to be stayed, and jurisdiction to be declined, in certain circumstances.[5]

Where the parties to a contract have agreed to submit the contract to the *exclusive* jurisdiction of a foreign court, the English court will stay proceedings brought in England unless the plaintiff proves that it is just and proper to allow the proceedings to be brought.[6] Where exclusive submission is to the court of a contracting state, the English court has no jurisdiction.[7]

The English court also has no jurisdiction in matters such as those concerning the validity of entries in public registers maintained in a contracting state other than the UK, where the Conventions confer exclusive jurisdiction on the court of that other contracting state.

It is impossible to address the entire range of litigation that might in theory be brought in the English courts in connection with global custody. Rather than attempt to do so, this chapter will consider the general principles of choice of law before turning to the English private international law aspects of those issues that were considered under English domestic law in chapter 3, and which concern the impact of computerisation on the nature of securities. These are: integrity of transfer, formalities of transfer and negotiability.

---

[1] Now codified in the State Immunity Act 1978, implementing the European Convention on State Immunity of 1972.

[2] There is an exception in relation to commercial transactions: section 3(1) of the Act, according with the earlier common law rule reflected in *Trendtex v Central Bank of Nigeria* [1977] QB 529, CA.

[3] See *Spiliada Maritime Corpn v Cansulex* [1987] AC 460 and *Re Harrods (Buenos Aires) Ltd* [1992] Ch 72.

[4] See *Dicey and Morris*, vol 1, p 274.

[5] See article 8 of the Conventions.

[6] See *Dicey and Morris*, vol 1, pp 31 et seq.

[7] Unless neither party is domiciled in a Contracting State, in which case the English court has jurisdiction only if the chosen court has declined jurisdiction: article 17 of the Conventions. This restriction applies where submission is in customary written form. This is the corollary of the exclusive jurisdiction provisions of article 17.

C   Choice of law: general principles[1]

1   The issue

Once it has been established that the English court has jurisdiction in a matter, it is necessary to determine whether it should apply English domestic law or foreign law.

2   Approach

(a)   Categories and connecting factors

English private international law's approach is (firstly) to place cross-border scenarios into categories, and (secondly) to identify factors in those scenarios that connect them to particular jurisdictions.[2] Categorisation is determined by English law as the law of the forum or *lex fori*. Thus, in a matter before the English courts concerning foreign securities, English domestic law would determine the legal location or *situs* of the securities.

(b)   Terms

The terms for the connecting factors are customarily given in Latin.[3]

3   Approach to foreign law

Foreign law must be proved as fact.[4] If foreign law is not pleaded and proved, English law will be applied.[5]

4   Renvoi

'The problem of renvoi arises whenever a rule of the conflict of laws refers to the "law" of a foreign country, but the conflict rules of the foreign country

---

[1] The importance of choice of law in financial and securities transactions is discussed by Guynn and Tahyar, *The Importance of Choice of Law and Finality*, Journal of Financial Regulation and Compliance, iv 2, 1996, p 170.

[2] See *Dicey and Morris*, vol 1, p 30.

[3] 'The *lex causae* is a convenient shorthand expression denoting the law (usually but not necessarily foreign) which governs the question. It is used in contradistinction to the *lex fori*, which always means the domestic law of the forum, *ie* (if the forum is English) English law. The *lex causae* may be more specifically denoted by a variety of expressions, usually in Latin, such as … *lex loci contractus* (law of the country where a contract is made), *lex loci solutionis* (law of the country where a contract is to be performed or where a debt is to be paid), … *lex situs* (law of the country where a thing is situated), … *lex loci actus* (law of the country where a legal act takes place), *lex monetae* (law of the country in whose currency a debt or other legal obligation is expressed).' *Dicey and Morris*, vol 1, p 30.

[4] 'In any case to which foreign law applies, that law must be pleaded and proved as a fact to the satisfaction of the judge by expert evidence or sometimes by certain other means.' *Dicey and Morris*, rule 18(1). See also *Baker v Archer-Shee* [1927] AC 844, HL, per Lord Blanesburgh at 874.

[5] See also *Baker v Archer-Shee* [1927] AC 844.

would have referred the question to the "law" of the first country or to the 'law' of some third country.'[1] When English law refers a matter to, say, the law of France, does that mean the domestic law of France, or French private international law, which may well refer the matter on somewhere else (or back to England again, creating a hall of mirrors)?

Although renvoi has long enchanted commentators, 'The history of the renvoi doctrine in English law is the history of a chapter of accidents.'[2] It originated in nineteenth century cases concerning the formal validity of wills. It is excluded by the Rome Convention on the Law Applicable to Contractual Obligations.[3] In the light of recent judicial comments, renvoi should be treated as inapplicable in commercial matters.[4]

D   Integrity of transfer

Chapter 3 considered the impact of computerisation on the legal nature of securities, and argued that, under English domestic law, it involved the loss of negotiable status. That chapter also indicated that some of the problems caused by this under domestic law may be cured under private international law. This section returns to these questions, starting with the approach of the English courts to conflict of laws issues relating to the integrity of transfers of securities held in global custody. The following sections will consider conflicts of law in relation to ease of transfer and negotiability.

As section B, above, indicated, the first step is to establish jurisdiction.

1   Jurisdiction

According to the jurisdiction rules discussed in section B, above, the English courts would have jurisdiction, for example, to hear an action against a London-based global custodian and/or its London-based client, by a third party victim of fraud who claims an interest in custody securities that were brought from or through a fraudster. In this example, no bad faith on the part of the custodian or the client is alleged. The securities in question are French bonds held through Cedel, and the fraudster, who is based in London, has transferred the securities to the custodian under an English law transfer, with settlement through Cedel into the account of the sub-custodian ('the Example').

The English courts would have jurisdiction to hear the matter (on the basis of the domicile or presence in England of the defendant(s)) and London would be a likely forum for the claim.

---

[1] *Dicey and Morris*, vol 1, p 71.
[2] *Dicey and Morris*, vol 1, p 77.
[3] Article 15.
[4] See the first instance of *Macmillan Inc v Bishopsgate Investment Trust plc (No 3)* [1995] 3 All ER 747, per Millett J at 766. See also ibid at 777.

2   Categorisation

It was seen (in section C, above) that, after jurisdiction has been established, the next step in conflicts of laws is to categorise the matter. The leading case on the issues raised in the Example is *Macmillan Inc v Bishopsgate Investment Trust plc (No 3)*.[1]

Macmillan, a company in the Maxwell group and a Delaware corporation, brought an action to recover shares in a New York subsidiary, Berlitz ('the Shares'). The shares had been held by BIT as nominee for Macmillan and (without Macmillan's authority) were put up by BIT as security to various financial institutions (the defendants in the action) to secure borrowings by the Maxwell group. By the time of the hearing all the shares had been transferred to those financial institutions in order to perfect their security interests. By agreement between the litigants all the shares had been sold. 'The question for determination now is whether Macmillan retained an interest in the shares superior to that of any of the Defendants and is accordingly entitled to the corresponding part of the proceeds of sale.'[2] 'Each of the Defendants claims to have been, or ... to have derived title through, a bona fide purchaser for value of the shares without notice of Macmillan's interest.'[3] At first instance, judgment was given for the defendants, on the basis that they were bona fide purchasers for value without notice. This judgment was upheld in the Court of Appeal.[4]

The initial question of characterisation was disputed.[5] However, the approach of the court was clear. 'In my judgment the Defendants have correctly characterised the issue as one of priority.'[6]

(a)   Undestroyed proprietary base

More precisely, the issue fell into a particular class of priority, relating to the concept of the 'undestroyed proprietary base'. In his judgment, Millett J distinguishes this from '*Dearle v Hall*' type priority issues, and from tracing.

The natural analysis of the present case is '... as a claim by the original owner to recover his property from a third party who claims to have acquired an interest in the property superior to that of the claimant.'[7]

(b)   Dearle v Hall

In contrast, the type of priority dispute governed by the rule in *Dearle v Hall* relates to '... successive assignments of the same debt or fund.'[8] In other words, the undestroyed proprietary base type of dispute concerns the contest between a transferee and a predecessor in title; *Dearle v Hall* type claims concern a contest between successive assignees.[9]

---

[1] [1995] 3 All ER 747 (first instance).
[2] Per Millett J at first instance, at 752.
[3] At 752.
[4] Although the reasoning relating in particular to the correct connecting factor differed: see below.
[5] See Millett J at first instance, at 757.
[6] At 759.
[7] At 762.
[8] At 761.
[9] At 762.

(c) Tracing

Millett J also distinguishes questions of priority from tracing. He refers to his earlier judgment in *El Ajou v Dollar Land Holdings*,[1] and comments: 'In my judgment there is no similarity between the two cases.'[2] In other words, 'undestroyed proprietary base' type priority disputes concern relative claims of title; tracing concerns identifying the assets to which such title can attach.

If the correct categorisation is priorities, the question remains, priorities in relation to what? The appropriate category for matters concerning securities other than negotiable instruments[3] is that of intangible movables.[4]

The position is governed both by statute and by case law.

3   Statute

(a) The Rome Convention

The Contracts (Applicable Law) Act 1990 implements the Rome Convention[5] in the UK. The Rome Convention applies 'to contractual obligations in any situation involving a choice between the laws of different countries,'[6,7] subject to various exceptions including ones in favour of negotiable instruments and trusts. Chapter 4 argued that the interest of a client in the custody securities is that of a beneficiary under a trust. However, the terms of the exception for trusts are confined to the internal constitution of the trust and do not extend to the question of whether transfers of trust units are subject to third party equitable interests.

Article 12 of the Rome Convention provides as follows:

'**Voluntary assignments**[8]

1. The mutual obligations of assignor and assignee under a voluntary assignment of a right against another person ("the debtor") shall be governed by the law which under this Convention applies to the contract between the assignor and assignee.
2. The law governing the right to which the assignment relates shall determine its assignability, the relationship between the assignee and the debtor, the conditions under which the assignment can be invoked against the debtor and any questions whether the debtor's obligations have been discharged.'

To apply these provisions to the integrity of transfers of securities one must look at the nature of transfers.

---

[1] [1993] 3 All ER 717; see also the appeal of the case at [1994] 2 All ER 685 and *El Ajou v Dollar Land Holdings plc (No 2)* [1995] 2 All ER 213. The case is discussed briefly in chapter 3, section B. 7(d), above.

[2] At 758, 759.

[3] Conflicts of law are discussed in relation to negotiable instruments in section F, below.

[4] See *Dicey and Morris*, vol 2, chapters 22 and 24. 'It is, of course, somewhat artificial to describe an intangible as a movable, for a thing that occupies no physical space cannot actually be moved from place to place. However, the distinction between movables and immovables is the leading distinction in conflicts of law' (see *Dicey and Morris*, vol 2, p 916) and serves (however notionally) to divide land-related property from other types of property.

[5] The Convention on the Law Applicable to Contractual Obligations.

[6] Whether or not the countries in question are party to the convention: see article 2.

[7] Article 1.

[8] These questions of course concern with contractual, voluntary assignments, rather than with assignments arising by operation of law, for example on insolvency or pursuant to a court order.

(b)   Contractual and proprietary aspects

A transfer or assignment has two aspects; it is both a contract and a conveyance. The Rome Convention distinguishes between these. Thus, article 12(1) indicates that the contractual aspects of an assignment, as between the assignor and the assignee, will be governed by the proper law of the contract of assignment;[1] in accordance with articles 3 and 4, this will be the law chosen in the assignment[2] or, in the absence of such choice, the law of the country with which the contract is most closely connected,[3] generally the country of central administration of the corporate obligor (transferor).[4]

On the other hand, article 12(2) indicates that the aspects of the assignment that apply as between the debtor and the assignee are governed by the proper law of the transferred property. It is convenient to refer to these aspects as proprietary.[5]

The application of article 12 to the Example must be considered. The legal issue in the Example, and in the whole question of the integrity of transfers, is proprietary: is the transfer subject to pre-existing adverse proprietary claims, or does it overreach them? Article 12(1) cannot be relevant, as the Example is not concerned with the mutual obligations of the assignor and assignee.[6] Neither, however, is it clear that article 12(2) is relevant.

(c)   Different proprietary relationships

Dicey and Morris extrapolate from article 12(2) the following rule: '... the validity of the assignment and the obligations of third parties – in other words, all the property aspects of the transaction – are governed by the law under which the right [assigned] was created.'[7] This suggests that article 12(2) governs the position in the Example. However, the terms of article 12(2) may not be so wide.

Chapter 2 argued that property is relative. Different persons may have

---

[1] This accords with the common law rule in *Lee v Adby* (1886) 17 QBD 309 and *Re Anziani* [1930] 1 Ch 407.
[2] Article 3(1).
[3] Article 4(1).
[4] Article 4(2).
[5] See chapter 2, section 3(b), above, for a discussion of the personal and proprietary aspects of choses in action. Under section 3(3)(a) of the Contracts (Applicable Law) Act 1990, the *Giuliano and Lagarde Report* on the Rome Convention may be considered in interpreting the Convention. This report indicates, on p. 10, that '... since the Convention is concerned only with the law applicable to contractual obligations, property rights ... are not covered by these provisions.' However, since article 12(2) concerns the relations between the debtor and the assignee, and since that relationship is proprietary in the sense of being the subject matter of the assignment, the article must be taken to be an exception to this comment.
[6] See the first instance decision in *Macmillan*, in which Millett J refers to '... the intrinsic validity of any of the assignments, its contractual effect as between the immediate parties thereto, or the mutual obligations of assignor and assignee. All such questions are governed by the proper law of the assignment. ... Such questions must be distinguished from questions of priority which are concerned with the proprietary effect of the assignment on the assignor and third parties such as Macmillan claiming under him. An assignment is only a species of contract, and the parties to it can choose the system of law by which they indent their contract to be governed; but they cannot by their contract choose the laws which will govern its effect upon third parties.' (at 760).
[7] Vol 2, p 980.

competing proprietary rights in an asset.[1] The means by which the courts address competing claims to assets is by considering the priorities between them. In the Example, the claimant does not argue that the transfer to the custodian was invalid but that the property of the custodian is subject to the competing property of the claimant. As *Macmillan* indicates, the issue is one of priorities.

In other words, the issue in the Example is wider than the proprietary relationship between the custodian and the 'debtor'.[2] The issue is the contest between that relationship on the one hand, and on the other the proprietary relationship between the debtor and the claimant.[3] Because property is relative, the proprietary position of the custodian (and its client) cannot be determined by reference only to the custodian's relationship with the debtor. Third party interests have to be taken into account, as in the Example.

The application of article 12(2) to these questions is dubious.[4] It refers to 'the relationship between the assignee and the debtor', and not the relationship*s* between the debtor, the assignee *and third parties*.

4 Case law

Until recently, the non-statutory rules for determining *lex causae* for questions of priority in relation to intangible movables were highly uncertain.[5] However, the position has now been clarified by *Macmillan*, in which the Court of Appeal held that the position is governed by *lex situs*.[6]

5 *Lex situs*

Because *lex situs* governs the possible vulnerability of the custody portfolio to fraud in this way, it is vital to identify the *situs* or legal location of the custody securities. The Court of Appeal indicated that, in the case of shares, *situs* will usually be the place of incorporation of the company to which the shares relate. However, where securities are intermediated through global custodial arrangements, and in particular immobilised in a central clearing

---

[1] See chapter 2, section 1(e), above.

[2] This is the term used in article 12 to denote the obligor of the right which is the subject of the transfer.

[3] This is the position where there has been no breach of duty by the defendant. If the defendant had defrauded the claimant, the position would differ, for the basis of the claim would rest upon an equitable claim of the claimant as against the defendant. This point is brought out in *Macmillan* at first instance by Millett J, at 758.

[4] The *Giuliano and Lagarde* Report on the Rome Convention does not shed light on this issue.

[5] 'The assignment of intangible things, such as debts, has long been one of the most intractable topics in the English conflict of laws. The writers on the subject are fundamentally divided and the little case law that exists is old, confused and inconclusive.' Mark Moshinsky, *The Assignments of Debts in the Conflict of Laws*, (1992) LQR 591. See the cautious suggestions in *Dicey and Morris*, vol 1, p 182 and vol 2, p 981.

[6] Rejecting the first instance reasoning of Millett J that *lex loci actus* applies. See a discussion of this judgment in 1996 (111) LQR 198–202.

system, chapter 7, section C.6, below, will argue that *situs* is the location of the intermediary.

E   Formalities of transfer

Chapter 3 considered section 53(1)(c) of the Law of Property Act 1925,[1] which requires a disposition of an equitable interest to be in writing. It argued that, because of intermediation, the interest of the custody client in its securities will in most cases be equitable. However, the secondary markets in intermediate securities do not use written transfers. A number of domestic law arguments were cited to show that compliance with section 53(1)(c) may not be necessary. Private international law provides another line of defence against that section.

1   Jurisdiction

The first issue in conflicts is jurisdiction. A French fraudster (acting through its Belgian agent) might transfer French bonds held through Euroclear to a London-based global custodian for the account of its London-based client under an English law oral transfer ('the first transfer)'. The fraudster then purports to transfer the same bonds to a third party under a written English law transfer ('the second transfer'). The first transfer is settled through Euroclear and the bonds are credited to the Euroclear account of the sub-custodian. The transferor goes into insolvent liquidation, and the third party brings an action in England against the global custodian and/or its client for delivery of the bonds, on the basis that the first transfer is invalid by virtue of section 53(1)(c) ('the question').

The English courts would have jurisdiction to try the Question on the basis of the domicile or presence in England of the defendant(s).[2]

2   Substance and procedure

The next problem is whether these formal requirements raise matters of substance or merely of procedure. If matters of substance are involved, the next step in the conflicts analysis will be, as usual, to categorise the matter in order to identify the body of rules that will determine *lex causae*. However, if these are merely matters of procedure, no categorisation is necessary, for '[a]ll matters of procedure are governed by the domestic law of the country to which the court wherein any legal proceedings are taken belongs (*lex fori*).'[3]

---

[1] In section 6.
[2] Belgium would not necessarily be a more likely forum to be chosen by the claimant, in view of the fact that the claim is based on English law formal requirements.
[3] *Dicey and Morris*, Rule 17, vol 1, p 169.

On the basis of available case law,[1] it is submitted that the requirements of section 53(1)(c) are substantive and that English law as *lex fori* does not therefore necessarily apply. In order to determine applicable law, the next stage in the conflicts analysis is categorisation.

3 Categorisation

The Question concerns the form and validity of the First Transfer. This is a contract for the assignment of intangible movables. *Lex causae* of the formal validity of contracts of assignment of intangible movables must be established.

4 Formal validity

Article 9 of the Rome Convention[2] includes the following provisions:

---

[1] Indirect authority on the question of whether section 53(1)(c) raises matters of substance or procedure, is arguably provided *obiter dicta* in the case of *Rochefoucauld v Boustead* [1897] 1 Ch 196. The case concerned section 7 of the Statute of Frauds 1677, which required declarations of trusts of land to be evidenced in writing, and which has been replaced by section 53(1)(b) of the Law of Property Act 1925. It might be argued that the drafting of section 53(1)(b) is comparable to that of section 53(1)(c), and that the drafting of section 7 of the Statute of Frauds is comparable to section 9 of that Act, which was replaced by section 53(1)(c). In *Rochefoucauld*, Lindley LJ comments (at 207): 'The statute relates to the kind of proof required in this country to enable a plaintiff suing here to establish his case here. It does not relate to lands abroad in any other way than this. It regulates procedure here, not title to land in other countries.'

However, this is not conclusive. The Statute of Frauds imposes formal requirements on a range of different transactions. These requirements fall into two categories, depending upon the sanctions specified for their breach. The penalty for non-compliance with section 4 (parole promises) is merely a bar to enforcement. However, in the case of a larger number of the requirements ('the Second Class'), non-compliance affects the validity of the transaction. Certain transactions '... shall be utterly void and of none effect' (sections 5, 7 and 9); others 'shall not either in law or equity be deemed or taken to have any other or greater force or effect [than that specified]' (section 1); yet others shall not '... be allowed to be good ...' (section 17), or are simply prohibited (section 3).

The difference between the two categories for the purposes of conflicts of law is brought out in *Leroux v Brown* ((1852) 12 CB 801, affirmed in *Royal Exchange Assurance Corpn v Vega* [1901] 2 KB 567; affd [1902] 2 KB 384. For the same distinction, see the judgment of Scrutton LJ in *Republica de Guatemala v Nunez* [1927] 1 KB 669 at 690 and 691), which concerned section 4. In this case an action was brought by a proposed employee for damages after the repudiation by a proposed employer of an oral contract of employment concluded in France. Under French law the agreement was enforceable although not in writing; section 4 of the Statute of Frauds required a written agreement.

Thus, section 4 goes to procedure and not substance, and is therefore governed by *lex fori*. However, the basis of this decision is the wording of the statutory provisions: 'Looking at the words of the 4th section of the Statute of Frauds, and contrasting them with those of the 1st, 3rd, and 17th sections this conclusion seems to me to be inevitable.' Section 4 is procedural because its terms distinguish it from those other sections falling into the second class. Section 9 falls into the second class, and section 53(1)(c) replaces it.

[2] Implemented in the UK by the Contracts (Applicable Law) Act 1990.

'Formal validity

1. A contract concluded between persons who are in the same country[1] is formally valid if it satisfies the formal requirements of the law which governs it under this Convention or of the law of the country where it is concluded.
2. A contract concluded between persons who are in different countries is formally valid if it satisfies the formal requirements of the law which governs it under this Convention or of the law of one of those countries.
3. Where a contract is concluded by an agent, the country in which the agent acts is the relevant country for the purposes of paragraphs 1 and 2.'[2]

These requirements are disjunctive, and compliance with the formal requirements of any of the specified laws will obviate need for compliance with any other. Renvoi is not relevant.[3]

Thus, in the Question, in accordance with Article 9(2) and 9(3), the first transfer is formally valid if it satisfies the formal requirements of English law (as the governing law of the transfer or the law of the location of the transferee) or Belgian law (as the law of the location of the agent of the transferor).

Belgian[4] law does not require a written transfer, and so the first transfer is valid. Thus the formal requirements of section 53(1)(c) may be avoided, by concluding transfers through agents located in jurisdictions with no equivalent requirements.

5   Mandatory rules

In the Convention, article 9 is subject to article 7(2), which contains a reservation in favour of the application of mandatory rules of the forum.[5]

'...Of course, under the system established by Article 7, it will be for the court hearing the case to decide whether it is appropriate to give effect to these mandatory provisions and consequently to disregard the rules laid down in Article 9.'[6]

The issue is then whether the English court will regard the requirements of section 53(1)(c) as a mandatory rule of the forum for the purposes of article 7(2), and apply them irrespective of the more liberal approach indicated by article 9(2) and (3) of the Rome Convention.

In the case of *Re Fry*,[7] share transfers were executed in New Jersey by

---

[1] '...it is first necessary to describe exactly what is meant by persons being or not being in the same country. ... If the parties' agents (or one party and the agent of the other) meet in a given country and conclude the contract there, this contract is considered, within the meaning of paragraph 1, to be concluded between persons in that country, even if the party or parties represented were in another country at the time.' *Giuliano and Lagarde Report*. This indicates that the test is presence and not domicile.

[2] Articles 5 and 6 contain disapplications in favour of consumer contracts and contracts relating to immovable property.

[3] 'Renvoi must be rejected as regards formal validity as in all other matters governed by the Convention' *Giuliano and Lagarde Report* (cf article 15).

[4] Under the Royal Decree No 62 of 1967, which establishes the regime of fungibility which is the basis of Euroclear.

[5] 'Nothing in this Convention shall restrict the application of the rules of the law of the forum in a situation where they are mandatory irrespective of the law otherwise applicable to the contract.'

[6] *Giuliano and Lagarde Report.*

[7] *Re Fry, Chase National Executors and Trustees Corpn v Fry* [1946] Ch 312. This case applied the comments of Turner LJ in *Milroy v Lord*.

way of gift. The transferor died before consent required by English domestic law for registration of the transfer under the English Defence (Finance) Regulations 1939 was obtained. The argument that the transfer was valid in equity because *lex causae* was *lex loci actus* (New Jersey), was rejected.[1] Romer J[2] applied the comments of Turner LJ in *Milroy v Lord*:[3]

> 'I take the law of this Court to be well settled that, in order to render a voluntary settlement valid and effectual, the settlor must have done everything which, according to the nature of the property comprised in the settlement, was necessary to be done in order to transfer the property and render the settlement binding upon him. ... there is no equity in this Court to perfect an imperfect gift.'

However, the rejection of *lex loci actus* in this judgment does not seem to be based on the court's discretion in relation to mandatory rules of the forum, but rather on the rule of equity in relation to voluntary assignments, which is not relevant in the secondary securities markets, where consideration is routinely given.

Overall, the position is unclear. However, the requirements for written evidence of transactions was imposed by statute in the 17th century[4] and last addressed by statute at a time[5] when Parliament may not have been able to conceive of a form of information that was neither documentary nor oral. It is therefore to be hoped that the courts would consider that section 53(1)(c) is anachronistic in the electronic era, and does not form part of the mandatory rules of the forum. If so, the requirements for written transfers of intermediate securities can readily be avoided under the rules of private international law.

F Negotiability

Chapter 3 considered the concept of negotiability under English domestic law in the context of global custody. It concluded that the electronic arrangements through which debt securities are held in global custody may have cost them negotiable status under English domestic law. This section will consider how the rules of English private international law affect the position.

1 Jurisdiction

Section D, above, considered a scenario ('the Example') in relation to the integrity of a transfer of securities. In the Example, a third party victim of fraud brings an action in England against a London-based global custodian and/or its London-based client, claiming an interest in French bonds held by the global custodian for the client through a sub-custodian's Cedel account, on the basis that the securities were bought from or through a fraudster. It was seen that the English courts have jurisdiction.

One defence that might be advanced is that the bonds are negotiable, so

---

[1] At 318.
[2] At 315.
[3] [1861–73] All ER Rep 783 at 789.
[4] In the Statute of Frauds 1677.
[5] In the 1920s, with the Law of Property Act 1925.

that the transfer to the sub-custodian was made free of the interest of the claimant. The complication here is that the bonds are immobilised through Cedel. The following sections will take this issue in two stages, starting with the approach of the courts to bearer bonds which are not so immobilised or otherwise computerised ('traditional bearer securities') before turning to immobilised or otherwise computerised bearer bonds ('bearer computerised securities').[1]

2   Traditional bearer securities

Certain provisions of the Bills of Exchange Act 1882 relate to conflicts of law.[2] However, these provisions are not relevant to this discussion, as they do not concern the proprietary aspects of secondary market transactions.[3]

The common law conflicts rules for determining *lex causae* for the negotiability of a bearer instrument are as follows. Private international law proceeds by categorisation. As documentary intangibles, bearer instruments are categorised as choses in possession (or tangible movables) and not as choses in action (or intangibles). As choses in possession, the general principle is that the law determining negotiable status is *lex loci actus*.[4,5]

3   Transaction not instrument

It follows that the status of negotiability may be said to attach, not to instruments, but to transactions in them, for an instrument may move from country to country, and the question of whether a transaction in it is protected by negotiability depends upon the country in which that transaction takes place.[6]

---

[1] For the full definitions of these terms, see chapter 3, section A, above.

[2] Section 72 ('... the United Kingdom is one country for the purposes of the law of negotiable instruments [Bills of Exchange Act 1882] ...' *Dicey and Morris*, vol 1, p 26).

[3] Section 72 concerns formal validity, interpretation, duties of holder and due date of payment.

[4] *Dicey and Morris, The Conflict of Laws*, p 369. *Alcock v Smith* [1892] 1 Ch 238 and *Embiricos v Anglo-Austrian Bank* [1905] 1 KB 677.

[5] 'In the conflict of laws, negotiable instruments are therefore treated as chattels, ie as tangible moveables. Whether they are "negotiable" is a question to be determined by the law of the country where the alleged transfer by way of "negotiation" takes place and this is, in the nature of things, the country in which the instrument is situated at the time of the delivery.' *Dicey and Morris*, vol 2, p 1420.

[6] Thus, in *Picker v London and County Banking Co* (1887) 18 QBD 515, Prussian bonds without the coupon sheets attached were held not to be as negotiable in England, although they were negotiable by mercantile custom in Prussia. Equally in *Lang v Smyth* (1831) 7 Bing 284, Neapolitan bordereaux were held not to be negotiable in England because they did not pass from hand to hand *in England* like money or bank notes. In relation to transfers taking place in England, 'I think that both upon principle and upon authority, whether the instrument in question be an English instrument or a foreign instrument, the usage necessary to support a claim to rank as negotiable must be in either case a usage in England.' (*Bechuanaland v London Trading Bank* [1898] 2 QB 658, per Kennedy K at 672).

Conversely, if the transaction in question takes place in a foreign country, the negotiable status of the instrument for the purposes of that transaction will be determined by the English courts by reference to the law of that foreign country. In *Alcock v Smith* [1892] 1 Ch 238 an instrument was sold in Norway at a time when it was negotiable under the law of Norway, but not under the law of England (as it was overdue and, under the Bills of Exchange Act 1882, could only be transferred subject to equities). It was held that Norwegian law governed and the transfer was not subject to the plaintiff's equities.

On this basis, the crucial issue is not where the underlying bonds were issued, but where the transaction takes place.[1]

4 Computerised bearer securities

It must be established how this rule applies to bearer computerised securities such as the bonds in the Example.

(a) The problem of categorisation

There are special conflicts rules for negotiable instruments. This raises the following problem. If a matter is categorised as one of negotiability it must be referred to the special rules on negotiable instruments. These rules may indicate that the security in question is not a negotiable instrument, and suggest in turn that a different categorisation may have been more appropriate. In other words, categorisation contains an element of prejudgment. This problem may have been less important when all the securities which were candidates for negotiable status were clearly distinguishable from those which were not (because they were in physical bearer form) and the only variable to be considered was (broadly) the presence or absence of mercantile custom (or statute) conferring negotiable status. However, with the computerisation of the Eurobond markets[2] this rule of thumb may have broken down.

It would therefore be helpful to be able to show that miscategorisation will have no adverse result, because the rules for negotiable and non-negotiable securities are the same.

The conflicts rules for integrity of transfer in relation to securities other than negotiable instruments were considered in section D, above. The leading case in that context is *Macmillan*,[3] which concerns shares. Under English law, shares are intangibles, and they are not negotiable.[4]

The first instance decision in *Macmillan* was based on a rule in favour of *lex loci actus*; the Court of Appeal upheld the judgment, but on the basis of an alternative rule in favour of *lex situs*. On the facts of that case, the two coincided. It will be submitted that, in the case of intermediate securities, the two always coincide, just as they always coincide in the case of traditional bearer securities.

(b) Situs of intangible

Chapter 3, section 4, above, argued that the interest of a participant in an immobilised clearing system such as Cedel is not the same as the underlying

---

[1] This 'transaction specific' approach may be compared to the statutory 'several laws' approach to Bills of Exchange: 'It is important to realise that a bill of exchange does not contain a single contract but a series of promises to pay made by the acceptor, the drawer and each subsequent indorser, all of which are contained in the same instrument. Section 72 clearly treats each of these contracts as a separate one for the purposes of the conflict of laws and thus adopts what has been called the "several laws" doctrine as opposed to the "single law" doctrine which at one time found favour with English courts in cases decided before the acts.' *Dicey and Morris*, p 366.

[2] See chapter 3.

[3] [1995] 3 All ER 747; on appeal [1996] 1 All ER 585, CA.

[4] Although shares are negotiable under the law of the State of New York. See the NY UCC article 8–105 and the first instance decision in *Macmillan* [1995] 3 All ER 747 at 759 and *Colonial Bank v Cady* (1890) 15 App Cas 267.

bond. Rather, as an intermediate security, it is an interest under a trust. Chapter 7, section C.6, below, will argue that the *situs* of such a trust interest is the jurisdiction of the clearer. On this basis, *lex situs* is Luxembourg law.[1]

(c) Lex loci actus

The discussions of the New York DTC in the first instance decision in *Macmillan* provide clear authority that *lex loci actus* of settlement by book entry is the law of the jurisdiction of the clearer.[2]

On this basis, *lex situs* and *lex loci actus* necessarily coincide in the case of bearer computerised securities as in the case of traditional bearer securities. In this way, the old rules may continue to apply in the computerised environment, and the problem of prejudgment referred to in section 4(a) above is more apparent than real.

In the Example, the issue of negotiability will be determined by Luxembourg law. In practice, as the approach of Luxembourg law to integrity of transfers generally within its clearing systems is robust. It was seen in chapter 3, section 7(e), above that, under Luxembourg law,[3] the transferee of securities through a depository system such as Cedel is protected against adverse proprietary claims as effectively as if the security in question were a negotiable instrument.[4]

5 Conclusions

As discussed in chapter 3, the computerisation of the bearer bond markets has cost negotiable status. However, under private international law, the benefits of negotiability may still be available in practice, particularly where the European international clearing systems are involved. This result has been achieved by the convergence of the conflicts rules for negotiable and computerised securities. The usefulness of a separate body of conflicts rules relating to negotiable instruments may be over.[5]

---

[1] Luxembourg domestic law does not have the concept of an Anglo-Saxon type trust; however, the notional location of the trust in Luxembourg rests on English private international law. See chapter 7, section C.6, below.

[2] '... my own inclination would be to apply the *lex loci actus*, with the result that the effect on Macmillan's pre-existing interest in the shares of ... the entries on the books of DTC ... would be governed by the law of New York because that is where the entries were made', at 763, 764. See also 768.

[3] Article 7 of the Grand Ducal Regulation of 17 February 1971 Modifying the Circulation of Securities.

[4] Although adverse claims are not necessarily defeated, but rather borne by the depository.

[5] The discussion in this section has concerned the proprietary aspects of transactions in bearer computerised securities. The contractual aspects of transactions in negotiable instruments attract different conflict rules as the Rome Convention is disapplied in respect of 'obligations arising under bills of exchange, cheques and promissory notes another negotiable instruments to the extent that the obligations arising under such other negotiable instruments arise out of their negotiable character', article 1(2)(c). However, if bearer computerised securities are not negotiable, this difference drops away also.

Chapter 7

Cross-border proprietary rights: taking security and insolvency[1]

A   General

This chapter considers the challenge presented by two important trends informing the global custody industry: the use of securities as collateral, and intermediation.[2] Market participants are concerned to know with certainty that their collateral is good, and that their assets will survive the insolvency of an intermediary. Such certainty is generally far from achievable and disquiet at this legal uncertainty has been expressed at senior levels for several years;[3] some jurisdictions have led the way with clarifying and reforming legislation.[4] However, the problem is precisely international, and national reform will never provide an adequate solution.

Insolvency and the enforcement of collateral are the two chief occasions when the strength of proprietary claims on assets are tested. The heart of the problem is that different jurisdictions conceive of property in fundamentally different ways, at least where the property in question is intangible, unallocated, intermediated and held cross-border, as are the interests of custody clients in their securities. This chapter will consider the nature of the interest of

---

[1] '... the ... claims of customers of a securities intermediary are marked by a lack of control and knowledge and an almost exclusive reliance on the integrity and solvency of the intermediary ...' CW Mooney, *Beyond Negotiability*, [1990] Cardozo Law Review, vol 12, 305 at 354.

[2] 'The many tiers of intermediaries that are typically involved in processing a single securities transaction pose a challenge to the market participant that seeks to be well-informed regarding risk.' Bank for International Settlements, *Cross-Border Securities Settlement*, May 1994, Basle, p 55.

[3] See the G10 Report, *Cross-Border Securities Settlement*, May 1995, Basle: 'Choice of law and conflict of laws problems might create uncertainty regarding the finality of transfer, ownership interests or collateral rights. In particular, such problems might complicate the use of collateral to mitigate credit exposures arising in cross-border transactions. In addition, differences in bankruptcy law could result in uncertain or conflicting outcomes regarding the disposition of securities in the event of a counterparty's or intermediary's insolvency. Predictability of outcome is essential in efforts to contain financial problems, but widely divergent legal frameworks make predictability hard to achieve in a cross-border context.' Recommendation 5 of the *Morgan Guaranty Report* of 1994, *Cross-Border Clearance, Settlement and Custody: Beyond the G30 Recommendations*, provides: 'Each country should modernise its securities pledging laws to ... include categorical choice-of-law rules assuring respect of the validity of pledges at each tier of a multi-tiered holding system, including tiers governed by foreign laws.'

[4] In *Modernising Securities Ownership Transfer and Pledging Laws*, IBA Discussion Paper (1996) Randall Guynn identifies New York, Belgium and Luxembourg as model jurisdictions for this purpose.

the custody client under English law, before discussing the wider cross-border issues relating to collateral and intermediation.

B   Nature of property interest

Chapter 4 argued that the relationship between the client and the global custodian in respect of securities is likely to be that of beneficiary and trustee.

Private international law as it relates to global custody is very complex. In order to simplify the analysis, certain assumptions will be made. The first is that both the global custodian and its sub-custodians offer fungible custody.[1] Secondly, fungible custody raises issues of allocation, discussed in chapter 5 under the term, 'the allocation problem'. It will be assumed that the allocation problem is overcome by the co-ownership of the commingled property by the custody clients, under a tenancy in common that arises either under the express terms of the global custody documentation or by operation of law.[2]

On the assumed bases[3] the custody trust asset under English domestic law is in all cases an interest under a trust. Because of the administrative duties of the intermediaries through whom the securities are held, this trust is active and not bare. As the custody trust asset arises under a trust and by way of co-ownership, it is indirect and unallocated. It is, nevertheless, proprietary in the sense that it would not be defeated by the insolvency of the nominee, sub-custodian or depository through whom it is held.

It should be stressed that this is merely the analysis under English domestic law, on the assumed bases. The treatment of the custody assets in the insolvency of a sub-custodian or other local entity in the global network will be determined by the local law of the insolvent entity, which may or may not recognise the English law position, even under English law sub-custody documentation. As a matter of reasonable prudence the global custodian should seek local legal advice as to the effect of the insolvency of a sub-custodian on the custody assets. The analysis in this section is not conclusive, or appropriate for risk management; it is rather the basis for the analysis under English private international law that follows, and in particular the discussion of situs in the next section.

C   Taking security

1   Generally

This section considers the conflicts aspects of the use of securities held in global custody as collateral.

---

[1] Ie that there is segregation of house positions from client positions, but that the positions of different clients are commingled. This arrangement is, generally speaking, customary, although not the invariable practice.

[2] These assumptions are artificial; there will be cases where client-specific segregation is offered, and there is some remote risk that the allocation problem is not addressed in the manner outlined above.

[3] Ie on the assumption of co-ownership between clients under fungible custody.

Bonds and shares collateralise much international financing,[1] as well as the securities settlement systems.[2] An important growth area is derivatives margin, and new products are being developed by the clearing systems to deliver securities as margin.[3]

The granting of security interests over assets held in global custody raises special legal challenges. The secured property often consists of a pool comprising securities issued in different jurisdictions. This pool is usually held through the intermediary clearing systems. In many cases the pool changes from time to time, under substitution provisions[4] and market to market provisions.[5]

It is important to determine which law will govern the security interest, and whether that law will uphold the security arrangements. This second issue may be divided into four component parts, namely, attachment, perfection, priorities and enforcement.

2 What law will govern?

(a) Problem with local jurisdiction

Suppose a Euroclear participant wishes to take security over investments held by another participant in Euroclear. The portfolio consists of French bonds. If the chargee[6] is well advised, it will require the security interest to be perfected in accordance with the requirements of Belgian law. If it is cautiously advised, it will also require perfection in accordance with French law, on the basis that the involvement of the French courts may be necessary to enforce the security interest, or defend it against third parties.[7] However, such cautious advice may be harder to follow where the charged property consists of a mixed portfolio of French, Italian, Spanish, German, Hong Kong and New York bonds. The delay and expense of local perfection may be impracticable. It may be commercially impossible in the case of derivatives margining, where collateral turnover may be rapid. The risk that the law of the issuer may govern security interests in the view of courts of competent jurisdiction is a major concern in international secured finance.

---

[1] 'Charges over investment securities are of immense importance in international finance, mainly because of the marketability and ease of valuation of the collateral, and also the facility with which investment securities can be made available, usually with a minimum of formality and fuss – in sharp contrast to, say, mortgages of land.' Philip Wood, *Comparative Law of Security and Guarantees*, Sweet & Maxwell, London, p 58.

[2] 'As more payment systems look to securities collateral to control credit risk in the settlement process, those systems also become dependent on the ability to acquire and maintain an enforceable interest in securities.' Bank for International Settlements, *Cross-Border Securities Settlement*, March 1995, Basle, p 46.

[3] Ie as collateral for derivatives exposures.

[4] Ie provisions that the chargee will release charged securities upon the chargor putting up substitute securities.

[5] Ie provision for new collateral to be called and existing collateral to be released to reflect increases and diminutions in the value of the secured obligations. Such provisions are characteristic of derivatives margining.

[6] In this section, 'chargee' is used in the widest sense of any person to whom a security interest is granted, and 'chargor' is used to mean any person granting a security interest, whether by way of charge, mortgage, pledge or otherwise.

[7] Such as the liquidator of the chargor, or other creditors, who may seek to attach the charged asset in the hands of the local depository of Euroclear, or even directly against the issuer.

(b) Intermediary jurisdiction

The obvious solution to this problem would be to determine that the charged property, and therefore the security interest, are governed by the law of the intermediary clearer, and not by the law of the local issuer. This approach ('the intermediary jurisdiction approach') informs the concept of a 'securities entitlement' in the new article 8 of the US Uniform Commercial Code.[1] It is advocated more widely in Randall Guynn's paper, *Modernising Securities Ownership, Transfer and Pledging Law*[2] and developed in section 6, below.

(c) Defence of security interest

However, the benefit of the intermediary jurisdiction approach may be limited in practice. It may be possible to rely on the cooperation of a clearing organisation in enforcing a security interest over assets held in the clearer and perfected in accordance with the law of the clearer's jurisdiction. Nevertheless, the danger remains that a third party wishing to challenge the security interest (eg the liquidator of the chargor or another creditor having a competing security interest in the same assets) may claim the assets in the courts of the underlying issuer, which in turn may make an order against the assets in the hands of the local depositary. The risk, of course, is that while the courts of the clearer's jurisdiction may adopt the intermediary juris-diction approach, the courts of the issuer may not. For the intermediary jurisdiction approach to be entirely reliable, it must be adopted in every juris-diction in which the clients of global custody invest. While an EC measure in this context would be most welcome, it would not cure the problem as investment is not confined to the EC. Investment in the emerging markets may increase the risk that security interests perfected at clearer level may be defeated locally.

The ability to defend a security interest at local level may depend on four criteria of local law: attachment, perfection, priority and enforcement procedure. The following sections will consider each of these in general terms.[3]

3 Attachment

(a) Managed collateral

Chapter 2 discussed the difference between personal and proprietary rights. A convenient form of shorthand is to consider personal rights as legal relations between persons, and proprietary rights as legal relations between persons and things. Attachment is the legal process whereby a personal right arising under the agreement to grant security is enlarged into a proprietary right,

---

[1] Article 8-110 (Transfers) and 9-103(6) (Pledges).

[2] February 1996, Capital Markets Forum, Section on Business Law, International Bar Association, p 35. See also Tyson Quah, *Cross Border Collateralisation Made Easy*, (1996) 11 JIBFL 117.

[3] 'The process by which a security interest is made to fasten on an asset so as to be enforceable against the debtor as respects that asset is conveniently termed *attachment*. Attachment is concerned only with relations between creditor and debtor and their respective representatives. It is to be contrasted with *perfection*, that is, the taking of any additional steps prescribed by law for giving public notice of the security interest so as to bind third parties. Perfection requirements are in turn to be distinguished from *priority* rules, ie rules declaring the ranking of the security interest in relation to rival claims to the asset, eg by a prior or subsequent encumbrancer.' Goode, *Commercial Law*, pp 673, 674.

by notionally fixing on the charged asset. Attachment confers a proprietary right on the chargee.

However, this proprietary right is less than full title. The chargor retains a residual proprietary right in the asset, which is the right to have it back upon discharge of the secured obligation. Under English law, this residual property is called the equity of redemption. Thus both the chargor and the chargee have concurrent proprietary interests, legally linking each of them to the same asset.

Broadly speaking, an actively managed portfolio is considerably more profitable than an unmanaged portfolio. If the huge volumes of securities that serve as collateral could not be traded in response to market changes, significant profits would be foregone. It is therefore often provided that collateral securities are not frozen, and that either the chargor or the chargee may deal in them.[1] The chargor is customarily permitted to deal in the collateral securities by substitution provisions, whereby it is allowed to withdraw securities from the collateral pool upon providing substitute securities of equal value and of a type acceptable to the chargee.[2] The chargee is customarily permitted to deal in the collateral securities by equivalent redelivery provisions, whereby its duty upon the discharge of the secured obligation is not to redeliver the very securities that were delivered to it by way of collateral, but to deliver securities of the same number and type. However, both substitution and equivalent redelivery are legally problematic.

English law has the concept of a floating charge, whereby security may be given over a changing pool of assets, with the chargor retaining freedom to deal in the ordinary course of its business. However, floating charges are generally registrable,[3] and rank lower in priority to fixed charges.[4] It is possible to create a fixed charge over a changing pool of assets by conditioning the right of substitution of the chargor, but this is incompatible with an unrestricted freedom to deal. Other jurisdictions[5] have no concept equivalent to the floating charge; a security interest purportedly given over a changing collateral pool might simply not attach. The risk, therefore, of permitting the chargor freedom to deal in the collateral is that the security may be defeated, for want of attachment under civil law, and for want of registration under English law.

For these reasons, it is more customary for the title to economic asset represented by the management potential of the collateral pool to be conferred on the chargee, through equivalent redelivery provisions. On-pledging has a long history, and is customary in the United States. However, under English law, it raises the following problem. If the chargee may deliver back securities which are different from those provided by the chargor, and may dispose of the original securities free of any interest of the chargor, the chargor can

---

[1] The chargee often wishes to use the collateral securities for 'on-pledging' (or, in US parlance, rehypothecation), ie as collateral to third parties to secure its own obligations. US law is more comfortable with these arrangements than English law because of the liberal provisions of article 9 of the UCC.

[2] For a discussion of substitution rights in relation to collateral, see Philip Wood, *Comparative Law of Security and Guarantees*, p 63.

[3] Under the Company Act 1985, section 395. In many security arrangements, the formality and publicity involved in registration would be commercially unacceptable. UK banks are prevented from giving floating charges by the Bank of England.

[4] And are frozen on administration together with other disadvantages.

[5] Particularly civil law jurisdictions.

retain no equity of redemption. If the securities it receives back are or may not be the same ones it put up, it has no continuing proprietary interest in them. The transaction is not the granting of security, but an outright transfer. This means that the chargor may not get back the excess value of the collateral in the insolvency of the chargee.

To summarise, the problem with permitting the chargor to deal is that the chargee's rights may not attach; the problem with permitting the chargee to deal is that the chargor's rights may not persist. For ease of reference, these two problems together will be referred to as the 'attachment problem'. A security interest involves the creation of concurrent proprietary interests in the chargor and the chargee; the need for a proprietary interest to be linked to an asset requires the charged asset in effect to be frozen between them. Thus, traditional concepts of security will inevitably be problematic in an environment where the freezing of large portfolios of securities is uneconomic.

The markets have therefore sought out ways of providing collateral otherwise than by way of security. The chief example is the growth of repurchase agreements ('repos'). Under these arrangements, collateral is provided by way of outright transfer, subject to contractual redelivery obligations. No security interest is taken, and counterparty risk is addressed by a set off mechanism that is triggered by default. The same structure is adopted in stocklending and sale and buy back arrangements.

The phenomenal growth of the repo market in recent years is certain to continue, as repos provide the natural answer to the attachment problem by substituting contractual for proprietary rights. In some respects the attachment problem (which arises when security is taken) is akin to the allocation problem[1] (which arises when proprietary rights are intermediated). Both derive from the need for property to inhere in particular assets, and both present difficulties in modern custodial practice where the trend is generally away from allocation and towards pooling. Chapter 5 considered how the allocation problem can be addressed by the concept of co-ownership. Co-ownership cannot cure the attachment problem, because of the need for collateral assets to be sold free of any encumbrance. The contractual set-off route adopted in repos cannot cure the allocation problem, for the simple reason that the exposures of investors to the intermediaries holding their securities are not matched by mutual obligations capable of set off. With intermediation, the exposure is all one way, so the concept of property is necessary to address insolvency risk.

(b)   English law

The English conflicts rules for the attachment of security interests may be summarised as follows.

The contractual aspects of an agreement to grant security are governed by the Rome Convention.[2] However, the Rome Convention does not cover proprietary rights.[3] The effect of attachment of a security interest over the custody portfolio is to transfer to the chargee a proprietary interest in the

---

[1] Discussed in chapter 5.

[2] The Convention on the Law Applicable to Contractual Obligations, implemented in the UK by the Contracts (Applicable Law) Act 1990.

[3] '... since the Convention is concerned only with the law applicable to contractual obligations, property rights ... are not covered by these provisions,' p 10, *Giuliano and Lagarde Report*.

portfolio. The position is likely to be governed by the non-statutory conflicts rules for the assignment of intangibles.[1]

While these are complex, Dicey and Morris, *The Conflict of Laws*, indicate that they produce the same result as the Rome Convention.[2] This is summarised as follows: '. . . the mutual obligations of the assignor and assignee are governed by the law applicable . . . to the contract between them while the validity of the assignment and the obligations of third parties – in other words, all the property aspects of the transaction – are governed by the law under which the right was created.'[3] On this basis, while the contractual validity of a security interest[4] will be determined by the governing law of the contract,[5] the attachment of a security interest to French traditional bearer securities will be governed by French domestic law. The law governing the attachment of a security interest to such securities when they are immobilised in Cedel will depend upon whether the charged asset consists of French law bonds or a Luxembourg law interest in such bonds. This issue is discussed in detail in section 6, below. An alternative view is that the position is determined by *lex situs*.[6] The two will often coincide in practice.

4 Perfection

(a) Generally

An attached security interest generally survives the insolvency of the chargor[7] and therefore addresses credit risk. However, it may not address the risk the chargee may double deal, and that a third party may claim the charged assets, for example under a court order or pursuant to a sale or a subsequent security interest. In order to bind third parties, different systems of law prescribe certain acts of perfection, or the giving of public notice.

The perfection requirements of English domestic law are few, although the Companies Act 1985 imposes strict registration requirements on corporate security interests.[8] However, other countries, particularly civil law jurisdictions, may impose expensive and time-consuming formalities, including notarisation.

Where security is taken over an international portfolio, it would often be impracticable to perfect in the jurisdiction of each issuer of the component securities. Where the collateral pool changes, so that securities of any one

---

[1] 'The assignment of intangible things, such as debts, has long been one of the most intractable topics in the English conflict of laws.' Mark Moshinsky, *The Assignment of Debts in the Conflict of Laws*, The Law Quarterly Review, 109, p 591.

[2] Vol 2, p 979.

[3] Pp 979, 980. See *Re Fry* [1946] Ch 312.

[4] Or at least one created by contract.

[5] Ie the contract creating the security interest.

[6] 'The *lex situs* is the basic choice of law rule for property in the conflict of laws, applying to tangible movables and immovable property alike. The *lex situs* has the virtue of simplicity in having the same rule apply for all types of property . . . The *lex situs* would in general seem to provide a satisfactory and appropriate rule to govern the transfer of property in a debt from the assignor to the assignee.' Moshinsky, op cit, pp 607, 609. It is clear that *lex situs* governs transfers of negotiable instruments: *Alcock v Smith* [1892] 1 Ch 238; *Embiricos v Anglo-Austrian Bank* [1905] 1 KB 677.

[7] Assuming of course that it is a valid and enforceable security interest. This is because, as between the chargor (and its representatives including its liquidator) and the chargee, the security interest is proprietary and not merely contractual.

[8] Section 395. Breach of these requirements defeats the security interest against the liquidator or any creditor of the chargor, so the requirements go both to attachment and perfection.

jurisdiction may enter and leave it from time to time, compliance with all local perfection requirements may be out of the question.

However, the risk cannot be excluded that the courts of any issuer jurisdiction would treat its local perfection requirements as applicable. The important question then is, will the chargor be exposed to the decision of such courts? It might, either if their cooperation is required in enforcing the security interest, or in defending the security interest against the competing claims of other creditors or the liquidator of the chargor.[1]

(b)   English law

The position under English conflicts rules has been clarified in the *Macmillan* judgment. Perfection is governed by the *lex situs*.

5   Priorities

(a)   Generally

Once a security interest has cleared the hurdles of attachment and perfection, it may then need to compete with other security interests that have also done so. The outcome of that competition depends on rules of priority. Chargees may routinely take representations of no prior encumbrance and negative pledges against subsequent encumbrances. However, these may not be entirely reliable,[2] and the rules of priority will therefore be of concern.

It would be prudent to assume that local courts may apply the rules of the forum to questions of priority. Where security is taken over an international portfolio, it is important to seek to identify the courts in which the security interest may require to be defended, and to consider the priority rules of those jurisdictions. The issuer jurisdiction is obviously important, as third parties might seek to attach the charged assets there.

(b)   English law

Priority rules under English private international law were considered in chapter 6, section D, above. Two different rules apply, depending on whether the claim of the plaintiff in the action concerns double dealing, or breach of fiduciary duty. In the first case, where security interests in the same property are granted first to A and then to B, the general rule is to apply *lex fori*.[3] However, where the charged property is a debt or (probably) other choses in action such as an interest in a security, the position is less clear. There is authority that priorities are governed by the law governing the chose in action.[4] There is conflicting authority that priorities are determined by *lex situs*.[5] Thus, if A charges French bonds held in Euroclear first to B and then

---

[1]   See the discussion in section 2, above.

[2]   Breach of representation and negative pledge will not necessarily defeat a competing interest.

[3]   *Ex p Melbourn* (1870) 6 Ch App 64; *The Tagus* [1903] P 44; *The Colorado* [1923] P 102, CA; *Bankers Trust International Ltd v Todd Shipyards Corpn, The Halcyon Isle* [1981] AC 221, 230–231. These cases concern the priorities in relation to a marriage settlement, and ships.

[4]   *Le Feuvre v Sullivan* (1855) 10 Moo PCC 1; *Kelly v Selwyn* [1905] 2 Ch 117; *Republica de Guatemala v Nunez* [1927] 1 KB 669.

[5]   See *Re Queensland Mercantile and Agency Co* [1891] 1 Ch 536 (North J); affd [1892] 1 Ch 219, CA, quoted at p 622 of Moshinsky, *Assignment of Debts*, Law Quarterly Review, (1992) 108, 591.

to C, priorities between B and C will (in an English court) be determined either by French law or by Belgian law, depending on the view taken by the court of the nature or location of the asset charged. For further discussion of this question, see section 6, below.

In the second case, A holds the bonds as fiduciary for B, and charges them to C in breach of fiduciary duty. As discussed in chapter 6, section D above, the position is governed by the rule in *Macmillan*, which is that priorities are determined by *lex situs*.

6 Intermediary jurisdiction approach

Section 2 above considered the problem of taking security over international portfolios, and the consequent exposure to the demands of a number of different legal jurisdictions. It suggested that the intermediary jurisdiction approach, whereby the charged asset is treated as being located in the jurisdiction of the intermediary, would help by consolidating the legal requirements for taking good security into those of the law of the clearer (although all courts of competent jurisdiction must recognise this approach before it is entirely reliable). This section will argue that the intermediary jurisdiction approach is already implicit in English law, and may not require to be introduced by legislation.

Section B of this chapter considered *what* the interest of the custody client is, and suggested that the English courts will characterise this interest as being, or as being akin to, an interest under a trust. This section will consider *where* it is.

(a) Lex situs

This section will argue that, where securities are held by intermediary custodians and clearing systems, the situs of the interest held by the intermediary is the jurisdiction of the intermediary. Such a situation would be important in addressing conflict of law risk, as under many systems of private international law proprietary interests including security interests are determined by *lex situs* of the charged asset. Under English conflict rules, *lex situs* is also important, for a number of reasons.

Firstly, jurisdiction must be considered. Broadly speaking, in matters involving European defendants, the English courts generally have jurisdiction in claims concerning a trust domiciled in England.[1] Where the defendant is domiciled in Scotland, Northern Ireland or outside Europe,[2] the English courts have jurisdiction over matters concerning moveable property situated in England.[3] These rules may assist in avoiding litigation in issuer jurisdictions. Secondly, and more importantly, attachment and priorities may be determined by *lex situs*.[4]

In the English courts, *lex situs* will be determined in accordance with English law.[5]

---

[1] See chapter 6, section B.1(d), above.
[2] And, in the latter case, leave for service outside the jurisdiction is granted.
[3] See chapter 6, sections B.1(d) and B.2(c), above.
[4] See sections C3 and C4, above.
[5] 'In the conflict of laws the *situs* of a thing is ascertained by reference to the rules of the *lex fori* because all concepts signifying connecting factors must be interpreted by reference to that system.' *Dicey and Morris*, vol 2, p 923.

(b)   Intangibles and securities

Attributing a location to an intangible such as an interest under a trust is a notional exercise. Of course, the intangibility of some securities predated computerisation and global custody. As discussed in chapter 3, traditional registered securities have always been intangible. That section also argued[1] that securities held through computerised clearing systems are a form of registered security, the register being the database of the clearer. Traditionally, *situs* of registered securities is the location of the register.[2]

(c)   Interest under a trust

Global custody and more generally the computerisation of securities involves intermediation, so that the interest of the custody client in the custody securities is no longer direct. Section B argued that the process of intermediation changes the legal nature of the client's proprietary interest, so that on the assumed bases[3] the custody trust asset is an interest under a trust. The *situs* of such an interest must be established.

This question was considered in the context of a trust of a portfolio of securities in *Re Cigala's Settlement Trusts*.[4] In this case, under a marriage settlement executed in England, a wife settled a portfolio of French and English securities on trust, after the death of the survivor of husband and wife, for their children. The trustees were English. Succession duty would have been payable if the property to which the children became entitled was English property. It was held that succession duty was payable.[5] The case suggests that the interposition of a trust between underlying property and its beneficial owners may move the situs of that property to the location of the trustees.

Further support for this view is provided by *A-G v Johnson*.[6] The slightly simplified facts are as follows. An English domiciled testator left a tea estate in Assam on trust with English resident trustees. Two of the beneficiaries died, thereby increasing the share of the survivors. It was necessary to determine the situs of this increased share for taxation purposes. It was held that the increase did not constitute property situate out of the United Kingdom so that succession, estate and settlement estate duty were payable. The decision was based on the fact that English trustees stood between the beneficial owner and the underlying property.[7]

The theme is continued in the case of *Favorke v Steinkopff*.[8] English trustees were directed to invest a certain sum in German securities. The beneficiaries were German nationals. It was held that the interests of the beneficiaries were charged under the Treaty of Peace Order 1919 as being 'property, rights and interests' in the United Kingdom.[9]

---

[1] Section D.
[2] *Dicey and Morris*, p 931.
[3] On the assumption of co-ownership between clients under fungible custody.
[4] (1878) 7 Ch D 351.
[5] See Jessel MR at 355.
[6] [1907] 2 KB 885.
[7] 'I think it is clear that, but for the intervention of the trustees and the special directions and powers given to them, the property would have been situate out of the United Kingdom.' per Bray J at 893.
[8] [1922] 1 Ch174.
[9] See Russell J at 177.

In all of these cases, the situs of the interest of a beneficiary under a trust is the location of the trustee.

(d) Enforcement procedure

Chapter 2 considered the nature of proprietary rights. It argued that property is, in origin, a remedy, and that the legal nature of property is deeply coloured by the court procedures whereby proprietary remedies may be obtained.[1] It should therefore be no surprise to find that the basis for the above judgments is procedural. The right of the beneficiary in respect of the underlying property is (in the absence of breach of trust)[2] not directly enforceable against that property. It is only enforceable through the trustee.[3] More generally, an important jurisprudential basis for the rule that proprietary rights are determined in accordance with *lex situs*, is the pragmatic consideration that the cooperation of the courts where the assets are located will be required for enforcement. In practice, the primary recourse of the custody client is against the trustee. These are arguments in favour of identifying *lex situs* as the jurisdiction of the trustee.

(e) Nature of interest under a trust

Chapter 2 considered the difference between personal and proprietary rights. It argued that the question of whether a right is proprietary makes little sense when considered in abstract terms, and is meaningful only in the context of concrete situations, the most important of which (in the modern era) is insolvency. It also argued that equitable interests arising under trusts lie on the border between personal and proprietary rights. Trusts comprise a broad category of legal arrangements, ranging from bare trusts (where the beneficiary has allocated property rights in the trust assets)[4] to unadministered estates (where no property rights in favour of the beneficiary can arise because of want of allocation), and the right of the beneficiary is merely personal against the trustee.[5] However, all trust interests are proprietary in the important sense that the beneficiaries' rights are not vulnerable to the insolvency of the trustee. However, these rights are indirect, for (in the absence of breach of trust) they are not enforceable by the beneficiary directly against the trust assets.[6]

---

[1] See chapter 2, section 1(f), above.

[2] When tracing may be available to beneficiaries.

[3] 'Maak's right is a right against the trustees, a right to call on them to do their duty under the will, and, if they do not, to come to the Court here and ask to have the estate administered according to the trusts of the will. That right seems to me to be a chose in action, and a chose in action must be regarded as situate in the country where it is enforceable.' *Favorke v Steinkopff*, per Russell J at 178. This is again emphasised in *A-G v Jewish Colonization Association* [1901] 1 KB 123: '... where property is found to be legally vested in a person subject to the jurisdiction of English Courts, ... the title to the beneficial interest in that property is regulated and capable of being enforced by the laws of England ...' (per Stirling LJ at 142).

[4] See also *A-G for Hong Kong v Reid* [1994] 1 All ER 1, where a trust interest is held to be proprietary and cautionable against underlying land.

[5] See *Webb v Webb* [1994] 3 All ER 911 for the characterisation of trusts interest as personal rights. *Baker v Archer-Shee* discusses the difference between a mere chose in action against the trustee and rights *in rem* against the underlying assets. See also Hayton, *The Law of Trusts*, pp 161–163. See also *Marshall v Kerr* [1994] 3 All ER 106 at 119.

[6] Enforcement must generally be through the trustee as legal owner of the assets. Thus, the beneficial owner of shares generally cannot compel the issuer to pay the dividends to him, without joining the trustee of the shares.

It might be said that trust interests are proprietary in the trustee's insolvency, and personal in enforcement against third parties. All trust interests share this hybrid nature. In locating their situs with the trustee the cases discussed in this section, the English courts have been guided by the nature of trust interests in third party enforcement.[1]

(f)   Allocated and unallocated interests

This chapter has assumed fungible custody at the level of the sub-custodian, with the result that the custody trust asset is unallocated. This is important, as it is arguable that the rules for attributing situs to an interest under a trust differ depending on whether the interest is allocated or unallocated.

Lord Sudeley v A-G[2] begins a long line of cases concerning the situs of another class of unallocated trust interests, namely interests in unadministered estates. In *Lord Sudeley*, an English domiciled testator left one-quarter of his residuary estate to his wife absolutely. His wife died domiciled in England before the husband's estate was fully administered or the residue ascertained. The residue included mortgages on real property in New Zealand. It was held that estate duty was payable on that part of the wife's estate referable to the mortgages as the property was an English asset. This was because the wife's interest in the residuary estate was unallocated.[3]

In this case, it was held that the interest was not merely unallocated, but that it was not proprietary at all, being merely a personal right of enforcement against the trustee.[4] In this respect, the cases differ from fungible custody, under which (on the basis assumed in this chapter) the interest of the client is proprietary.

Lord Sudeley was directly followed in the cases of *Re Smyth*[5] and *Stamp Duties Comr (Queensland) v Hugh Duncan Livingston*.[6] In these cases, the interest in question also arose in an unadministered estate, and there was no indication that the interest in question was proprietary.[7] However, in the case of *Baker v Archer-Shee*,[8] the position more closely accorded with that under fungible custody, as the case concerned an estate that had been administered.

In this case, a US testator left foreign securities under a US trust for his daughter for life. The trustees were a US trust corporation. Income was not remitted to England but held in an account in New York. Archer-Shee, the husband of the daughter, was assessed to income tax on the income of his wife on the basis that it was income arising from foreign securities (which was taxable whether or not received in the UK). Archer-Shee argued that, because of the interposition of the trust, it was income from a foreign possession

---

[1] The English courts have also been guided by the nature of trust interest in third party enforcement in determining the question of jurisdiction.
[2] [1897] AC 11, HL.
[3] Per Lord Davey at 21.
[4] 'I do not think that they [the wife and her executors] have an estate, right, or interest, legal or equitable, in these New Zealand mortgages so as to make them assets of her estate.' per Lord Herschell at 18. See also Lord Davey at 21.
[5] *Re Smyth, Leach v Leach* [1898] 1 Ch 89.
[6] [1965] AC 694. The reasoning in *Lord Sudeley* and *Stamp Duties Comr (Queensland) v Livingston* is endorsed by Lord Browne Wilkinson in *Marshall v Kerr* [1994] 3 WLR 299 at 312.
[7] Chapter 2, section 1(h), above argued that the interest under a beneficiary in an unadministered estate is merely an equitable chose in action and not an equitable chose in possession.
[8] [1927] AC 844, HL.

other than stocks and shares (which was only taxable to the extent it was remitted to the United Kingdom).

The House of Lords held that the income was taxable.[1] The daughter was specifically entitled to the income and had an allocated interest in the underlying property under the terms of the trust. The Master of the Rolls in the lower court had relied on the principle of *Lord Sudeley* to hold that tax was not payable. However, *Lord Sudeley* was distinguished, because in this case the estate had been administered.[2]

There is *obiter* authority that, had the daughter's interest been proprietary but unallocated, the judgment would have differed.[3] Also of interest are the dissenting judgments of Viscount Sumner and Lord Blanesburgh, who argue that, even though allocated, the daughter's interest is indirect and therefore not the same as a direct proprietary interest in the underlying property.[4] The trust in question was a New York law trust, and New York law was presumed to be the same as English law. However, further assessments to tax were made on Archer-Shee, and in a later case (*Archer-Shee v Garland*[5]) he adduced expert evidence that New York law differed from English law in that his wife did not have an estate or interest in the underlying securities, but only a chose in action against the trustees. On this basis it was held that tax was not payable.

These cases help to formulate the rule that the situs of trust interests which are unallocated but proprietary (as in fungible custody on the assumed bases), is the jurisdiction where the trustee is located.

(g) Situs of underlying property

A different approach is suggested in *Dicey and Morris*. This approach seeks to distinguish between trust interests which are proprietary interests in the trust assets, and those which are mere choses in action against the trustee. (This chapter has argued that all trust interests are both of these things.) *Dicey and Morris* argue that the rule for the situs of a trust interest differs according to which class it belongs:

> 'If the beneficiary is given a beneficial interest in the trust property then his interest under the trust is located in the country where the trust property is situated. If the beneficiary is given merely a right of action against the trustees then his interest under the trust is located where the action may be brought, ie at the trustees' place of residence.'[6]

---

[1] Viscount Sumner and Lord Blanesburgh dissenting.

[2] 'My Lords, with great respect to the Master of the Rolls, I do not think either his own reasoning or the quotations he relies upon have any application to a case such as the present when, as I have already pointed out, we are dealing with "a definite and specific trust fund".' Per Lord Carson at 871. See also Lord Atkinson at 862 and Lord Wrenbury at 866.

[3] '... had the share to which Lady Archer-Shee was entitled been a proportion only of the income or profits of the residue other questions would, no doubt, arise.' Per Lord Carson at 869.

[4] 'All that she has is a right, in the forum of the trustee and of the trust fund, to have the trust executed in her favour under an order to be made for her benefit by the appropriate Court of equity, and this "possession" neither consists in the trust's investments or any of them nor is it situated here. It is "foreign".' Per Viscount Sumner at 856. Again, 'Her interest is merely an equitable one, and it is not an interest in the specific stocks and shares constituting the trust fund at all' per Lord Blanesburgh at 877, quoting Rowlatt J.

[5] [1931] AC 212, HL.

[6] Rule 114(9) at p 933.

Only two cases are cited in support of the first part of the rule (that situs of the interest coincides with that of the underlying property), namely *Re Berchtold*[1] and *Phillipson-Stow v IRC*.[2] Both of these concern the private international law of succession. The outcome of each case depended on whether, upon succession, an interest in land held on trust for sale was movable or immovable property. In both cases such interests in freeholds were held to be immovable. As the scope of the definition of immovable property is extremely wide and somewhat arbitrary,[3] these cases do not provide clear authority for location of any proprietary interest under a trust in the jurisdiction of the underlying assets.[4]

A larger number of cases are cited in *Dicey and Morris* in support of the rule that situs of the trust interest coincides with that of the trustee. This chapter has argued that this rule is correct, and applies to all trust interests, on the basis of the manner in which they are enforceable.

(h)   Conclusions

In conclusion, it is argued that *lex situs* of an unallocated trust interest such as the interest of the custody client in the custody trust asset, is the law of the jurisdiction of the trustee.[5] In other words, the way in which securities are held determines not only their legal nature but also their legal location.

This approach is clearly advantageous in the context of global custody, for there will be only one trustee (and therefore only one *lex situs*). In contrast, identifying *lex situs* with the situs of the underlying assets, will produce a fragmented approach in the case of mixed portfolios that are characteristic in global custody.[6]

However, the benefit of the approach remains limited by forum risk.

The intermediary jurisdiction approach accords with the approach of the revised article 8 of the US Uniform Commercial Code. The unallocated interest

---

[1] [1923] 1 Ch 192.

[2] [1961] AC 727.

[3] 'A mortgage debt secured by land is immovable property': *Re Berchtold*, per Russell J, at 201.

[4] It may be proper to distinguish between movable and immovable property; the importance of the location of the underlying property is greater in the latter case. See DWM Waters, *The Law of Trusts in Canada*, (1974), Carswell, Toronto, p 969: '... where immoveables are concerned, the *lex situs* will continue to have an overwhelming and inevitable influence ... where a trust comprises both movables and immoveables ... there is good reason for not giving such an influence to the *lex situs* ... because it should be a matter of importance that the trust should be seen as a unit and its issues dealt with accordingly ...'.

[5] Support for this view is found in Philip Wood, *Comparative Law of Security and Guarantees*, (1995), Sweet & Maxwell, London, p 190: 'The lex situs of fungible securities deposited with a custodian ought to be the office of the custodian where the securities account is kept'. See also ibid, p 81.

[6] This sort of fragmented result was judicially rejected in the slightly different context of integrity of transfer. In the first instance judgment of *Macmillan v Bishopsgate Investment Trust plc (No 3)* [1995] 3 All ER 747, Millett J refers to '... cases like the present in which portfolios of securities are delivered which consist of shares of companies in many different countries ... when it comes to considering whether any and if so what inquiries the recipient ought to make in order to verify the right of the transferor to deliver the portfolio, it would in my judgment be absurd to distinguish between the different components of the portfolio unless and until the recipient himself differentiates between them by attempting to perfect his security', at 763. See also Moshinsky, op cit, pp 605, 611 and 613.

of the client in securities held through an intermediary (a 'securities entitlement')
is located with the intermediary: article 8–110.

> 'Because [the client's] property is "located" at Custodian, it is clear, as a matter
> of general principle, that the only proper subject of legal process by [the client's]
> creditors would be Custodian'.[1]

7   Forum risk

While the intermediary jurisdiction approach may be the way forward for
the use of custody securities as collateral, the problem remains that a forum
such as that of the issuer of the securities may assume jurisdiction, and adopt
a different approach.

The difficulty of the legal position, and the commercial imperative of using
securities as collateral, call for a pragmatic approach. Chargees will often have
to tolerate some measure of legal risk, and should focus upon practical issues
relating to enforcement. Possession is of primary importance. Will the intermediary clearer or custodian cooperate in enforcing the security interest
sufficiently rapidly, so that challenge at issuer level may come too late? Does
the clearer have more than one local depositary, so that a third party claiming
a competing right in the charged assets would be unable to identify and therefore
attach the charged assets through the local courts? Finally, and subject to the
need to avoid illegality, does the chargee have any assets of its own in the issuer
jurisdiction against which adverse claims or penalties might be enforced?

D   Insolvency[2]

1   Cash and securities

Custodian insolvency is complicated by the fact that global custodial
arrangements are intermediated and cross-border. However, this is only true
in relation to the securities in the custody portfolio. As discussed in chapter
6, section A.2, above, custody cash balances are neither intermediated nor
cross-border, for they are not proprietary.[3]

Where the global custodian becomes insolvent, the client's cash balances
will generally[4] be at risk as unsecured debt. However, if a sub-custodian becomes
insolvent, the client's cash balances will not generally[5] be affected, as the

---

[1] SJ Rogers, *Policy Perspectives on Revised UCC, Article 8*, UCLA Law Rev, June 1996, p 1431,
at 1457.
[2] The author is grateful to Dermot Turing of Clifford Chance for his help in reviewing this
section.
[3] In general, the custody cash balance represents the unsecured debt of the custodian to the
client. Because the client's claim is personal against the custodian and not proprietary, the
client takes the custodian's credit risk. The legal analysis is simple, as the client does not
look beyond the custodian to other persons in other jurisdictions in order to assert proprietary
rights against them.
[4] Unless a special arrangement has been established, such as a client money trust with a third
party bank, a 'near cash' arrangement such as a short-term investment fund, or comparable
arrangements rendering the claim of the client proprietary. Following the Barings crisis,
innovative work was done in developing such arrangements.
[5] In the absence of contractual provision to the contrary in the global custody agreement.

global custodian's obligation to pay is not conditional on its ability to recover from sub-custodians.[1]

The comments in the remainder of this section relate to custody securities.

2   Intermediation

The growth in cross-border investment implies greater use of intermediaries in the custody of securities, as the need for liaison with local issuers and tax authorities necessitates the use of local sub-custodians. A second reason for the growth of intermediation is settlement. Much of the risk and inefficiency in the securities markets is associated with settlement. The need to address settlement difficulties is one of the driving forces for innovation in the securities markets. The problem is simple. On the one hand, transferring securities in certain markets involves risk, expense and delay. On the other hand, investors need to be able to buy and sell their beneficial interests in securities safely, cheaply and quickly. One solution has been used again and again: the removal of settlement from the problematic forum of the issuer of the underlying securities, to the safe and convenient forum of an intermediary. Whether securities are repackaged in depositary receipt form[2] or immobilised in a clearing system,[3] the fundamental idea is the same. Large numbers of securities are transferred into the name of an intermediary institution and held by it for participating investors; transactions between participants are settled by amending the records of the intermediary, thereby avoiding the need for settlement in the local markets. One level of intermediation may be introduced by repackaging, another by immobilisation, and yet others by the need to have a lead custodian in the jurisdiction of the client, and a further custodian in the jurisdiction of the issuer of the underlying securities. The investor may be separated from the underlying securities by a chain with a significant number of links.

However, if intermediation reduces settlement risk, it introduces risks of its own: investors' securities may be lost in the hands of intermediaries for a variety of reasons, including fraud.[4] However, a study of the London markets[5] has shown that losses of client securities in the hands of intermediaries have not been caused by fraud alone,[6] but by the combination of fraud and insolvency.[7] In the worst case, the assets are not there, and there is no one to sue for their recovery. Both the investor's proprietary rights and its personal rights[8] in respect of its investment are valueless.

---

[1] Although its inability to recover from sub-custodians may trigger its own insolvency. In commercial effect, the global custodian guarantees the cash positions with the sub-custodians. Legally, of course, it is not a guarantee but a primary obligation.

[2] See chapter 10.

[3] See chapter 11.

[4] '... the involvement of intermediaries in the holding of securities and the settling of trades necessarily creates new legal relationships and new risks. Perhaps the most basic difference in risks is that the non-resident faces custody risk – the potential loss of the securities held in custody in the event that the local agent becomes insolvent, acts negligently or commits fraud.' Bank for International Settlements, *Cross-Border Securities Settlement*, May 1995, Basle, p 22.

[5] *Custodianship and the Protection of Client Property*, July 1994, London Business School.

[6] Presumably because, provided the intermediary is solvent, there will be an enforceable obligation on the intermediary to make up the shortfall.

[7] See *Custodianship and the Protection of Client Property*, p 3.

[8] Against the custodian.

Intermediary risk is the risk that custody securities in the hands of the insolvent intermediary may be available to its general creditors; this is a question of law. Shortfall risk is the risk that there is a shortfall in the intermediary's holding of custody securities; this is a question of fact. Sections 3 to 6, below, will look at intermediary risk and section 7 will consider shortfall risk. Sections 8 and 9 will address other risks to the custody assets on insolvency (liens and liquidator's costs). Finally, section 10 will consider insolvency conflicts of law.

3 Intermediary risk

Chapter 2 indicated[1] that the chief practical difference between personal and proprietary rights is that personal rights may become valueless in the insolvency of the obligor. In the context of custody, it is important to establish that the client enjoys proprietary rights in the custody securities, so that it is not exposed to the credit risk of any intermediary. Proprietary rights link a person to an asset. In order to be linked to the underlying custody securities, the client must demonstrate that its property runs through each link in the chain of intermediaries through which the securities are held. Its proprietary claims are as weak as the weakest link.

Suppose an English investor appoints a London global custodian to hold its Italian bonds. The bonds are held through Euroclear, of which the global custodian is not a participant. This means that the custody chain will have four links. The investor delegates safekeeping to the global custodian. The global custodian sub-delegates custody to a Belgian sub-custodian which is a Euroclear participant. The sub-custodian delegates to Euroclear. Euroclear does not hold the bonds itself, but sub-delegates custody to an Italian depositary, which holds the bonds in its vaults. The global custody agreement is governed by English law. The sub-custodian agreement, Euroclear's general terms and conditions and the depositary agreement are governed by Belgian law. The bonds are governed by Italian law.

In order for the client to own the bonds, each link in the chain must pass proprietary rights upwards to the next intermediary. It may be assumed that the depositary will own the bonds under Italian law, by virtue of possession (in the case of bearer bonds) or registration (in the case of registered bonds). Whether Euroclear enjoys proprietary rights under the depositary agreement that would be recognised in the insolvency of the depositary will depend on the terms of that agreement and Italian law.[2] It is understood that the international clearers obtain the opinion of local counsel that their proprietary rights would survive the insolvency of a depositary. The proprietary link between Euroclear and its participants is supported by legislation.[3] Whether the assets would be safe from the general creditors of the sub-custodian in its insolvency will be determined by the terms of the sub-custodian agreement

---

[1] In section 3, above.
[2] On the likely assumption that the depositary's insolvency would be governed by Italian law.
[3] Royal Decree No 62 of 10 November 1967, as amended by an Act of 7 April 1995. Similar provision is made for Cedel under Luxembourg law in a Grand Ducal Decree of 17 February 1971, as amended by a Decree of 8 June 1994.

and Belgian law.[1] Finally, the client will be able to recover its assets in the insolvency of the global custodian if, as a matter of English law, they are held for it on trust.[2]

If any link in the chain fails, the client has only a personal claim and therefore bears the credit risk of the intermediary immediately above the failed link.[3] Issuer (or market) risk is compounded by intermediary risk, and the value of the investment is reduced accordingly. The following sections will consider reasons why a link might fail in this way.

4 Civil law jurisdictions

Global custody involves intermediation, or the separation of ownership from possession or control. Under English law, two legal relationships permit property to be held by one person yet owned by another: bailment and trust. Chapter 4 argued that bailment is of limited relevance in the modern securities markets,[4] so that the concept of trusts is the main basis for intermediated proprietary rights under English law.

The function of the custody chain is to cross borders. The trust is an Anglo-Saxon concept, and not generally recognised in civil law jurisdictions. An alternative basis for conferring intermediated proprietary rights must therefore be identified in those jurisdictions. As noted above, the European international clearers have legislative support. Article 8 of the New York US Uniform Commercial Code provides for proprietary rights in favour of purchasers of fungible securities held by financial intermediaries.[5] In the absence of such legislation, how will civil law jurisdictions treat the custody assets? The position is complicated by the fact that the choice of law of the contracts governing the intermediary chain is not always the law of the jurisdiction of the intermediary. For example, the European clearers may require their local law to govern their depositary agreements. Also, some English global custodians require their sub-custody contracts to be governed by English law. Would an intermediated proprietary relationship purported to be created under such contracts be recognised in a jurisdiction having no such concept under its local law?

'In civil law jurisdictions ... major problems arise because the trust concept is alien to their domestic law.'[6] An English law trust may be recognised if the jurisdiction is bound by the Hague Trusts Convention.[7] 'The Convention *does not* introduce the trust concept into the domestic law of countries lacking the concept ("non-trust countries"). ... The Convention *does* make non-trust

---

[1] On the assumption that its insolvency is governed by Belgian law. Where local custody is provided in Luxembourg through a branch, the position might differ as Luxembourg law applies the insolvency rules of the jurisdiction of incorporation.

[2] See chapters 4 and 5, above.

[3] Subject to any contractual or general law duty on the custodian to make good any losses associated with sub-custodian insolvency; see chapter 8, below.

[4] Because bailment necessarily implies tangible and allocated property.

[5] Article 8-313(1)(d)(ii) and (iii), and 8-313(2). Of course, New York is not a civil law jurisdiction.

[6] DJ Hayton, 'International Recognition of Trusts', ed J Glasson, *International Trust Laws,* Chancery Law, London, C.1.1.

[7] The UK, Italy, Luxembourg, United States, Canada, Australia and France have signed the treaty; the UK, Italy, The Netherlands, the provinces of Canada, other than Ontario and Quebec, and Australia have gone on to ratify it. Signing without more merely indicates an intention to implement in due course by legislation upon ratification.

countries, like trust countries, recognise trusts of property as a matter of private international law (subject to significant safeguards).'[1]

The Convention provides as follows:

'Such recognition shall imply, as a minimum, that the trust property constitutes a separate fund ... In so far as the law applicable to a trust requires or provides, such recognition shall imply, in particular–

(a) that personal creditors of the trustee shall have no recourse against the trust assets;

(b) that the trust assets shall not form part of the trustee's estate upon his insolvency or bankruptcy; ...'.[2]

However, certain provisions in the Convention may defeat the recognition of a trust arising under a contract governed by the law of a trust state, in the courts of a non-trust issuer jurisdiction. Article 13 may obviate the need for recognition where the underlying securities are issued in a non-trust state.[3] Arguably, article 15 may cut across recognition in the context of insolvency (and, incidentally, taking security).[4]

Alternatively, the local courts may follow the approach of the Swiss Federal Court in *Hunter v Moss* securities.[5, 6] Swiss law being the applicable law of a trust created by an American, it held that 'it is necessary to examine to which legal institutions of Swiss law the legal relationship in dispute has the closest resemblance as far as its effects are concerned.' The court found that the trust was really a mixed contract depending on the law of obligations, since it contained aspects of a contract of mandate, of an agreement to make a fiduciary transfer of property, of a gift and of a contract for the benefit of a third party.[7, 8]

Where the Hague Convention and the principle in *Hunter v Moss* do not assist, the risk may remain that the custody assets are available to the creditors of an intermediary in its insolvency, unless the safekeeping arrangements clearly earmark the assets for the custodian's clients.

5 Local restrictions not met

Another source of intermediary risk is failure to comply with issuer jurisdiction formalities. The use of street names (or informal sub-delegations of custody

---

[1] Glasson, op cit, cl 5 and 6.

[2] Article 11.

[3] 'No state shall be bound to recognise a trust the significant elements of which, except for the choice of the applicable law, the place of administration and the habitual residence of the trustee, are more closely connected with States which do not have the institution of the trust or the category of trust involved.' Article 13 does not form part of English law: the Recognition of Trusts Act 1987, which implemented the Convention, omits article 13.

[4] 'The Convention does not prevent the application of provisions of the law designated by the conflicts rules of the forum, in so far as these provisions cannot be derogated from by voluntary act, relating in particular to the following matters–
... d. the transfer of title to property and security interests in property;
... e. the protection of creditors in matters of insolvency.'
    Article 15(1) (d) and (e) is excluded in implementing Dutch legislation so as to oust article 84 of Book 3 of the Dutch Civil Code, which does not recognise transfers to a person otherwise than as fully part of his patrimony.

[5] [1993] 1 WLR 934; affd [1994] 1 WLR 452, CA.

[6] AFT 96, 1970, II 79.

[7] Hayton and Glasson, op cit, C1.33.

[8] For an example of the equivalent process under English conflicts law, see *Macmillan v Bishopsgate (No 3)* [1996] 3 All ER 747 at 769, 770.

to local brokers to escape restrictions on foreign holdings) is widespread in some Far East jurisdictions.[1]

The historic and legitimate function of global custody is to address the inefficiencies and risks involved in cross-border investment. However, where the custodian goes further and seeks to assist the client in defeating the policy requirements of the issuer's jurisdiction,[2] care should be taken. The risk is that, by seeking to make the client's position invisible in the issuer's jurisdiction, it is unenforceable there. The rules of private international law may render local enforceability indispensable.

6   Commingling

Custody securities are generally commingled in the hands of each intermediary in the custody chain. In other words, each intermediary will hold any particular custody securities in a mixed account together with other like securities held for other beneficial owners. As property may be loosely described as a legal relationship between persons and assets, the general rule is that a proprietary right can only arise in relation to identifiable assets. The difficulty for the investor is that it cannot identify which of the securities within the pooled account belong to it. Chapter 5, above, considered this problem ('the allocation problem') under English law. It suggested that the answer is the concept of co-ownership, whereby all investors having interests in the pool together co-own all the securities in the pool. Such co-ownership may be implied under English law, but the position is uncertain, and express co-ownership provision is recommended in the custody documentation.[3] In Belgium and Luxembourg, it was felt necessary to pass legislation confirming proprietary rights in commingled (or fungible) accounts; a similar result is provided by article 8 of the New York Uniform Commercial Code.[4] The existence of this legislation suggests that the position at general law is uncertain.[5] Some doubt must therefore arise where custody securities are commingled in jurisdictions having no equivalent legislation. It would be prudent for the global custodian or its clients to obtain the opinion of local counsel that commingled securities will be safe in the insolvency of the local sub-custodian or other intermediary.

---

[1] Another example is investment in Russia. Although a civil law jurisdiction, Russian law has a limited statutory concept of trusts. The beneficial ownership of shares by a person other than the registered holder is recognised, provided that a note of the beneficial holding is entered on the register of the issuer or the registered holder is a financial intermediary. In order to benefit from a double taxation treaty between the Russian Federation and Cyprus, it is customary for much Western investment in Russian shares to be held through a Cyprus nominee. The nominee agrees to hold the shares for investors under the terms of a Cyprus trust, and opinion is taken from Cyprus counsel that the trust is constituted in accordance with Cyprus domestic law. However, no note of the trust customarily appears on the register of the Russian issuer. Therefore, depending on the status of the registered holder, the trust may not be enforceable in Russia, and the risk must arise that creditors of the nominee could claim the shares through the Russian courts. Further, there may be some risk that the trust would be vulnerable in the Cypriot insolvency of the nominee. Although good under Cyprus *domestic* law, it would not be good under Cyprus *private international* law if the latter applied *lex situs* (ie Russian law) to transfers of beneficial interests to third parties such as the investors.
[2] Such as taxation, or restrictions on foreign ownership of securities.
[3] See chapter 5, above.
[4] See section 3, above.
[5] It is uncertain in common law as well as in civil law.

7 Shortfall and contractual settlement

Even if a trust or similar arrangement is recognised in the insolvency of the intermediary, the client will still suffer loss if all its securities are not there:

'Shortfalls in custodial holdings may develop for a number of reasons, including the failure of trades to settle as anticipated, poor accounting controls, or intentional fraud. The shortfalls may be temporary or long-standing. Allocation of the risk of loss from a shortfall will vary depending on the circumstances under which the shortfall arose. Of course, if the custodian is solvent, no real problems arise; it may either replace the missing securities, or pay damages, or both. However, if the custodian is insolvent, or the shortfall arises from fraud or insolvency on the part of a sub-custodian or CSD, the investor's risk of loss may be severe. In a cross-border context, the involvement of multiple legal jurisdictions and multiple settlement intermediaries increases the importance of custody risks and greatly complicates their analysis.'[1]

A special risk associated with commingled accounts is that shortfalls attributable to the business of one client may be borne by other clients sharing the account. Where segregated accounts are not offered, therefore, prudent clients may wish to enquire whether the custodian engages in practices which heighten the risk of shortfall. An obvious example of such a practice is the contractual settlement of securities. Contractual settlement is a service offered by some global custodians in relation to cash or (more rarely) securities. It is agreed that, where moneys or securities are due to be received under a trade, those assets will be credited to the client's account on the date agreed for settlement with the counterparty, whether or not they are actually received on that date by the custodian. The custodian reserves the right to reverse the credit entry if the assets do not arrive within a reasonable period.[2] Contractual settlement amounts to lending of cash and/or securities.[3] Where contractual settlement of securities is offered in connection with commingled securities accounts, clear dangers arise. If 100 bonds are contractually settled, the client is free to sell them to a third party. If the original trade fails, the custodian cannot reverse the credit entry without causing a shortfall. Further, as the contractual settlement of securities amounts to securities lending, the question arises, from whom is the client borrowing? It will only be borrowing from the custodian if the custodian transfers new securities into the commingled account to support the transaction.[4] If the custodian does not do this, the client is borrowing securities from the other clients of the custodian, without their consent or knowledge. Under English law, such arrangements may involve the custodian in liability for theft. In the custodian's insolvency, the consequent shortfall would be handled in accordance with the equitable tracing rules.

8 Liens

A further risk to the custody assets is the possibility of liens or other security interests in favour of intermediaries in the global custody chain, such as sub-

[1] Bank for International Settlements, *Cross-Border Securities Settlement*, May 1995, Basle, p 20.
[2] Custodians only offer contractual settlement in markets where they are confident of settlement.
[3] Raising issues of authority to lend and borrow such assets, as well as taxation issues.
[4] As in prime brokerage.

custodians and settlement systems. For example, if a global custodian becomes insolvent, a sub-custodian may enforce a lien over the client assets it holds for the global custodian in respect of unpaid fees. Where fungible custody is offered, one client's assets may in effect be charged to secure exposures referable to the business of another client. The SFA rulebook restricts the ability of authorised firms to permit custodial liens to be taken over client assets.[1]

9   Liquidator's costs

The case of *Berkeley Applegate (Investment Consultants) Ltd*[2] established the principle that, where the assets of the insolvent company are insufficient to meet the liquidator's costs in administering property held on trust by the company for its clients, the court has discretion to award those costs out of the trust assets.[3]

This principle may pose a threat to the assets of custody clients where the custodian does not have substantial assets of its own, and where adequate records of the custody have not been kept, so that significant work is required to clarify the entitlements of clients.

10   Conflict of laws

Cross-border insolvency raises complex legal issues. However, not all of them are directly relevant to custody. Liquidation is the legal procedure for the collection, administration and distribution of the assets of the insolvent. In theory, the insolvent liquidation of the custodian should not affect custody assets, as these are the assets, not of the insolvent, but of its clients.[4] But, as indicated above, the courts of the different jurisdictions involved may take a different approach to the recognition of trusts and the allocation of shortfalls. The manner in which these differences will be handled is inherently unpredictable, partly because the English private international law of insolvency is uncertain, and partly because the international position is very far from being harmonised.[5] The following are a few very general comments on the subject.

---

[1] Rules 4.6.d and 4.7.d. The European clearers exempt participant client accounts from their security interests for this reason.

[2] [1988] 3 All ER 71.

[3] At 76, 82.

[4] These comments relate to custody securities and not custody cash.

[5] Lack of progress in harmonisation is perhaps due to the profound political and social differences that underlie the different provisions of nations' insolvency laws.

However, within Europe some progress is being made towards harmonisation with the Bankruptcy Convention and the Winding Up Directive (discussed in section (d), below). See also the Istanbul Convention of the Council of Europe which seeks to achieve co-operation in cross-border insolvencies.

(a) General principles

(I) JURISDICTION

Universality and plurality In the theory of the private international law of insolvency, two conflicting sets of principles determine the varying approach of different courts to jurisdiction. Under the principles of universality and unity, one set of insolvency proceedings in the jurisdiction of the insolvent governs the insolvent's assets worldwide. Under the principles of plurality and territoriality, each forum governs assets in its jurisdiction. In practice a compromise between the two is usually reached.

Global custody is international in two senses. Firstly, the arrangements involve *intermediaries* in different jurisdictions. Secondly, the arrangements relate to *assets* in different jurisdictions. While, generally, local assets will be held by local intermediaries[1] there will be circumstances where an intermediary holds international assets.[2] The question, therefore, arises whether the foreign assets of an insolvent English custodian will be subject to English or to foreign insolvency proceedings. Under the principles of unity and universality, the English courts would prevail; under the principles of plurality and territoriality, the foreign courts would deal with the assets.

In principle, English insolvency relates to assets wherever located.[3] However, this universal approach may in practice be limited by pragmatic difficulties of enforcement against foreign assets in circumstances where local creditors may assert claims against those assets under local law. Moreover, while the English courts may assume jurisdiction over foreign assets under the universal approach, they do not necessarily limit their jurisdiction over English assets of foreign companies in accordance with the same universal approach.[4] Because enforcement is more important than theory, in practice it would be prudent to assume that, in a custodian's insolvency, assets will be dealt with in accordance with the law of the jurisdiction in which the assets are located. The legal location of custody securities is often a nice question, as discussed in section C.6, above.

Jurisdiction of the English courts The English courts' jurisdiction to wind up companies depends on whether they are English registered and, if they are not, on whether there is a sufficient connection with the jurisdiction.

---

[1] So that, for example, French bonds are held by a French sub-custodian.

[2] For example, as between the global custodian and a French sub-custodian, the asset of the global custodian may be a proprietary right arising under French law, ie a French asset, enforceable and therefore located (for conflicts purposes) in France. On this basis, with a mixed portfolio, the assets held by the global custodian for its client may be legally located across all of the jurisdiction in which the client has invested.

[3] Section 144 of the Insolvency Act 1986.

[4] Ie the English courts may assume jurisdiction over the liquidation of a foreign company in certain circumstances (see below in this section). Where it does so, its jurisdiction is not limited to an English branch of the company or its English assets, but in principle may extend to the whole of the company (although, if there is also a home-state proceeding an English court is likely to order that the English liquidation be ancillary, ie territorial). Contrast this 'universal approach' to the 'ring fence' approach of Germany (local proceedings for a foreign company confined to local branch and local assets) and the 'no local proceedings' approach of Belgium (no local proceedings for a foreign company, but recognition of home state liquidation). Moreover, '[T]here is no rule of English law whereby the proprietary effects of a foreign liquidation are recognised as extending beyond the territorial limits of the jurisdiction in which the foreign liquidation has taken place.' Fletcher, op cit, p 763.

English registered companies   The English courts have discretionary jurisdiction to wind up any company registered in England.[1]

Unregistered company   That is a company not registered under the Companies Act.[2] The English courts have jurisdiction to wind up an unregistered company if, broadly, the company has ceased business, is unable to pay its debts or if it is just and equitable to do so. Case law[3] indicates that in practice the English courts will assume jurisdiction to wind up a foreign company if either the company at the time a petition is presented has assets in England or at any time has carried on business in England either directly or through an agent and in both cases where there is a reasonable possibility of benefit accruing to creditors in making the winding-up order.[4]

Civil Jurisdiction and Judgments Act 1982   This Act, which implements the Brussels and Lugano Conventions,[5] does not apply in respect of the winding up of insolvent companies.[6]

Forum non conveniens   Jurisdiction may be declined in order to prevent injustice where another forum of competent jurisdiction is more suitable, as discussed in chapter 6, section B.3, above.

(II)   PROPER LAW

As a general rule, insolvency is governed by the law of the jurisdiction in which it is conducted (*lex fori* or *lex concursus*) (although there are important exceptions to this[7]).

Under section 426 of the Insolvency Act 1986, the English courts may apply foreign law if so requested by certain (mainly) Commonwealth courts.[8]

---

[1] Insolvency Act 1986, section 117.

[2] Ibid, section 220. 'Company' for this purpose is widely defined.

[3] See *Banque des Marchands de Moscou (Koupetschesky) v Kindersley* [1951] Ch 112; *Re Matheson Bros Ltd* (1884) 27 Ch D 225; *Tovarishestvo Manufactur Liudvig-Rabenek* [1944] Ch 404; *Re Azoff-Don Commercial Bank* [1954] Ch 315; *Re Compania Merabello San Nicholas SA* [1973] Ch 75; *Re Eloc Electro-Optiecka and Communicatie BV* [1982] Ch 43; *Re a Company (No 00359 of 1987) (Okeanos)* [1988] Ch 210; *Re a Company (No 003102 of 1991), ex p Nyckeln Finance Co Ltd* [1991] BCLC 539.

[4] In practice it may also be necessary to show that there are no home state proceedings or that the home state liquidator agrees to the institution of an English liquidator, or alternatively that the foreign proceedings are prejudicial to English creditors.

[5] Discussed in chapter 6, section B.1, above.

[6] For the Act to be disapplied on the basis of proceedings concerning winding up it is necessary that they derive directly from the winding up and be closely connected with the winding-up proceedings: *Gourdain v Nadler* [1979] ECR 733.

[7] For example, where the Luxembourg branch of a foreign entity is wound up in Luxembourg, the Luxembourg courts will apply the law of the jurisdiction of incorporation.

[8] 'The courts having jurisdiction in relation to insolvency law in any part of the United Kingdom shall assist the courts having corresponding jurisdiction in any other part of the United Kingdom or any relevant authority or territory. The relevant designated territories are: Channel Islands, Isle of Man, Anguilla, Australia, Bahamas, Bermuda, Botswana, Canada, Cayman Islands, Falkland islands, Gibraltar, Hong Kong, Republic of Ireland, Montserrat, New Zealand, St Helena, Turks and Caicos Islands, Tuvalu, British Virgin Islands. The court may apply the insolvency law "applicable to either court in relation to comparable matters falling within its jurisdiction" but the court "shall have regard in particular to the rules of private International law". In other words, the courts must have regard to the English conflicts rules applicable to bankruptcy and not slavishly apply the laws of the foreign bankruptcy forum ...' Wood, *Principles of International Insolvency*, pp 255, 256.

(III)   CONCURRENT INSOLVENCY PROCEEDINGS

Clearly, if insolvency proceedings are also being taken out in other jurisdictions, some form of cooperation would have to be achieved, by recognition or otherwise:[1] 'Therefore, whenever the assets of an insolvent debtor are dispersed between two or more jurisdictions the effectiveness and efficiency of any insolvency proceedings centred in one country will be dependent upon the degree of recognition and co-operation accorded by the laws of the other jurisdictions involved.'[2]

(b)   Insolvency risk

Insolvency risk, or the risk that a local jurisdiction will not recognise the custody trust in respect of local custody assets (so that such assets are available to creditors of the custodian) is discussed above. Where an English custodian becomes insolvent, as a matter of English law the custody assets will be impressed with the custody trust wherever those assets are located.[3] However, in practice local courts may take a territorial approach, and hence the need to ensure that local assets (such as claims against sub-custodians and depositaries) are legally robust as a matter of local law, and that local law will not make the custody assets available to creditors[4] (or to rival insolvency officials where multiple insolvency proceedings are taken out).

(c)   Shortfall risk

Where there is a shortfall in the pooled client account of an insolvent custodian, the question arises what law will govern the manner in which that shortfall is borne by the respective clients. If the custodial relationship is governed by English law and the assets are governed by foreign law,[5] it may be argued that the English tracing rules would govern the allocation of the shortfall, as part of the law of trusts that governs the custodial relationship wherever the custody assets are located. Another possibility is that the local jurisdiction treats the allocation of shortfalls as a procedural matter, and therefore applies its law as the law of the forum. In any case, the question only arises where there is a conflict between English and foreign law; such conflicts may be less unlikely as many jurisdictions 'pro rate' losses among all clients, which appears to be the current approach of the English courts in active commingled accounts.[6]

---

[1]   '... most states will allow concurrent proceedings to be opened, whether an ancillary proceeding or a full bankruptcy ... the effect of the local proceedings is to allow the local jurisdiction to give effect to its own bankruptcy.' Wood, *Principles of International Insolvency*, p 242.

[2]   *Fletcher*, p 767.

[3]   This is because equity acts *in personam*; the jurisprudential basis of the trust is the relationship between trustee and beneficiary, so that the *lex situs* rule does not apply. Accordingly, the trust created over the assets of a company by a winding-up order extends to foreign assets: see *Fletcher*, pp 751, 752.

[4]   While the making of an English winding-up order stays all actions by unsecured creditors against the insolvent company or its assets under section 130(2) of the Insolvency Act 1986, this would not bind foreign creditors outside the jurisdiction.

[5]   Eg the assets consist of debts, shares or other choses in action whose governing law is foreign.

[6]   See *Barlow Clowes International v Vaughan* [1992] 4 All ER 22. However, the pro ration adopted in this case may not be the invariable practice.

(d)   The European Bankruptcy Convention and Winding-Up Directive

Two proposed European measures may be of relevance to insolvency conflict of laws for global custodians. The aim of both the Bankruptcy Convention and Winding-Up Directive is to harmonise the rules relating to insolvency jurisdiction and choice of law within the EC.

(I)   THE BANKRUPTCY CONVENTION

The Convention applies to all collective insolvency procedures (ie liquidation and administration but not receivership). It provides that the courts of the state of the insolvent's 'centre of main interests' ('home state') have jurisdiction to open insolvency proceedings. The place of the company's registered office is rebuttably presumed to be its home state. Secondary winding-up proceedings are permitted in other member states only if the insolvent has a local establishment; any such secondary proceedings must be 'ring fenced' to that local establishment and limited to assets in the second member state. These jurisdiction provisions are supported by recognition provisions.

The law of the state in which proceedings are taken out governs them, and determines among other things which assets are available to creditors.

However, the Convention may be of limited relevance to custody insolvency, for the following reasons. It does not apply (broadly) to banks or investment firms providing custody. This may exclude most custodians, but not necessarily the affiliate nominees who may hold client assets.

There is a carve out for third party proprietary rights (or rights *in rem*) at least in respect of assets within the EC. The natural reading of this provision is that the validity of the custody trust will be determined under normal conflicts rules. (The same is true of the validity of security interests.)

---

[1]   Articles 1(1) and 2(a) and Annex A.
[2]   Article 3(1).
[3]   Article 3(2) and 3(3). 'Establishment' is defined as 'any place of operations where the debtor carries out a non-transitory economic activity with human means and goods.' (Article 2(h)).
[4]   Article 27.
[5]   Chapter II.
[6]   Articles 4(1) and 28.
[7]   Article 4(2)(b). This law also determines who bears the costs of liquidation (Article 4(2)(1)); this can be relevant to custody clients in view of the rule in *Berkeley Applegate*: see section 9, above.
[8]   'This Convention shall not apply to insolvency proceedings concerning insurance undertakings, credit institutions, investment undertakings which provide services involving the holding of funds or securities for third parties, or to collective investment undertakings.' Article 1(2).
[9]   Article 5 provides as follows:
'(1) The opening of insolvency proceedings shall not affect the rights in rem of creditors or third parties in respect of tangible or intangible, movable or immovable assets belonging to the debtor which are situated within the territory of another Contracting State at the time of the opening of proceedings.
(2) The rights referred to in paragraph 1 shall in particular mean:
    (a) the right to dispose of assets or have them disposed of and to obtain satisfaction from the proceeds of or income from those assets, in particular by virtue of a lien or a mortgage;
    . . .
    (d) a right in rem to the beneficial use of assets.'
The wording of article 5(2)(d) is curious, but should be interpreted to include interests under trusts.
[10]   Although it might be argued that the Convention does not indicate which law will determine whether clients' rights are rights *in rem* or not, posing the threat that the foreign liquidator will not be obliged to recognise the English law trust.

In the case of custody assets not situated within a member state, the position seems to be governed by the general provision[1] that the law of the state in which proceedings are taken out governs the availability of assets to the creditors of the insolvent (although this is limited to home state proceedings).[2]

There is a further carve out for payment systems and financial markets within the EC.[3]

(II) THE WINDING-UP DIRECTIVE

The Winding-Up Directive applies to credit institutions, and is closely modelled on the Bankruptcy Convention. However, it is somewhat simpler in that no secondary proceedings are permitted. It is still in draft form.

(III) TIMETABLE

The initiative for the Convention began in the 1960s but encountered long delays. The unsatisfactory conflicts position following the collapse of BCCI in 1991 led to progress being made in the mid-1990s. The text was finalised in 1995 but Britain missed the May 1996 signature deadline because of the beef crisis. It will come into force six months after the last signature. The ratification process will take longer. The draft of the Winding-Up Directive is well advanced and the Directive will probably be made in 1997. Implementation may take a further three years, so that both measures may be in force by the new millennium.

It is proposed that separate measures will cover the insolvency of EC investment firms,[4] but these have not yet been published.

11 Insolvency risk in practice

Cross-border insolvency is problematic, for historical[5] and political[6] reasons. Much theoretical material has been written. However, in practice a pragmatic

---

[1] In article 4(2)(b).
[2] Article 27. In relation to secondary proceedings, non-EC assets are outside the scope of the Convention.
[3] Article 9 provides as follows:
'(1) ... the effects of insolvency proceedings on the rights and obligations of the parties to a payment or settlement system or to a financial market shall be governed solely by the law of the Contracting State applicable to that system or market.
(2) Paragraph 1 shall not preclude any action for voidness, voidability or unenforceability which may be taken to set aside payments or transactions under the law applicable to the relevant payment system or financial market.'
[4] And insurance companies, which are also not covered by either the Bankruptcy Convention or the Winding-Up Directive.
[5] Firstly, civil law and (to a lesser extent) common law is still dominated by Roman law, and the operation of insolvency law is based on the old Justinian distinction between rights of persons and rights of things, which is probably obsolete in relation to an electronic product such as global custody. Secondly, law follows political regimes, and England has not been invaded since 1066; the trust (on which custody rests) has developed in Anglo Saxon jurisdictions, but is unknown in continental Europe.
[6] Insolvency law, and in particular jurisdictions' differing for ranking creditors, reflect differing political priorities (eg whether employees should be postponed to secured bank creditors).

approach is called for.[1] If sub-custodial arrangements are supported by reasonably clean legal opinions, it may be unnecessary to enquire further in practice.

E   Conclusions

Conflicts of law will never be certain, and the doubts associated with the proprietary aspects of global custody are inexhaustible. This is particularly true where custody securities are used as collateral. However, legal uncertainty in commercial affairs is not new. Commercial law has always followed practice, and legal consensus may eventually follow the increasing harmonisation of practice.[2]

In the meantime, risk can be managed by focus on operation controls (in particular the speed with which collateral can be realised). Beyond that, it may properly be borne. Investment business is risk business, and a measure of legal risk may be tolerated, provided it is understood.

[1] 'The rules of cross-border insolvency tend to establish boundaries rather than lay down rigid and detailed procedures to be applied in all cases, and within those boundaries the practitioner is free to work towards the most advantageous solution for his or her client. In addition, the need for flexibility is underlined by the broad range of issues which fall to be determined by the English court in the exercise of its discretion.' Philip Smart, *Cross-Border Insolvency*, p vii.

[2] Offered by the growing use of central depositaries and initiatives such as G30.

Chapter 8

The custodian's duties[1]

'To describe some one as a fiduciary, without more, is meaningless.'[2]

Operational failures in the holding and administration of a portfolio of securities can cause significant losses to clients. Where such losses occur, global custodians may choose to make them good irrespective of legal liability, in order to preserve the client relationship. However, losses may be so great that liability would have severe consequences for the global custodian. Very broadly speaking, the custodian will be liable where client losses are attributable to its breach of duty.[3] Duty is the measure of potential liability. Control of levels of legal duty is therefore an essential part of risk management for the global custodian.

The chief method of controlling levels of duty is the use of duty defining and limitation of liability clauses in the global custody contract; as indicated below, these are highly effective in modifying the level of duty implied by general law. Indeed, such clauses are arguably the real reason for the global custodian to put a global custody contract in place.[4] These contractual techniques are discussed in section B, below. Section A provides the context of duty at general law.

A General law

1 Is the custodian a fiduciary?

The interrelation of fiduciary duties and financial arrangements has been much discussed in recent years.[5] While fiduciary duty is a very uncertain area of

---

[1] This chapter focuses on fiduciary duty and liability. For liability for breach of contract or tortious liability (such as negligence), the general principles of the law of contract and tort apply to the global custodian. These are touched on only very briefly in section F, below.
[2] *Re Goldcorp Exchange Ltd (in receivership)* [1994] 2 All ER 806, per Lord Mustill at 821.
[3] For a fuller discussion, see section A, below.
[4] Conversely, the practice of offering undocumented global custodian services exposes the global custodian to the risk of unmodified general law duties, implying commercially unacceptable levels of potential liability.
[5] Debate has been stimulated by a May 1992 Law Commission Consultative Paper, *Fiduciary Duties and Regulatory Rules* and a subsequent report having the same title and published in December 1995 (Cm 3049).

law, it is possible to make the following generalisations. Fiduciary relationships are relationships of special trust:[1] 'The "fiduciary" standard for its part enjoins one party to act in the interests of another – to act selflessly and with undivided loyalty.'[2] The significance of fiduciary status here is that fiduciaries owe special implied duties to their beneficiaries.[3] Fiduciary duties are summarised in four basic rules:

- the no conflict rule,
- the no profit rule,
- the undivided loyalty rule, and
- the duty of confidentiality.[4]

Beyond these rules (which are derived from the general duty to act in the interests of the beneficiary) fiduciary status does not prescribe positive duties. Thus, the particular services that a custodian must render are determined by its agreement with its client, and not by implied fiduciary status. Fiduciary status does not determine the content of the relationship between the parties; rather it is (in essence) merely a judicial remedy for want of loyalty where loyalty is owed.[5]

The argument that a global custodian is not a fiduciary is considered to be untenable. Because of its safekeeping role, the custodian is either a trustee

---

[1] 'Broadly speaking, a fiduciary relationship is one in which a person undertakes to act on behalf of or for the benefit of another, often as an intermediary with a discretion or power which affects the interests of the other who depends on the fiduciary for information and advice ... in determining whether a relationship was fiduciary, and if so, the extent of the fiduciary duties, a court would look at the substance of a relationship and not merely its description in the contract.' Law Commission Report, pp 1, 11.

[2] PD Finn, *The Fiduciary Principle, Equity, Fiduciaries and Trusts*, ed Youdan, (1989), Carswell, Toronto, p 4.

[3] More generally, in certain common law jurisdictions including England, '... to designate someone a fiduciary is to expose that person to the full rigour of equity both in method [for example, in reversal of the onus of proof, in presumptions of wrongdoing and in disregard of notions such as causation, foreseeability and remoteness] and in remedy [from avoidance through damages and the account of profits to the constructive trust] ...' PD Finn, *The Fiduciary Principle*, p 2.

[4] 'The exact scope of the fiduciary's obligations and the consequences of breach vary according to the particular circumstances but the duties may conveniently be summarised in the following basic rules:
   (i) *The "no conflict" rule*   A fiduciary must not place himself in a position where his own interest conflicts with that of his customer, the beneficiary. There must be a "real sensible possibility of conflict";
   (ii) *The "no profit" rule*   A fiduciary must not profit from his position at the expense of his customer, the beneficiary;
   (iii) *The "undivided loyalty" rule*   A fiduciary owes undivided loyalty to his customer, the beneficiary, not to place himself in a position where his duty towards one customer conflicts with a duty that he owes to another customer. A consequence of this is that a fiduciary must make available to a customer all the information that is relevant to the customer's affairs;
   (iv) *The "duty of confidentiality"*   A fiduciary must only use information obtained in confidence from his customer, the beneficiary, for the benefit of the customer and must not use it for his own advantage, or for the benefit of any other person.'
   Law Commission Report, pp 1, 2.

[5] See Finn, *The Fiduciary Principle*, p 28.

JB

Possession ⟵ denoted ...

Sister

Velupe — pat. of Laur
~ . intej ⟶ 4e

or a bailee.[1] A trustee is always a fiduciary.[2] Whether or not a bailee is a fiduciary will depend on all the circumstances and the terms of the bailment.[3] However, because the custodian role actively combines safekeeping with administration and settlement on behalf of the client, it would be prudent to assume that the global custodian is a fiduciary.[4]

2 Bailee

The traditional legal characterisation of the custodian of securities is as bailee of the client. Chapter 4 argued that this characterisation may no longer be appropriate.[5] However, there may still be cases where the global custodian is a bailee.[6] What then are a custodial bailee's duties at common law?

'A bailee for reward must take reasonable care of any articles in his possession: *British Road Service Ltd v Arthur V Crutchley Ltd* [1968] 1 All ER 811. The degree of precaution must be gauged according to the value of the goods, their disposability and portability, their vulnerability to theft, and to such other factors as the overall risk to them and the prevalence of crime in the vicinity. In the case of a bank the duty is to take such care as a reasonably prudent banker would take, in like circumstances, of the property of his clients.'[7]

From the discussion of a trustee's duties that follows, it will appear that the recharacterisation of the global custodian as trustee does not significantly alter the level of its duties, for the following reason. Although the level of

---

[1] See chapter 3. As discussed in that chapter, trustee status is the more likely characterisation of global custodians in respect of most of their current business.

[2] '... it is possible to divide fiduciaries into two categories, status-based fiduciaries and fact-based fiduciaries. ... [The latter] include people who, by virtue of their involvement in certain relationships are considered, without further inquiry, to be fiduciaries. Such relationships include those between trustee-beneficiary, solicitor-client, agent-principal, director-company, and partner-partner.' Law Commission Consultation Paper, pp 27, 28.

[3] *Re: Andrabell Ltd (in liquidation), Airborne Accessories Ltd* [1984] 3 All ER 407 per Peter Gibson J.

[4] 'a "fiduciary relation" exists ... wherever the plaintiff entrusts to the defendant property ... and relies on the defendant to deal with such property for the benefit of the plaintiff or for purposes authorised by him, and not otherwise ...' *Reading v A-G* [1949] 2 KB 232.
See also *Re Brooke Bond & Co Ltd's Trust Deed* [1963] Ch 357, in which a custodian trustee is held to be subject to the fiduciary 'no profit' rule.
See also Finn, *The Fiduciary Principle*, p 35: 'In many instances property is a subject of a legal relationship with one party having custodial or other rights in or to that property. To the extent that party has limited or indeed no rights to its beneficial use and enjoyment, that person's position is incipiently fiduciary.'
In a writ issued on 5 June 1992 by MGN Pension Trustees Limited against Bank of America National Trust and Savings Association and Credit Suisse, the trustees of the Maxwell pension fund sued Bank of America as custodians of the pension fund assets, asserting that they should not have settled instructions from the managers whereby the pension fund assets were lost. The writ asserted that Bank of America was a fiduciary: 'In the premises, and by reason of the [custody] Agreement and by reason of its position as custodian of assets of the [pension fund], BA owed fiduciary duties to the Trustee and the [pension fund].' (p 25).

[5] In view of the electronic and fungible basis of modern custodial arrangements, the global custodian will in general hold securities as trustee.

[6] Where documents of title are physically held by custodian for a client and segregated from instruments held for other clients, so that in specie redelivery is possible.

[7] Palmer, *Liability of Bankers as Custodians of Client Property*, (1979), pp 9, 10.

duty implied at common law for a trustee is higher than that so implied for a bailee, the shared fiduciary status of both trustees and bailees imposes the same restrictions on their ability contractually to limit their duties. Therefore, assuming that the customary limitation clauses are included in the global custody agreement, the same core level of inexcludable fiduciary duty will be owed by the global custodian, whether as bailee or as trustee.

3   Trustee

Trusteeship is 'the most intense form of fiduciary relationship'.[1] The level of implied duty imposed on a trustee is higher than that imposed on a bailee. The test for non-professional trustees is the level of care with which an ordinary prudent man of business would conduct his own affairs.[2] However, a higher duty of care is expected from professional trustees (who advertise themselves as such). The rule in *Re Waterman's Will Trusts*[3] provides that the trustee holding itself out as possessing special skills and which is paid for its services must observe a higher standard of diligence and knowledge than an unpaid trustee; and will be expected to exercise a greater degree of care. This rule was expanded in the case of *Bartlett v Barclays Bank*[4] in which Brightman set the test as 'the special skill and care which [the professional trustee] professes to have'.[5]

B   Contract

The global custody contract should contain an exhaustive list of the services that will be provided, and as much operational detail as possible should be included.[6] These duty defining clauses delimit the extent of the contractual duties of the global custodian.

Perhaps even more importantly, limitation clauses delimit the liability of the global custodian who fails to perform its contractual or fiduciary duties.[7]

---

[1] Law Commission Consultation Paper, p 84.

[2] *Speight v Gaunt* (1883) 9 App Cas 1, per Lord Blackburn: '... as a general rule a trustee sufficiently discharges his duty if he takes in the managing of trust affairs all those precautions which an ordinary prudent man of business would take in managing similar affairs of his own' (at 19).

[3] [1952] 2 All ER 1054 per Harman J: 'I do not forget that a professional trustee is expected to exercise a higher standard of diligence and knowledge than an unpaid trustee and that a bank which advertises itself largely in the public press as taking charge of administrations is under a special duty' at 1055.

[4] [1980] Ch 515.

[5] The ordinary trustee is required 'to be prudent and exercise the degree of care he would in conducting his own affairs but mindful, when making investment decisions, that he is dealing with another's property' while 'a professional person, a trust corporation ..., held out as an expert, will be expected to display the degree of skill, care and diligence such an expert would have.' Per Lord Nicholls (1995) 9 TLI 71, 73–76.

[6] It is customary to specify detailed provisions in a service level agreement or service annex, which is incorporated by reference in the global custody agreement.

[7] While duty-defining clauses specify what the client can expect, limitation clauses specify the client's recourse if it is disappointed.

The case law relating to limitation clauses[1] indicates that they are extremely effective, although limitation clauses are subject to certain limits.[2]

1 Case law

Contract is generally effective in modifying fiduciary duty, as well as imposing particular restrictions on liability.

(a) Contract and fiduciary duty

The position of the global custodian seeking to rely on contractual limitation provisions is enormously strengthened by the case of *Kelly v Cooper Associates*,[3] in which it was stated[4] that a fiduciary relationship arising in the context of a contractual deal should not change the nature of the deal. Lord Browne-Wilkinson quoted an earlier case[5] as follows:

'That contractual and fiduciary relationships may co-exist between the same parties has never been doubted. Indeed, the existence of a basic contractual relationship has in many situations provided a foundation for the erection of a fiduciary relationship. In these situations, it is the contractual foundation which is all important because it is the contract that regulates the basic rights and liabilities of the parties. The fiduciary relationship, if it is to exist at all, must accommodate itself to the terms of the contract so that it is consistent with, and conforms to them. The fiduciary relationship cannot be superimposed upon the contract in such a way as to alter the operation which the contract was intended to have according to its true construction.'

The Law Commission discusses *Kelly* in the following terms:

'It confirmed that where a fiduciary relationship arises out of a contract, a clearly worded duty defining or exclusion clause will circumscribe the extent of the fiduciary duties owed to the other party.'[6]

The report summarises the conditions that must be satisfied before the principle in *Kelly* may be relied upon[7] and draws attention to its

---

[1] It is understood that the regulatory authorities in Dublin and Luxembourg are cautious in their approach to limitation clauses.

[2] As well as statutory limits indicated in section 2 below, equity imposes certain limits. For example, 'The duty to act in good faith (ie honestly and consciously) in respect of any trust matter cannot, of course, be excluded. To do so would make a nonsense of the trust relationship as an obligation of confidence.' David Hayton, *The Irreducible Core Content of Trusteeship*, [1996] JTCP p 3.

[3] [1993] AC 205. This was a Privy Council decision, on appeal from the Court of Appeal of Bermuda. The case concerned the practices of an estate agent and its failure to notify one vendor client that it also acted for a vendor of an adjoining property.

[4] *Obiter*, by Lord Browne-Wilkinson.

[5] Mason J in the case of *Hospital Products International Pty Ltd v United States Surgical Corpn* (1984) 156 CLR 41.

[6] p 4 of the 1995 Report.

[7] '*Kelly* will provide a solution where the following conditions are satisfied. First, the duty defining and exclusion clause must clearly cover the transaction in question: it will have to do so unambiguously since it will be subject to the *contra proferentum* rule of interpretation. Secondly, in those situations where the relationship between the firm and client has altered over time, this altered relationship will also have to be caught by the clause. And thirdly, it must be the substance of the relationship between the client and the firm that is covered by the clause and not what the parties call it. If these three conditions are satisfied, then *Kelly* provides a way of solving the problems that arise from any mismatch between fiduciary rules, regulatory rules and market structure.' pp 85, 86.

limits.

This approach was endorsed in the case of *Clark Boyce v Mouat*. 'A fiduciary duty ... cannot be prayed in aid to enlarge the scope of contractual duties.' Similar sentiments are expressed *obiter* in *Target Holdings Ltd v Redferns*. However, while fiduciary duties must conform with the contract, they are not entirely subsumed within it, for '... the essence of a fiduciary relationship is that it creates obligations of a different character from those deriving from the contract itself.'

(b)   Limitations of liability

There is longstanding authority that the terms of a fiduciary's appointment may limit its duties. However, it is also clear from case law that trustees, as other fiduciaries, have a core minimum level of duty that cannot be excluded by any relieving provisions. Old authority indicates that liability for gross negligence and wilful default are inexcludable but modern authority indicates that liability for negligence and even gross negligence can be excluded if the exclusion is clearly brought to the attention of the settlor (client).

In any case, the minimum level of core duty that cannot be excluded is lower than that which global custodians customarily seek contractually to exclude, ie negligence and wilful default. Any limitation clause will be restrictively construed by the court and any doubt or ambiguity resolved against the fiduciary seeking to rely on it. It may also be prudent to draw clients' attention to exclusion clauses prior to the execution of the custody agreement

---

1   In relation to conflicts of interest 'However, there are three situations of conflict in which, despite *Kelly*, it will be necessary either to make appropriate provision in the contract or obtain the informed consent of the customer in order to avoid breaching a fiduciary duty. The first is where the firm is acting for two customers in the same transaction. The second is where there is a conflict between the firm's own interest and the duty which it owes to a customer and that conflict is more acute than that which arose in *Kelly*. ... The conflict would be more acute if, for example, (i) a firm has a direct beneficial interest in a transaction with a customer, such as where it sells its own property to a customer, ... The third situation is where there has been "iniquity".' p 24.

2   [1994] 1 AC 428. This was another Privy Council decision, on appeal from the Court of Appeal of New Zealand. The case concerned a claim against a solicitor; the plaintiff mortgaged her house to secure a loan to her son, and the solicitor acted for both of them.

3   Per Lord Jauncey of Tullichettle, at 437.

4   [1995] 3 WLR 352, per Lord Browne-Wilkinson at 795: 'But in my judgment it is important, if the trust is not to be rendered commercially useless, to distinguish between the basic principles of trust law and those specialist rules developed in relation to traditional trusts which are applicable only to such trusts and the rationale of which has no application to trusts of quite a different kind.'

5   *Re Goldcrop Exchange Ltd* [1994] 2 All ER 806 at 821. See also *Henderson v Merrett* [1994] 3 All ER 506 at 543.

6   See *Wilkins v Hogg* (1861) 66 ER 346.

7   Ibid at 348.

8   The difference between negligence and gross negligence is indicated in *Midland Bank Trustee (Jersey) Ltd v Federated Pension Service* (21 December 1995 unreported), at 44: the trustee's conduct 'was not mere negligence consisting of a departure from the normal standards of conduct of a paid professional trustee, but a serious, unusual and market departure from that standard which amounted to "gross negligence".'

9   In the case of *Pass v Dundas* (1880) 43 LT 665 Bacon VC held that the effect of the decision in *Wilkins v Hogg* was that an appropriate exemption clause 'does protect a trustee from loss that may have been sustained in the course of administering the trust estate, unless you can impute to him gross negligence or personal misconduct.'

10 In *Midland Bank Trust (Jersey) Ltd v FPS* (1995) the Jersey Court of Appeal held that liability for gross negligence may be excluded unless prohibited by statute.

in cases where the client is not legally represented, particularly where it is sought to exclude gross negligence.[1] However, provided they are adequately drafted, it may generally be assumed that these clauses are effective, subject to the comments below.[2, 3]

2   Statutory restrictions

(a)   Unfair Contract Terms Act 1977 ('UCTA')

In accordance with section 3 of UCTA, exclusion clauses relating to business liability for breach of contract contained in one party's written standard terms of business are subject to a test of reasonableness.

An exemption may be available as follows. Paragraph 1 of Schedule 1 to the Act provides that 'sections 2 to 4 of this Act do not extend to ... any contract so far as it relates to the creation or transfer of securities or of any right or interest of securities'. This exclusion was designed primarily to assist brokers and not custodians. It does not clearly exempt the terms of the global custody agreement, as of course this relates to the holding and administration of securities as well as their transfer. However, this exemption may protect the settlement side of the global custody service.[4]

To the extent that the exemption is not available, the custodian's limitation clauses are subject to a statutory reasonableness test.[5] It might be argued

---

[1]   '...there needs to be full frank disclosure ... so that a fully informed consent can be given, because a fiduciary relationship exists even before the trust instrument is finally executed.' David Hayton, *The Irreducible Core of Trusteeship* [1996] JTCP p 3.

[2]   See the unreported High Court judgment of Harman J in *Galmerrow Securities Ltd v National Westminster Bank* (20 December 1990, unreported), in which a trust deed is considered which contained relieving provisions limiting trustee liability to losses resulting from its fraud and negligence: 'However high a standard of skill and care is imposed by the general law, and I would wish to impose the highest standard on Trustee departments of major clearing banks, the duty has still to be defined by reference to the actual trust deed in the case before the Court. In *Bartlett*'s case (supra) no terms like those in the Trust Deed constituting the 22nd PAUT existed.' (p 35).

   This view is endorsed by the Law Commission: 'We stated in the consultation paper that a fiduciary could not exclude liability for fraud, deliberate breach of duty and, possibly, gross negligence. Beyond that, our provisional view was that, in general, no restriction operated as a matter of fiduciary law to prevent a fiduciary from contracting out of or modifying his fiduciary duties, particularly where no prior fiduciary relationship existed and the contract sought to define the duties of the parties.' Law Commission Report No 236, December 1995, Cm 3049, *Fiduciary Duties and Regulatory Rules*, p 11.

[3]   Compare the position in Jersey, clarified in the recent decision of the Jersey Court of Appeal in *Midland Bank Trustee (Jersey) Ltd v Federated Pension Services* (21 December 1995, unreported). This case confirmed that higher standards are required from professional than non-professional trustees and that limitation clauses may be valid if they comply with statutory restrictions (article 26(9) of the Trusts (Jersey) Law 1984 as amended prohibits exclusions of liability for fraud, wilful misconduct or gross negligence). Limitation clauses will be construed against the trustee.

[4]   The view that UCTA applies to a limitation clause in some circumstances and not others may be supported by the case of *Micklefield v SAC Technology* [1991] 1 All ER 275. In this case the court emphasised that the exception applies to 'any contract *insofar as* it relates to the creation or transfer of securities' at 281.

[5]   This is defined in section 11 as the requirement 'that the term shall have been a fair and reasonable one to be included having regard to the circumstances which were, or ought reasonably to have been, known to or in the contemplation of the parties when the contract was made.'

that this test is satisfied in cases where terms in question are in market standard form.[1]

(b) Unfair terms in Consumer Contracts Regulations 1994[2]

These regulations apply (in addition to UCTA) to terms which have not been individually negotiated, in contracts for the supply of goods or services by businesses to consumers. For this purpose, a consumer is a natural person (ie not a company or, probably, partnerships or unincorporated associations) who is acting for purposes which are 'outside his business'. Thus, terms in standard form global custody contracts with high net worth individuals who are not involved in investment business may be prima facie caught.

The regulations impose requirements of fairness and plain English.

3 Particular clauses

Certain additional exclusions are customary in global custody agreements. Precisely what is included depends on the concerns and negotiating strengths of the parties. The following are important examples.

(a) Force majeure

The global custodian's ability to discharge its duties may be particularly vulnerable to computer failure. Force majeure clauses (excusing performance where it is rendered impossible or impracticable) are very important. However, they cannot substitute practical measures such as disaster recovery systems and insurance.

(b) Consequential damages

In view of the judgment in *Target Holdings Ltd v Redferns*[3] it is important for fiduciaries contractually to exclude liability for consequential damages; such provision must, however, be brought clearly to the attention of clients.

C Liability for third parties

The global custodian is at the centre of a communications and service network. When losses occur to a client's portfolio, they will often be attributable, not to the global custodian itself, but to a third party. This section will consider two topical issues, namely the liability of the global custodian in respect of sub-custodian default and fraudulent instructions from managers.

---

[1] Section 2(2) of UCTA subjects exclusions of liability for negligence to the reasonableness test. It is fairly unusual for custodians to seek to exclude liability for negligence.

[2] These came into force on 1 July 1995, implementing the EC Directive on Unfair Terms in Consumer Contracts (93/13/EEC).

[3] [1995] 3 All ER 785, per Lord Browne-Wilkinson at 794, 798: '... the common law rules of remoteness of damages and causation do not apply ... The plaintiff's actual loss as a consequence of the breach is to be assessed with the full benefit of hindsight. Foreseeability is not a concern in assessing compensation...'.

1 Liability for sub-custodians

One of the most commercially sensitive issues facing the global custodian is the extent to which it should stand behind its sub-custodians.

Many clients mistakenly believe that the law imposes strict liability upon custodians for the defaults of their delegates, but this is far from true. Where the sub-custodian is a nominee or close associate of the global custodian, it may be unrealistic for the global custodian to expect to escape liability. However, for independent sub-custodians, liability is much more limited. The Trustee Act 1925 contains important relieving provisions in respect of liability for third parties.

Section 30(1) limits liability for sub-custodians to the personal wilful default of trustee custodians. The term 'wilful default' has been the subject of much debate. The term appeared in the statutory precursors to section 30, in which it was construed as meaning want of common prudence or negligence. However, a narrow interpretation was given in *Re Vickery* where the term was held to mean conscious breach of duty or recklessness as to whether there was breach of duty. This narrow interpretation has been criticised and in the later case of *Bartlett v Barclays Bank Trust Co* Brightman LJ held wilful default to cover 'a passive breach of trust, an omission to do something which, as a prudent trustee, he ought to have done.' Therefore it would be prudent to take wilful default for this purpose to mean lack of ordinary prudence. On this basis, to escape liability under this section for third party losses, the global custodian must show ordinary prudence in the appointment and supervision of its global custodial network.

---

[1] The power to sub-delegate safekeeping should be expressly reserved in the global custody agreement: 'At present there is no general power to put trust investments into the name of a nominee otherwise than under section 7 of the Trustee Act 1925' (which relates to bearer securities). Law Reform Committee, *Twenty-Third Report, The Powers and Duties of Trustees*, p 39.

[2] In 1996 the ICB 6th annual global custody matrix indicated that about 75% of custodians offer indemnities for sub-custodians losses.

[3] This position is reflected in the SIB's proposals in its 'Custody Review'.

[4] 'A trustee shall be chargeable only for money and securities actually received by him notwithstanding his signing any receipt for the sake of conformity, and shall be answerable and accountable only for his own acts, receipts, neglects, or defaults, and not for those of any trustee, nor for any banker, broker, or other person with whom any trust money or securities may be deposited, nor for the insufficiency or deficiency of any securities, nor for any other loss, unless the same happens through his own wilful default.'

[5] Section 31 of the Law of Property Amendment Act 1859 and section 24 of the Trustee Act 1893.

[6] *Underwood v Stevens* (1816) 1 Mer 712; *Re Brier* (1884) 26 Ch D 238, 243; *Re Chapman* [1896] 2 Ch 763, 776; *Speight v Gaunt* (1883) 9 App Cas 1, 13–15, 22–23. These references are given in paragraph 2.1.6 of Trust Law Commission, *Collective Delegation of Trustees' Powers and Duties*, internal paper of the Trust Law Commission, October 1995. See also *Underhill and Hayton*, p 623.

[7] [1931] 1 Ch 572.

[8] The term was held to mean '... either a consciousness of negligence or breach of duty or recklessness in the performance of a duty' per Maugham J at 584. The narrower interpretation was followed by Hoffmann J in *Steel v Wellcome Trustees Ltd* [1988] 1 WLR 167, 174.

[9] 'It will shortly be seen that the traditional equitable meaning of 'wilful default' extends to negligent conduct and such traditional meaning should have applied in section 30.' *Collective Delegation of Trustees' Powers and Duties* (above), paragraph 4.1.5. See also *Underhill and Hayton*, p 623.

[10] [1980] Ch 515, 546.

Section 23(1) permits the appointment of agents, and exempts the trustee from liability from agents' default if employed in good faith.[1] Again, global custodians should be cautious in relying on this provision in the light of *Bartlett v Barclays*, as its terms may be construed strictly against them.[2] Moreover, it applies to the defaults of a trustee's *agents*. In characteristic global custodial arrangements, the sub-custodians are not agents but principals.[3] Moreover, the prudent interpretation of this sub-section is that it relates only to *vicarious* liability[4] and does not affect the *personal* liability of the custodian, which remains governed by section 30.

Accordingly, the position implied by statute is probably that the global custodian is liable for losses caused by sub-custodian default only where the loss is due to the failure of the global custodian to use ordinary prudence in appointing and supervising the sub-custodian, or where the loss is otherwise due to the global custodian's negligence (or, possibly, gross negligence) or wilful default. This assumes that the appointment of the sub-custodian was authorised by the terms of the global custody agreement; if it was not, it is unlikely that the global custodian will escape strict liability.

Global custodians should, therefore, take care in the initial choice of the members of their network, and in reviewing that choice from time to time. Criteria should include all matters affecting the safety of client assets, including local custodial and administrative arrangements and staff controls. These should be considered in the light of local law and market practice. In particular, the global custodian should consider the impact of local insolvency law on its ability to recover client assets in the event of the third party's insolvency. Delegation by third parties should be carefully controlled.[5]

Global custodians sometimes take indemnities from sub-custodians. However, the usefulness of any such indemnity might be limited for the

---

[1] 'Trustees or personal representatives may, instead of acting personally, employ and pay an agent, whether a solicitor, banker, stockbroker, or other person, to transact any business or do any act required to be transacted or done in the execution of the trust, or the administration of the testator's or intestate's estate, including the receipt and payment of the money, and shall be entitled to be allowed and paid all charges and expenses so incurred, and shall not be responsible for the default of any such agent if employed in good faith.'

[2] See Law Reform Committee Twenty-Third Report, Cmnd 8733, p 36: 'We think that the standard of care presently found in section 23(1) is not stringent enough.' See also *Underhill and Hayton* at pp 623, 624.

[3] Any agency between the global custodians and sub-custodians is avoided, in order to prevent a direct contractual relationship between the third parties and the global custody clients, which might in turn undermine the commercial position of the global custodian.

[4] Contrast the wording of section 23(2), which relates to personal liability. The interpretation that section 23(1) is limited to vicarious liability accords with the pre-1925 position under the general law: 'Before the Trustee Act 1925, while trustees were vicariously liable for the acts of unauthorised agents (and still are), it was clear that trustees who were authorised to delegate the carrying out of specific tasks to an agent were not *vicariously* liable for the acts of that agent but could be *personally* liable for their own acts in failing to select or supervise the agent with good faith and common prudence' *Collective Delegation of Trustees' Powers and Duties*, internal paper of the Trust Law Committee, October 1995, paragraph 4.1.1. See *Fry v Tapson* (1884) 28 Ch D 268 and *Re Brier* (1884) 26 Ch D 238, per Lord Selborne LC at 243.

[5] Under the general rule, *delegatus non potest delegare*, the custodian must act personally and delegation and sub-delegation are not permitted, unless expressly provided for in the global custody contract, on the basis that the client is deemed to have chosen the custodian personally to carry out its duties.

For US clients, sub-delegation of custody of pension assets is restricted by regulations made under section 404(b) of ERISA and sub-delegation of custody of mutual fund assets by rule 17(f)(5) under the Investment Companies Act 1940.

following reasons. The major risk associated with sub-custodians may be their credit risk; their insolvency would clearly affect the enforceability of an indemnity issued by them. Moreover, if the global custodian's exposure is due to its breach of duty, an indemnity in respect of it may be unenforceable, as discussed in section F.4, below.

2   Fraudulent instructions

An important potential exposure to the custodian is the arrangement, customary in pensions business, where instructions come not from the client, but from a fund manager.

(a) Bank America writ

Following the Maxwell scandal, the pension trustees sued Bank America as custodian for implementing the manager's instructions to make the free deliveries that led to the loss of the pension assets. Bank America has now settled the claim. It was not disputed that the instructions were technically valid.[1] The basis for the claim was that the custodian's suspicions should have been raised and, as a fiduciary, it should have reviewed the instructions and enquired into the circumstances surrounding them. This claim raises the suggestion that the custodian's duties may extend to oversight of the manager, or even co-management.[2] As the claim was settled out of court, these issues have not been judicially clarified.

The suggestion that the custodian is obliged to vet manager's instructions is worrying for the custodian. Firstly, it is contractually obliged to obey instructions, so that any obligation to decline to obey certain instructions might put it in breach of contract.[3] Secondly, in view of the high level of automation that is increasingly customary in settlement operations, any duty to review or subjectively appraise particular instructions may be impractical to discharge. In any case, the staff involved in settlement may be trained for administrative duties, and not in a position to exercise judgments as to the propriety of instructions.

There are strong arguments that the custodian is not under a general duty to review manager's instructions,[4] as follows.

---

[1] Although it may be argued that fraudulent instructions cannot be valid instructions under a custody contract.

[2] The writ alleged that a number of terms were implied into the custody agreement, including the following:
'...(5) that BA would immediately inform the Trustees and if necessary each of the directors thereof of any instructions that it received in relation to the funds, which might involve risks to the assets under their management or alter the nature of their rights and duties and/or their performance thereof or which were abnormal, suspicious or otherwise out of the ordinary. (6) that BA would not deal with the funds and securities that it held in any way which put them at risk or allowed them to be stolen or used for improper purposes or lost to the MGPS ...' p 27.

[3] As delayed settlement may put the manager into default and also prevent it from taking advantage of investment opportunities, damages may be significant.

[4] Although it can be liable for dishonest assistance in breach of fiduciary duty: *Royal Brunei Airlines v Tan* [1995] 3 All ER 97.

(b)   Galmerrow

The unreported case of *Galmerrow Securities Ltd v National Westminster Bank plc* (1990) considered the position of the trustee of an unauthorised unit trust scheme. Mr Justice Harman noted that the trust deed conferred exclusive power of and responsibility for management on the managers. 'Plainly these terms are inconsistent with NatWest as Trustee exercising a general supervision over the choice of property.'[1] On this basis, the trustee was held not to be liable for losses attributable to bad management.

(c)   Goode Report

During September 1993 the Pension Law Review Committee, chaired by Professor Roy Goode, published its report on pension law reform. There is a section discussing the custody of pension assets and the desirability of using a custodian independent of the sponsor and the manager.[2] The report concludes as follows '. . . whilst recognising the value of custodianship services, we do not consider that it would be right to require trustees . . . to place pension funds assets with independent custodians'.[3] Part of the basis for this conclusion is '. . . the fact that the custodian exercises ministerial rather than managerial functions and has no duty to investigate the propriety of instructions given to it, which appear to be in order, unless it has specifically undertaken a monitoring function'.[4] 'The use of custodians may well give the semblance of protection without the reality.'[5]

(d)   Conclusions

Contractual provisions should be included in the global custody agreement confirming the ability to assume that technically valid instructions are in order and that there is no duty of oversight of the manager. However, it would be prudent for global custodians to assume that they may not escape liability for acting on evidently fraudulent instructions, and for this reason may consider implementing controls that alert them to free deliveries or possibly large transfers.[6] Timely transaction reports to clients may also address risk.

---

[1] P 25.

[2] This is of course a crucial issue, as the success of custodians in the years ahead may depend on their ability to provide services to occupational pension schemes.

[3] P 369.

[4] P 367. 'The custodian will wish to see the provisions of the trust deed relating to the trustees' investment powers. When dealing with a fund manager the custodian should also verify the authority given to the fund manager, and, where that authority does not come direct from the trustees as a whole but from individual trustees or from a third party, the source of their power to confer that authority. But when these steps have been taken, the custodian is free to act on its instructions in the absence of circumstances putting it on enquiry that something may be amiss.' p 368.

[5] P 369.

[6] Because the contractual provision may not be wholly enforceable, care should be taken to ensure that 'partial invalidity' boilerplate is also included (ie provision that, if any part of the agreement is invalid, the remainder will remain in effect).

D   Secret profits

Section A.1, above, indicated that, as a fiduciary, the global custodian is generally not permitted to profit from its position at the expense of the client. One aspect of this is that the custodian cannot be remunerated unless fees are expressly agreed with the client, although there is an implied right to recover reasonable expenses. Another aspect of the rule is that in general no profit to the custodian indirectly derived from its service to the client can be retained. While this rule can be modified by the informed consent of the client, any 'secret profits' must be accounted for to the client.

Downward competitive pressure has reduced custodian fees to minimal levels, and the significant profits associated with global custody are no longer fee-based, but derived from 'cross selling'. The global custodian may undertake discretionary stocklending of the clients' portfolios, and provide foreign exchange and derivative services, retaining significant profits in each case. These profits are not always expressly disclosed.

Many custodians take a middle course, and include provision in the global custody contract giving general advance disclosures relating to cross selling and associated profits. In its Consultation Paper the Law Commission casts doubt on such general advances disclosures, arguing that in order to establish informed client consent, a much higher level of detail than was customary, was necessary. However, in its subsequent report the Law Commission is more robust. It argues that *Kelly* permits firms to rely on advance disclosures.

However, some clients who are trustees may fear that general advance consent may involve them in breach of trust to their beneficiaries. Further, a note of caution is sounded by the case of *Glynwill Investments NV v Thomson McKinnon Futures Ltd*, where a foreign exchange dealer was held liable for

---

[1] 'A trustee, even one rendering services of a professional nature, cannot charge for those services unless the trust instrument expressly so provides or a court authorises remuneration.' *Law Reform Committee, Twenty-third Report, The Powers and Duties of Trustees*, Cmnd 8733, October 1982, p 1.

[2] 'A trustee may reimburse himself or pay or discharge out of the trust premises all expenses incurred in or about the execution of the trusts or powers': section 30(2) of the Trustee Act 1925. Express provision is still customary, in order to avoid argument as to what is reasonable, and to specify 'flat rate' expenses such as transaction charges which are a reasonable estimate of the custodian's expenses, to obviate the need to demonstrate actual disbursements equal to the charge.

[3] Ie profits to which the client has not informedly consented.

[4] See *Re Brooke Bond Trust Deed* [1963] Ch 357. See also *Bray v Ford* [1896] AC 44: The trustee is under a duty not to place himself in a position where his trusteeship duties and his personal interests may possibly conflict.

[5] *Fiduciary Duties and Regulatory Rules*, May 1992.

[6] P 128.

[7] December 1995.

[8] 'We now believe that a sufficiently precise general advanced disclosure made in a contract will be effective provided that the contract clearly delimits the fiduciary duties owed to the customer and displaces the obligation to make full disclosure of all material facts, and the customer has not been misled as to the nature of the relationship between the parties' p 47.

[9] See Hayton, *Developing the Law of Trusts for the Twenty-First Century*, (1900) 106 LQR 87, 89.

[10] (13 February 1992, unreported), Tuckey QC.

breach of fiduciary duty, and was not able to rely on contractual provision which did not accord with the commercial realities of its client business.[1]

The prudent approach would be to treat profits from cross selling in the same way as custody fees, and assume that they may only be retained if expressly detailed in the global custody agreement.

E   Conflicts of interest

A trustee is under a duty not to place itself in a position where its trusteeship duties and its personal interest may possibly conflict.[2] An important and growing function of custody securities is collateral. For reasons of administrative convenience[3]custodians are often asked to act in two capacities, both as custodian for their clients and as collateral trustee for their client's secured creditors.[4] The arrangement may be documented by one tri-party contract.[5]

Section A.1, above, referred to the undivided loyalty rule, which prevents the fiduciary from placing itself in a position where its duty towards one customer conflicts with its duty to another. Clearly, to be acting as fiduciary for the parties on both sides of a security interest involves such a conflict. The general rule that fiduciary duties can be modified by informed contractual consent, and that commercial contractual terms prevail over fiduciary duty, should be treated with some caution in this context. Careful drafting may adequately address the conflict in circumstances where the custodian has no discretionary powers or duties in relation to the security interest, but is merely obliged to act on the express instructions of the chargee. However, where it has any discretionary powers in relation to the management or enforcement of collateral on behalf of the chargee, its position may be untenable.

F   Consequences of breach of duty

In order successfully to sue a global custodian, a client must establish liability. Apart from criminal liability, there are very broadly three general categories

---

[1] 'This case also considered the extent to which the contract can determine the scope of fiduciary duties. The defendant firm was a foreign exchange dealer. It acted for the plaintiff in currency transaction, charging a commission and also, in some cases, taking a mark-up on the price at which it had bought in the market. It did not disclose the mark-up to the plaintiff. The plaintiff contended that the defendant was acting as its agent and was therefore liable to account for the mark-up. The defendant claimed that it was acting, as the contract between it and the plaintiff specified, as principal. However, the deputy judge concluded that in the light of the other evidence, including the agreement of commission and the market order method used by the plaintiffs, the trading relationship was one of principal and agent. The plaintiff was therefore entitled to recover the amount of the mark-up from the defendant.' Law Commission Report, pp 29, 30.

[2] *Bray v Ford* [1896] AC 44.

[3] And because the transfer of securities can involve delay, expense and tax.

[4] In other words, the client both places its securities with the custodian, and charges them to the creditor, and the creditor appoints the custodian to act on its behalf in relation to the administration and enforcement of the charge.

[5] To which the client, the secured creditor and the custodian are parties.

of civil liability under English law. These are: breach of fiduciary duty, breach of contract and tortious liability (negligence).[1]

1   Breach of fiduciary duty[2]

Very broadly speaking, a custodian incurs liability to the client where it is in breach of its fiduciary duties to the client and this breach results in loss to the client. The measure of this liability is to make good such loss.[3] Remote or unforeseeable damages are not excluded,[4] but there must be some causal connection between the breach of duty and the loss to establish liability.[5] Liability is subject to contractual or statutory relieving provisions.

Statutory relief is in theory available under section 61 of the Trustee Act 1925, where the custodian has acted honestly and reasonably and ought fairly to be excused.[6] However, it is considered unlikely that such

---

[1] These are the traditional heads of liability. A possible additional head is unjust enrichment. See, for example, *Westdeutsche Landesbank Girozentrale v Islington Borough Council* [1994] 1 WLR 938. However, this additional head of liability is fairly speculative at the time of writing.

[2] The discussion of liability that follows assumes that the custodian is a trustee. Broadly similar general principles govern the liability of a bailee.

[3] This is essentially akin to the position at common law. See *Target Holdings v Redferns* [1995] 3 All ER 785, per Lord Browne-Wilkinson at 792: 'At common law there are two principles fundamental to the award of damages. First, that the defendant's wrongful act must cause the damage complained of. Second, that the plaintiff is to be put "in the same position as he would have been in if he had not sustained the wrong for which he is now getting his compensation or reparation" ... Although, as will appear, in many ways equity approaches liability for making good a breach of trust from a different starting point, in my judgment those two principles are applicable as much in equity as at common law.'

[4] Nor is there any duty on the plaintiff to mitigate its losses by litigation: see *Target*, at 799, quoting from the judgment of Hoffmann LJ *Bishopsgate Investment Management Ltd (in liquidation) v Maxwell (No 2)* [1994] 1 All ER 261: '... it is sound law that a plaintiff is not required to engage in hazardous litigation in order to mitigate his loss.'

[5] See *Target*, per Lord Browne-Wilkinson at 794: 'Even if the immediate cause of the loss is the dishonesty or failure of a third party, the trustee is liable to make good that loss to the trust estate if, but for the breach, such loss would not have occurred. ... Thus the common law rules of remoteness of damages and causation do not apply. However, there does have to be some causal connection between the breach of trust and the loss to the trust estate for which compensation is recoverable, *viz* the fact that the loss would not have occurred but for the breach.'

In *Target* the issue was breach of an equitable duty of care and not breach of core fiduciary duty. This latter issue is considered in the following cases.

The insistence on some causal connection alters the earlier rule that loss flowing from non-disclosure by a fiduciary attracts strict liability (*Brickenden v London Loan & Savings Co* [1934] 3 DLR 465 at 469). However, in respect of active misrepresentations, liability remains strict: *Bristol and West Building Society and May May & Merrimans* [1996] 2 All ER 801.

[6] '61. If it appears to the court that a trustee, whether appointed by the court or otherwise, is or may be personally liable for any breach of trust, whether the transaction alleged to be a breach of trust occurred before or after the commencement of this Act, but has acted honestly and reasonably, and ought fairly to be excused for the breach of trust and for omitting to obtain the directions from the court in the matter in which he committed such breach, then the courts may relieve him either wholly or partly from personal liability for the same.'

Similar provisions in relation to company directors are contained in section 727 of the Companies Act 1985 (directors etc).

relief would be granted to a professional trustee such as a global custodian.[1]

A custody client may have remedies against parties other than the global custodian in certain circumstances. Equitable tracing may be available. In addition a custody client may be able to sue persons holding or having held their custody assets as constructive trustees,[2] and (even where the defendant does and has not held the assets) there may be liability for dishonest assistance.[3] (This concept may impose liability on a fund manager who, for example, co-operates with a custodian in settling a purchase of securities into a street name, if it knows that such an arrangement is in breach of the terms of the custody agreement.)

2   Negligence

'Negligence as a tort is the breach of a legal duty to take care which results in damage, undesired by the defendant, to the plaintiff.'[4]

The measure of damages for negligence or other torts is the award which

---

[1] 'Although there is no doubt about the court's jurisdiction to grant relief under section 61 to a trustee who is remunerated, there appears from the cases to be a market reluctance to do so.' Law Commission Report, *Fiduciary Duties and Regulatory Rules*, December 1995, p 95.

The 23rd Report of the Law Reform Committee looked at the whole question of the powers and duties of trustees and considered the issue of whether it was desirable to incorporate the distinction between professional and voluntary trustees into statute. It concluded that this was not necessary, stating that section 61 was an adequate statutory provision to allow this difference to be recognised. The courts would be far more likely to give relief to a voluntary trustee under section 61 than to a professional trustee.

[2] 'A constructive trust of property is a trust imposed by equity in respect of property on proof of a variety of special circumstances ... where equity considers it unconscionable for the owner of particular property to hold it purely for his own benefit. It confers a proprietary right on the plaintiff ... It is now apparent that a constructive trust is a remedial institution which equity imposes to preclude the retention or assertion of beneficial ownership of property ... to the extent that such retention or assertion would be contrary to some principle of equity.' DJ Hayton, *Underhill and Hayton, Law Relating to Trusts and Trustees*, (15 edn, 1995) Butterworths, London, pp 42, 43.

The case of *Brinks Ltd v Abu-Saleh (No 3)* (1995) Times, 23 October considered the decision in *Brunei*; confirmed that in order for a person to be liable in equity as an accessory to a breach of trust it was necessary for him to have given the relevant assistance in the knowledge of the existence of the trust or, at least, of the facts giving rise to the trust. Mr Justice Rimer 'considered *Royal Brunei Airlines*, in particular p 76E, and said that he did not consider that the Privy Council intended to suggest that an accessory could be made accountable to the beneficiaries as a constructive trustee regardless of whether he had any knowledge of the existence of the trust.'

[3] See *Royal Brunei Airlines v Tan* [1995] 3 All ER 97, per Lord Nicholls at 109: 'A liability in equity to make good resulting loss attaches to a person who dishonestly procures or assists in a breach of trust or fiduciary obligation. It is not necessary that, in addition, the trustee or fiduciary was acting dishonestly ...'. Unlike in the criminal law, dishonesty for this purpose is an objective standard: see 105, 106.

[4] *Winfield and Jolowicz on Tort*, (14 edn 1994), Sweet & Maxwell, London, p 78.

is necessary to put the plaintiff back into the position it would have been in had the tort never occurred (ie it is retrospective).[1]

There are limits to the ability to recover damages for economic loss in negligence.[2]

The relationship between negligence and breach of fiduciary duty is discussed by Lord Browne-Wilkinson in *Henderson v Merrett*.[3] Liability in negligence is derived from fiduciary duties of care. The two heads of liability cannot be claimed as alternatives, for the tortious and fiduciary duties of care are in essence the same.[4] The judgment extends the principle in *Kelly v Cooper* to tortious liability: just as fiduciary duties may be limited and determined by contract, so tortious duties may be so limited and determined.[5]

However, contractual and tortious liability can be concurrent.[6]

3   Breach of contract

'Damages for a breach of contract committed by the defendant are a compensation to the plaintiff for the damage, loss or injury he has suffered through that breach. He is, as far as money can do it, to be placed in the same position as if the contract had been performed.'[7]

In other words, the approach is prospective (in contrast with the retrospective approach for assessing tortious damages).

Compliance with a contractual duty is not a defence to liability for breach of fiduciary duty, where the two conflict. Hence the importance, for example, of modifying the fiduciary duty of disclosure of all relevant information to one client, in view of the contractual and fiduciary duties of confidentiality to another client.

4   Nexus

Where a custody client suffers loss due to the default of a sub-custodian, its ability to recover damages (whether for breach of fiduciary duty, breach of contract or negligence) will depend on its ability to demonstrate that it is in a direct relationship with the defendant.[8] Such relationships can be established between the client and the global custodian, but no liability may arise there because the global custodian is not at fault (unless it was in breach

[1] 'The basic principle for the measure of damages in tort ... is that there should be *restitutio in integrum*. Apart from the special cases we have considered, 'where any injury is to be compensated by damages, in settling the sum of money to be given for reparation of damages you should as nearly as possible get at that sum of money which will put the party who has been injured, or who has suffered, in the same position as he would have been in if he had not sustained the wrong for which he is now getting his compensation or reparation' [*Livingstone v Rawyards Coal Co* (1880) 5 App Cas 25, 39 per Lord Blackburn, *Winfield and Jolowicz on Tort*, (14 edn, 1994) Sweet & Maxwell, London, p 645.
[2] See *Hedley Byrne v Heller* [1964] AC 465. A huge literature has been written on this topic.
[3] [1994] 3 All ER 506 at 543.
[4] At 543.
[5] At 544.
[6] See *Henderson v Merrett* and *White v Jones* [1995] 1 All ER 691 at 730.
[7] *Chitty on Contracts*, (27 edn, 1994), Sweet & Maxwell, London, p 1198.
[8] Because, under English law, fiduciary duties only arise where there is a relationship of special trust, contractual duties only arise where there is privity of contract, and negligence can only be established where duties of care are owed.

of its duty of care in appointing or supervising the sub-custodian). There may be fault at sub-custodian level, but no liability, because there was no relationship on which to establish duty owed to the client. In an intermediated product such as global custody, the client has no direct nexus with the sub-delegates responsible for losses; therefore duty and fault may be unlikely to coincide in the same person, and the client is more exposed than in a service where there is no sub-delegation.

5   Indemnities for breach of duty

Where a manager wishes the global custodian to act in breach of its duties to its client (for example by appointing a sub-custodian in a jurisdiction where it cannot prudently do so) the manager may offer the global custodian an indemnity in respect of the global custodian's exposure for that breach. The global custodian should treat this with caution, as such an indemnity may be unenforceable.[1]

---

[1] See *Chitty on Contracts*, (27 edn, 1994), Sweet & Maxwell, London, Vol 1, p 868.

Chapter 9

Depositary receipts[1]

The depositary receipt is originally a US development. This chapter considers depositary receipts from a European perspective, focusing on the customary European structures used to avoid the full impact of US securities regulation.

A Introduction

1 DRs and global custody

Depositary receipts are repackaged securities. The depositary receipts industry is closely associated with the global custody industry.[2] Many banks which act as global custodian also act as depositary in depositary receipt programs, as each role is complementary to the other, requiring similar systems and procedures. Depositary receipts constitute a growth area generating significant profits. Global custodians not currently operating DR programs may be actively considering doing so.

Like global custody, depositary receipts represent the effort by the US banks (and more recently, banks in other jurisdictions including the UK) to facilitate cross-border investment by their clients. Both global custody and depositary receipts address the inefficiencies of international settlements, currency exposures and securities administration. The influence of US securities regulations and the structure of the major clearing systems[3] on both has been profound.

While a global custody service may relate to a wide range of securities, a depositary receipt program is confined to a single underlying security.[4] Other superficial differences between the two products are clear. While in global custody clients' securities are held *through* the bank, with depositary receipts they are repackaged, so that the investor holds securities issued *by* the bank. However, at a deeper level of legal analysis, the similarities outnumber the differences. A depositary receipt program is expressly structured as an equitable

---

[1] The author is grateful to Paul Giordano and Ed Bradley of Clifford Chance for their help with this chapter. Any errors are her own.

 The provisions of this chapter are intended for guidance only; legal advice should be sought in connection with any depositary receipt proposals.

[2] The American depositary receipt grew out of US custody and regulation.

[3] The DTC, Euroclear and Cedel.

[4] This is almost invariably the case. UK tax and regulatory problems arise if it is not: see below.

tenancy in common, so that different investors co-own the underlying security pool under a trust.[1] Chapters 4 and 5 have argued that global custody is probably so structured by operation of law. The interest of investors in both products are examples of a class of securities that are discussed in chapter 3, section B.4, above, as intermediate securities, where underlying securities are issued to an intermediary entity (the custodian or depositary), which holds them on a commingled basis for the investor, so that the investor's interest is unallocated, intangible and generally enforceable, not directly against the underlying issuer, but only through the intermediary.[2]

There is a further similarity. The chief motive for repackaging securities in DR form is to change their jurisdiction, so that for example Indian equities are transformed into US DRs where there is a US depositary. Chapter 7, section C.6, above, argued that *situs* of the interest of the client of global custody is the jurisdiction of the global custodian. Thus DR programs make use of a feature (the relocation of situs) that they may share with global custody, and which global custodians have yet to exploit.

2 An overview of DRs

Originally developed in the United States as American depositary receipts (ADRs), depositary receipt programs permitted US persons to invest indirectly in non-US securities where direct investment in such securities was not possible or attractive for currency, administrative, settlement, taxation, or regulatory reasons. Underlying securities are legally acquired by a depositary (and held on its behalf by a custodian in the jurisdiction of the underlying issuer[3]). The depositary holds its interest in the underlying securities beneficially for holders of depositary receipts.[4]

The underlying securities are shares or (less frequently) debt securities.[5] The underlying securities can generally be withdrawn at any time upon cancellation of the DR.[6]

The DRs are issued by the depositary which is usually a US bank.[7] The services of the depositary include paying dividends to holders, passing on information about corporate actions, answering enquiries and liaising with brokers making markets in the issuer's securities to ensure smooth settlements.

Settlement is usually through the DTC in New York, and/or Euroclear in Brussels and Cedel in Luxembourg. In the clearing systems, DRs are generally represented by one or more master global depositary receipt or master certificates. These are issued to Cede, the nominee of DTC, or to the common

---

[1] This is the English law position; under New York law arrangements the depositary acts as bailee.

[2] For a discussion of the enforcement of investor's rights under DRs, see below.

[3] The role of the custodian in DR issues is characteristically limited to taking physical possession of the share certificate representing the underlying securities. Dividends are generally paid to the depositary.

[4] Under the terms of an express trust in the deposit agreement. Under New York law arrangements, a bailment rather than a trust is adopted.

[5] DRs represent the underlying shares in a ratio that varies from program to program to give the DRs an initial market price that is customary in the US or European markets where the DRs are traded.

[6] Although this may be affected by regulatory restrictions or restrictions in the issuer's jurisdiction.

[7] More recently, a UK bank has entered the market.

depositary of Euroclear or Cedel. More than one master certificate may be issued for US regulatory reasons.[1]

American depositary receipts or ADRs are the original form of DR program. The depositary is a US bank and the receipts are denominated in US$. Dividends are also paid in US$. ADRs trade on the New York Stock Exchange, NASDAQ or over the counter. Settlement is generally through the DTC. The global depositary receipt or GDR, while not substantively different from an ADR, is a development of it. It is used to raise capital simultaneously in two or more markets. GDRs are generally London or Luxembourg listed, and settle through Euroclear and Cedel. GDRs often include a US element which settles through the DTC.

DRs offer benefits to issuers[2] and investors[3] alike. Their history dates from the 1920s, but their most significant development has been in the 1980s and 1990s; in 1994 the relaxation of US regulatory requirements did much to encourage their growth.[4] Increases in cross-border investment generally has been matched by growth in DR programs.

B   US securities regulation

1   Generally

Most DR programs are registered in the US. However, from a European perspective, the structure of DR programs is largely driven by the form of two exemptions that are available from the requirements of the US Securities Act 1933 and the Securities Exchange Act 1934, under rule 144A and regulation S respectively. Very broadly, programs which do not involve public offers

---

[1] See below.
[2] DRs may offer a number of benefits to the underlying issuer. They may serve to attract capital unavailable at home and broaden the capital base in a cost-effective manner. DRs enhance the profile of the issuer in the markets where they trade. Listing is simplified, with minimum disclosure and attendant liability. Listing fees may be lower than those for underlying shares (as DRs generally represent multiples of the underlying shares). An issuer concerned about hostile takeovers can provide, in a sponsored program, for loss of voting rights if more than a specified number of ADRs are purchased or if a nominee refuses to identify the beneficial owner of an ADR. Finally, DRs may overcome prohibitions in certain countries on the appointment of foreign registrars, and restrictions on foreign investment (eg foreign investment in the shares of Indian companies is generally restricted to registered foreign institutional investors; however, DR issues are excluded from these restrictions).
[3] For the investor, DRs may be the first step into the emerging markets. They offer exposure to foreign securities without the disadvantages of local investment. They are a means of avoiding local trading and settlement problems (such as inconsistencies of timing and settlements between local and home markets). Some investors can only hold securities listed on a European or US exchange. The use of DRs avoids the need for currency conversions (as they are quoted in and pay dividends in US$ or sterling). They are a possible means of avoiding restrictions on foreign holdings. Where the underlying shares are in bearer form, DRs can be used to convert bearer securities into registered securities. This may be desirable as distributions on foreign bearer securities may be announced in foreign newspapers not read by US or European investors. Also, shares in bearer form are generally not eligible for US listing. A holder of DRs may be better informed about the issuer than if it held the securities directly, as costs and possible liability under federal securities laws mean that foreign issuers may be reluctant to transmit shareholder communications directly to US investors. DRs may be more liquid than the underlying shares. In addition there are possible tax advantages.
[4] See below.

in the US or US listing or quotation on NASDAQ should escape the full registration requirements under the 1933 Act.[1] By way of background, a very brief note of US securities regulation is necessary.[2]

The Securities Act 1933 regulates the offer and sale of securities. A public offering in the US must generally be registered with the SEC.[3]

The Securities Exchange Act 1934 requires periodic reporting by issuers of securities publicly traded in the US.[4] It requires filings to the SEC to ensure full and fair disclosure of financial data.[5] Financial statements are generally required to comply with US GAAP.[6]

2   Exemptions

To encourage DR programs, certain exemptions from US regulatory requirements are available where selling restrictions are observed.

(a)   US private offering (private placement via rule 144A) ('RADR')

Rule 144A permits resales to certain institutional investors, qualified institutional buyers or 'QIBs'.[7] It permits QIBs to resell such securities privately to other QIBs without a holding restriction.[8] Securities acquired by a QIB pursuant to this rule are deemed 'restricted securities'.[9]

(b)   Regulation S

The non-US element of GDRs usually relies on regulation S. The regulation was adopted by the SEC in April 1990 in conjunction with the adoption of rule 144A. It clarifies the conditions under which offers and sales of securities made outside the US are deemed to be in a 'safe harbour' and therefore not subject to SEC registration requirements.[10]

---

[1] The reporting requirements of the 1934 Act still apply if US ownership thresholds are exceeded, and US anti-fraud rules still apply.

[2] The following is a general note of US securities regulations as they relate to sponsored DR programs of shares of a 'foreign private issuer'. It is a brief indication of the major provisions only, and is not exhaustive. These statutory requirements are supplemented by state securities or 'blue sky' law requirements, which vary widely from state to state.

[3] For a note of registration requirements for a public offering of securities in the US, see Appendix 2, part a, below.

[4] Reporting is required for exchange listed or NASDAQ quoted securities. Securities traded OTC may be exempt under rule 12g 3–2(b) (see below).

[5] For details of periodic reporting requirements, see Appendix 2, part b, below.

[6] Ie generally accepted accounting principles (provided that financial statements may accord with local accounting principles if an explanation is provided and there is numerical reconciliation between results presented and results that would have been obtained under GAAP).

[7] QIBs *include* institutional investors having at least $100 million under management (although some may have substantially fewer assets: see rule 144A(a)(1)).

[8] The seller and its representatives must take reasonable steps to ensure the purchaser is aware of the seller's reliance on rule 144A. When the securities are issued, securities of the same class must not be listed on a US national securities exchange or quoted on a US automated inter-dealer quotation system. rule 144A(d)(4) imposes an information requirement.

[9] For further details of restricted securities, see the Appendix 2, part c, below.

[10] For further details of regulation S, see Appendix 2, part d, below.

C   Types of program

1   Overview

Programs may be sponsored[1] (ie involve the issuer) or unsponsored[2] (ie independent of the issuer).[3]

US registered ADR programs may be established in respect of shares trading in the secondary markets (levels I[4] and II[5]) or to raise new capital (level III[6]).

Programs which raise capital in two or more markets simultaneously are referred to as global depositary receipt programs ('GDRs').[7] GDRs may be unitary, dual or bifurcated in structure; the options relate to the status of the master certificate and are driven by US regulatory exemptions and clearing arrangements.

2   The GDR

The GDR is used to raise capital in two or more markets simultaneously. An initial restricted offer may be followed by a wider program.[8] Rule 144A DRs are restricted securities. Regulation S DRs are unrestricted after 40 days.[9]

---

[1] A sponsored program is implemented with the involvement of the company issuing the underlying securities. The issuer appoints the depositary bank. The issuer and the depositary are both parties to the deposit agreement. DR holders may be permitted to vote on certain corporate actions and receive shareholder information directly. A sponsored program may serve as preparation for the issuer to undertake a full equity offering in the US.

[2] In an unsponsored program, the issuer is not party to the deposit agreement. There may be several unsponsored programs in respect of the same underlying securities. Unsponsored DRs generally trade OTC. They are ineligible for New York and London listing. (Section 143(2) of the Financial Services Act 1986 provides that 'No application for the listing of any securities shall be made except by or with the consent of the issuer of the securities.' In accordance with section 142(7), 'issuer' for this purpose means the issuer of the underlying securities and not the issuer of the depositary receipts.)

[3] Rule 144A programs cannot be conducted on an unsponsored basis.

[4] See Appendix 2, part e, below, for details of level I DRs.

[5] See Appendix 2, part f, below, for details of level II DRs.

[6] See Appendix 2, part g, below, for details of level III DRs.

[7] Offerings with no US element may be called IDRs (international depositary receipts).

[8] Until recently GDRs were usually Luxembourg listed and quoted on SEAQ (The London Stock Exchange automated quotation system that links traders around the world). However, in 1994, a new regime for London listing was introduced. GDRs settle in DTC, Euroclear and CEDEL. They are represented in those clearing systems by master certificates; definitive certificates are issuable on issuer, depositary or clearer default and (sometimes) at the option of the investor.

[9] After 40 days regulation S DRs become unrestricted in the US because they are deemed to be 'seasoned'. (A seasoning period is required by section 4.3 of the Securities Act 1933, during which US public investors are precluded from buying the DRs which are the subject of the initial offer (although QIBs and non-US investors may trade amongst themselves). Thereafter transactions in the securities are treated as taking place in the secondary market, not on the basis of the terms of the initial offer.) Secondary market trades to any one in the US is permitted. Therefore in those programs that segregate regulation S DRs from rule 144A DRs (ie bifurcated programs: see below), contractual restrictions on regulation S DRs can drop away after the seasoning period. However, in those programs that fail to segregate regulation S DRs from rule 144A DRs (ie unitary and dual program: see below), contractual restrictions cannot drop away, and all DRs must remain subject to the higher contractual restrictions required for rule 144A DRs.

(a) Structures

(I) CHOICE OF STRUCTURE

GDRs are generally structured as a rule 144A private placement in the US and a public offering outside the US relying on regulation S. The relationship between the pools of DRs making up the two elements of the offering may vary, according to which of the following structures is adopted.[1]

(II) UNITARY (ONE MASTER, RESTRICTED)

This structure is not generally used nowadays. In a unitary structure, a single master certificate is issued by the depositary, evidencing all the underlying deposited shares. The master GDR is held in the DTC.[2] All DRs in the issue are subject to rule 144A restrictions. European investors hold their interests through Euroclear and Cedel, who in turn hold through the DTC. The master certificate is restricted. Unitary structures are going out of use, chiefly because of the disadvantage of having all DRs subject to US restrictions. However, the fungibility of all the DRs provides greater liquidity.

(III) DUAL[3] (TWO MASTERS, BOTH RESTRICTED)

In a dual structure, two master certificates are issued by the depositary, together evidencing all the underlying shares. The American master certificate is held in the DTC. The European master certificate is held by the common depositary in Euroclear and CEDEL. The terms of two global certificates are identical (except to reflect the requirement of the different clearers).

However, there is no segregation of the underlying shares held in respect of the two certificates, ie the *custodian* may hold only one certificate in respect of all the underlying shares.

American GDRs are sold to US QIBs in a rule 144A private placement. European GDRs are sold to non-US institutions in a regulation S offer and listed on the London or Luxembourg stock exchanges. Because the underlying shares are not segregated (and because continuing restrictions under rule 144A apply to underlying shares as well as to DRs), it is necessary contractually to limit holding of *all* DRs *in the US* to QIBs. Therefore both master certificates are restricted and carry the rule 144A legend.[4] Because want of segregation necessitates higher contractual restrictions than are necessarily imposed by

---

[1] Different terminology is used by different players in the market; the terminology in this discussion is not universally accepted.

[2] Ie registered in name of Cede & Co as nominee for the DTC, and held by the depositary as custodian for the DTC.

[3] English lawyers call this structure 'dual'; some US lawyers call this structure 'unitary'.

[4] As the higher restrictions apply to European GDRs as well as American GDRs, each type of GDR may be exchanged for the other without violation of US securities law. The two types are not fungible (ie different CUSIP, CIN or ISIN numbers identify the different pools of DRs), but US QIBs and non-US investors can sell to each other by exchanging their interests through the depositary.)

US securities law, this structure is not generally recommended.[1] The European clearers have objected to the dual structure.[2]

(IV)   BIFURCATED (TWO MASTERS, ONLY ONE RESTRICTED)

The bifurcated structure is akin to the dual structure, but segregation of underlying shares permits lighter contractual restrictions. Two master certificates are issued by the depositary, together evidencing all underlying deposited shares.

As with the dual structure, the regulation S master certificate represents those DRs originally sold to European investors, and the rule 144A master certificate represents those DRs originally sold to QIBs. Both may be held in the DTC. Non-US investors participate via Euroclear and Cedel which hold their interests through the DTC.

The bifurcated structure differs from the dual structure in that the underlying shares represented by each master certificate are segregated from each other.

The rule 144A master certificate is restricted and carries a rule 144A legend. The regulation S master certificate is restricted for 40 days.[3,4]

There are several advantages to the bifurcated structure, the chief of which is that European investors can generally resell into the US market after 40 days.

(b)   Level I

An initial offer (subject to restrictions under rule 144A and/or regulation S) is often followed by a level I program (ie an unlisted DR program in respect of existing shares).[5] According to SEC policy, a registration statement in respect of ADRs to be issued as part of a level I program may be filed no earlier than 40 days after the offer.

An SEC letter concerning depositary receipts dated 14 April 1993, establishes 6 principles governing concurrent restricted and unrestricted DR programs.[6]

---

[1] Unless there is no US retail interest in the program, in which case restriction to QIBs will not be onerous.

[2] Cedel and Euroclear are concerned that acceptance of DRs for clearing might involve responsibility under US securities law for monitoring compliance with holding restrictions imposed by US regulation. A bifurcated structure will be more acceptable to the European clearers.

[3] Ie only regulation S and 144A resales are permitted.

[4] During the 40-day restricted period, interests in regulation S master certificate may only be held through Euroclear and Cedel.

Interests in the rule 144A master certificate may be exchanged for interests in the regulation S master certificate only upon receipt by the depositary of a written certification from the transferor that such transfer is being made in accordance with regulation S. On or before the 40th day after the later of the commencement of the offering and the closing date, interests in the regulation S master may be exchanged for interests in the rule 144A master only upon receipt by the depositary of a written certification from the transferor that such transfer is being made in accordance with rule 144A. After the 40-day restricted period, in certain circumstances the regulation S master GDR becomes unrestricted and regulation S DRs may be sold freely in the US.

[5] See above.

[6] These principles were developed to address regulatory concerns including 'leakage', ie the withdrawal of underlying shares from a restricted facility and their redeposit in an unrestricted facility at a time when the underlying shares constituted 'restricted securities' within the meaning of rule 144 under the Securities Act. For a note of the principles, see Appendix 2, part g.

(c) Governing law

The documentation of about 50% of GDR programs is governed by English law, and that of about 50% of GDR programs is governed by New York law.[1] The following points distinguish English law and New York law documentation.

(I) SEC

At the time of writing it is understood that no English law program has been filed with the SEC.

(II) STRUCTURE

Under English law programs, the underlying shares are represented by GDRs. Under New York law programs the underlying shares are represented by global or American depositary shares, which are in turn evidenced by global or American depositary receipts.

(III) TRUST

Under English law programs, the depositary holds the underlying shares as trustee for receipt holders. The trust protects holders from the credit risk of the depositary, and is a requirement of the London Stock Exchange. Under New York law programs, the depositary holds the underlying shares as bailee.[2] Under English law programs, cash associated with the underlying shares may be available to the general creditors of the depositary on its insolvency.

(IV) ENFORCEMENT BY INVESTORS[3]

Under English law programs, the issuing company executes a deed poll to enable investors to enforce the obligations of the company under the deposit agreement (to which investors are not party). Under New York law deposit agreements, holders and beneficial owners of receipts are parties thereto by virtue of their acceptance of receipts or beneficial interests therein.

(V) ENFORCEMENT BY COMPANY

Under English law documentation there is no method for the underlying issuer company to enforce contractual obligations against holders. Problems may therefore arise in relation to disclosure of beneficial interests in shares and voting restrictions.[4]

(VI) JURISDICTION CLAUSE

Under English law documentation, the company (in respect of the deposit agreement and the terms and conditions of the GDRs) and the depositary (in respect of the deposit agreement) submit to the jurisdiction of the English and the New York courts. This allows proceedings to be brought in England

---

[1] Although all ADRs are governed by New York law. ADRs outnumber GDRs.
[2] Under New York law, share certificates are generally negotiable instruments.
[3] For more details see below.
[4] See below.

and New York without any further action by the parties. Under New York documentation, whether or not submission to jurisdiction is included in the deposit agreement will depend on the jurisdiction in which the issuing company is incorporated or operates. Often no such provision is included.

(d)   One or two deposit agreements

In dual and bifurcated structures, either one or two deposit agreements may be executed in respect of the two master GDRs. In bifurcated (but not dual) structures, two agreements are traditional in the US. One argument for the use of a single deposit agreement is that this arrangement makes it easier to ensure that the depositary will remain the same for both facilities during the life of the program (ensuring smooth interfacility transfers). This could of course be achieved by contractual restrictions in like form in two depositary agreements. In the case of bifurcated structures, it may be argued that the use of two deposit agreements assists in achieving segregation between the two pools of underlying shares.[1] However, segregation is more a function of the underlying arrangements (ie the use of two different entries on the books of the issuing company) than of the deposit agreement.

D   Tax

1   Withholding tax

Section 118A of the Taxes Act 1988 requires banks and other collecting agents in the UK to deduct tax at the lower rate (currently 20%) from dividends received on foreign shares or UK quoted Eurobond interests which they hold on behalf of the beneficial owners, unless either the beneficial owner confirms that it is not resident in the UK or another specific exemption is available. Thus where the depositary is in the UK, it will have to distribute net (of foreign tax and UK tax equal in total to a deduction of 20% from the gross dividend), unless investors are non-resident or payment of the foreign dividend is obtained outside the UK.

However, if the DRs are held in a recognised clearing system, for example Euroclear or Cedel, and foreign dividends or UK-quoted Eurobond interest are paid or accounted for by the UK collecting agent directly to the depositary for that recognised clearing system then, subject to compliance with certain conditions, the UK collecting agent may pay the foreign dividends without deducting UK tax.

Nevertheless, it is important to note that the UK tax treatment of parties involved in DR structures will depend on the nature of the transaction and the drafting of the documentation: the position is not always so clear-cut and the Inland Revenue are known to take the view that in certain circumstances a DR structure can involve a separate and independent obligation owed by a depositary trustee to the recipient holder which will give rise to different tax consideration. This is an area where professional advice should be sought.

---

[1] See SEC letter of 1993, discussed above.

2 H arrangements

Special tax arrangements for the purposes of obtaining UK tax credit at source are available with the Inland Revenue in respect of dividends paid by a UK issuer under an ADR facility to the depositary in connection with the UK/US and UK/Canada Double Taxation Convention (H arrangements). The combined effect of the Conventions and the H arrangement is that DR holders who are US or Canadian residents pay no more than 15% on the aggregate of any dividend paid on the shares represented by the ADRs and the advance corporation tax ('ACT') paid by the issuer. In practice, the issuer, on a dividend of £80 grossed up to £100 (with related ACT), instead of paying £20 to the Inland Revenue as ACT, will pay £15 to the Inland Revenue, and the remaining £85 to the depositary. Each beneficial owner of ADRs must be resident in the US or Canada, must make a declaration to this effect and must otherwise qualify for participation in the H arrangement. It is necessary to set up the H arrangements with the Inland Revenue, ensuring that the Inland Revenue is informed and that the depositary is required to comply with and effect the H arrangement in the deposit agreement. The effect of the H arrangement is to enable the US or Canadian beneficial owner of ADRs to receive the benefit of the tax credit at source; it does not confer any additional relief over and above that given by the applicable Convention.

3 Stamp duty

(a) Shares in UK incorporated companies

The Finance Act 1986 provides[1] for stamp duty to be payable at 1.5%[2] (of the consideration on a sale, otherwise on market value) on the transfer[3] of relevant securities[4] of a United Kingdom incorporated company into a depositary receipt scheme.[5]

(b) Shares in non UK incorporated companies

No UK stamp duty is payable provided the document of transfer is executed outside the UK.

(c) Dealings in DRs

No UK stamp duty is generally payable on transfers of DRs on the basis

---

[1] In section 67. See also sections 68 and 69.

[2] There is a reduced rate of 1% for transfers by qualified dealers: section 67(4).

[3] While it might be thought that stamp duty can be avoided by issuing securities directly to the depositary or its nominee, thereby avoiding a transfer, such arrangements would attract SDRT under section 93, which relates to issues and transfers.

[4] Ie shares or stock or marketable securities: section 69(3).

[5] Ie transfer to a depositary's nominee (sections 67(6) and 67(7)) or a depositary. Transfers to depositaries and certain nominees are only caught if the transferee is specified by Treasury SI. There is an obligation for a depositary or certain nominees to notify the Inland Revenue within one month of first issuing DRS in DR programs in UK relevant securities: section 68.

that they are usually registered, with the register being kept, and any transfer documents executed and kept, overseas.

4   Stamp duty reserve tax ('SDRT')

The issue of DRs in conjunction with the issue or transfer of chargeable securities[1] to a depositor or its nominee attracts SDRT of 1.5%.[2] However, liability to SDRT is reduced by any ad valorem stamp duty paid.[3]

E   Legal issues[4]

The following legal issues arise in relation to depositary receipts.

1   Prospectus liability

In most cases, an issue of DRs involves the issue of a prospectus. In sponsored programs, the responsibility of the depositary may be limited to statements concerning itself in the prospectus. In any event, an important legal issue is liability for misleading statements and omissions in the prospectus. The following heads of liability arise under English law.

(a)   Section 150 of the Financial Services Act 1986 ('the FSA')

Section 152(1) of the FSA specifies the persons responsible for listing particulars. These include the issuer of the securities to which the particulars relate.[5] However, it is provided[6] that in the case of repackaged securities such as DRs, 'issuer' means the issuer of the underlying securities. The depositary is not responsible for listing particulars unless (broadly) it is included in the responsibility statement in the listing particulars.[7] The London listing rules require information concerning the depositary to be specified in the listing particulars (although a request to the Stock Exchange for derogation from certain requirements explaining why such derogation would be reasonable ('a derogation letter') is usually accepted).

Section 150 provides (broadly) that persons responsible for listing particulars

---

[1] Ie (broadly) stocks, shares or loan capital, interests in or in dividends arising out of the above, allotment and subscription rights for or options to the above and units under a unit trust scheme (generally) issued or raised by a UK incorporated company: section 99(3), (4) and (5). Chargeable securities do not generally include DRs but section 93 of the Finance Act 1986 specifically brings them into charge in the circumstances outlined.

[2] Section 93 of the Finance Act 1986.

[3] Section 93(7).

[4] 'The legal status of these "quasi-securities" is not always clear. ... Depositary receipt programs can raise many issues independent of the underlying securities. While they may simplify the operational aspects of cross-border investment, they may also add new risks that are not fully understood.' Bank for International Settlements, *Cross-Border Securities Settlements*, May 1995, Basle, p 52.

[5] Section 152(1)(a).

[6] In section 142(7).

[7] Section 152(1)(d).

shall be liable to pay compensation to any person who has acquired the listed securities and suffered loss in respect of them, as a result of any untrue or misleading statement in the particulars or omission from them of any matter required by the FSA or the listing rules to be included. It is a defence to such liability to show (broadly) reasonable belief, having made reasonable enquiries, that the statement was true and not misleading and that the omission was proper.

(b) Section 47 of the Financial Services Act 1986

This section imposes criminal liability[1] for (very broadly) a person who knowingly or recklessly makes misstatements or material omissions for the purpose of (or recklessly as to whether) another person is thereby induced to enter into an investment agreement.

(c) Common law

General common law principles may impose liability upon issuers and underwriters for fraudulent and negligent misrepresentations.

2 Other English law issues

(a) Financial Services Act 1986 ('the FSA')

(I) COLLECTIVE INVESTMENT SCHEMES

DRs are exempted from the definition of collective investment schemes by section 75(6)(h).[2] However, the exemption is not available for programs having more than one type of underlying security.[3] The consequence of collective investment scheme status would be that marketing restrictions under section 76 would apply, and that establishing, operating and winding up the program would be investment business under paragraph 16 of Schedule 1 to the FSA.

In addition, a tax problem arises where a DR scheme is a collective investment scheme.[4]

---

[1] The maximum sentence is seven years' imprisonment and a fine: section 47(6).

[2] 'The following are not collective investment schemes –
... (h) arrangements under which the rights or interests of the participants are investments falling within paragraph 5 of Schedule 1 to this Act;
Paragraph 5 relates to certificates representing securities.
Therefore if DRs are fully dematerialised so that no certificates are issued, a DR program may become a collective investment scheme.

[3] A note to paragraph 5 provides: 'This paragraph does not apply to any instrument which confers rights in respect of two or more investments issued by different persons or in respect of two or more different instruments falling within paragraph 3 above [government and public securities] and issued by the same person.'
This means that a program having more than one type of underlying security may be a collective investment scheme. This may cause concerns for pre-release arrangements (see below) if securities are accepted as collateral.

[4] If a program is a collective investment scheme, it is likely to fall within the definition of 'unit trust scheme' in section 75(8) of the FSA. (The scheme would not escape the definition unless no trust were imposed over the underlying shares in favour of receipt holders, thus exposing them to the credit risk of the depositary.)

(II)   INVESTMENT BUSINESS

The operation of a DR program should not involve the depositary in investment business for the purposes of the FSA, on the following basis. Investment business is defined by reference to the activities listed in Part II of Schedule 1 to the FSA. These are as set out below.

Dealing in investments   The definition of dealing in investments in paragraph 12 of Schedule 1 is wide enough to catch both the purchase of the underlying shares and the issue of DRs. However, exemption may be available under paragraph 17 of Schedule 1 (dealing as principal) broadly on the basis that the depositary is not making a market in either the underlying securities or in the depositary receipts.

Arranging deals in investments   The depositary will not be involved in arranging deals as the definition of this activity[1] excludes arrangements with a view to a transaction to which the arranger will be a party.[2]

Managing investments   The activities of the depositary should not involve managing investments;[3] management implies discretion to deal, and the depositary has no such discretion in relation to the underlying securities.

One possible exception to this is pre-release collateral management. As discussed below, the depositary may receive collateral from brokers in relation to a pre-release program. If this is actively managed and may consist of or include investments, management may be involved. If conducted in the UK, this may amount to regulatable investment business.

Giving investment advice   Provided the depositary does not make buy/sell recommendations to holders and potential holders of DRs, giving investment advice[4] should not be involved. While it is possible that the depositary may give advice to issuers on sponsored programs, this would not be caught by paragraph 15, which relates only to investment advice to persons in their capacity as investors or potential investors.

Establishing etc collective investment schemes   The depositary will not be involved in establishing, operating or winding up a collective investment scheme provided that the DR program is not such a scheme. Generally it will not be, for the reasons indicated above.

(b)   Disclosure of interest in shares under the Companies Act 1985

Where the issuer is a UK public company, DR holders are treated as interested in the underlying shares for the purposes of Part VI of the Companies Act 1985.[5] DR holders are therefore obliged to notify the issuer when they acquire or dispose of any holding representing 3% or more of the shares of the

[1] Paragraph 13 of Schedule 1.
[2] Note (1) to paragraph 13.
[3] Defined in paragraph 14 of Schedule 1.
[4] Defined in paragraph 15 of Schedule 1.
[5] Interests in shares for this purpose includes an interest of any kind whatsoever in shares (section 208(2)). It includes interests under a trust (section 208(3)) and unallocated interests (section 208(8)).

underlying issuer under section 198. However, the depositary is exempt from the obligation of disclosure by section 209(4)(b). DR holders and the depositary can be required by UK plc issuers to provide information relating to their interests in the issuer's shares under section 212.[1]

Non-compliance with company investigation provisions may carry criminal sanctions,[2] and may entitle the company to seek a freezing order from the court.[3] Non-compliance with disclosable interest provisions may carry criminal sanctions.[4] Freezing orders are only available where there has been a criminal conviction.[5] Non-UK DR holders may not be subject to UK criminal sanctions. It may therefore be appropriate to include provision in the deposit agreement enabling the depositary to freeze the DRs of holders who fail to comply with disclosure obligations.

(c)   Irreconciliations

(I)   REASONS

In practice, shortfalls in the underlying securities are understood to be a major problem. Such shortfalls may arise through administrative error; bad transfers (ie inward transfers of underlying securities which are later reversed by the courts because of matters such as fraud or insolvency, or by the issuer because of such matters as nationality restrictions); and deliberate policy, through pre-release.

(II)   PRE-RELEASE

Where new DRs are issued against underlying securities bought in the secondary market, brokers typically sell DRs to their customers at the same time as they purchase the underlying security. The settlement cycle for the underlying security may be longer than that for the DR. Therefore the broker may request that DRs are issued by the depositary in advance of receipt by the depositary of the underlying shares. The resulting exposure of the depositary to the broker is usually collateralised by the deposit with the depositary of cash, or in some cases 'near cash' (ie highly liquid debt securities such as certificates of deposits) or other securities. It is understood that the volumes involved in pre-release are huge, and that it may be the most lucrative aspect of DR business for the depositary.

(III)   LEGAL PROBLEMS WITH PRE-RELEASE

Pre-release amounts to informal securities lending by the depositary to the broker. The depositary is lending, not its own securities, but securities held on trust by it for DR holders. Unless pre-release is provided for in the deposit agreement and the terms and conditions, the DR holders neither know of or consent to the arrangements, nor to the risks involved in them, nor to the retention by the depositary of the associated profits. The risks for DR

---

[1] In accordance with section 212(5), section 208 (defining interests widely to catch unallocated beneficial interests) applies for the purpose of construing references in section 212 to interests in shares, but section 209 (the exempt custodian provisions) does not.
[2] Under section 216(3) and Schedule 24.
[3] Under section 216.
[4] Under section 210(3).
[5] Under section 210(5).

holders may not be adequately addressed by the provision of collateral: unless the depositary places cash collateral in a segregated account, it would not be protected in the insolvency of the depositary.

(IV) BURDEN OF SHORTFALL

It may be prudent for the depositary to assume that it will bear the cost of making good any shortfall, in the absence of clear disclosures and risk warnings to DR holders. To the extent that the depositary does not make good any shortfall, it will be borne under English law by DR holders in accordance with equitable tracing rules. As the DR structure is an equitable tenancy in common,[1] any shortfall would probably be borne by all DR holders ratably, following the rule in *Barlow Clowes v Vaughan*.[2]

(d) Trust over cash

London listing requirements require the depositary to hold on trust not only the underlying securities but also associated cash.[3] The deposit agreement in customary form declares such a trust. However, there is no duty on the depositary to segregate cash it receives through, for example, dividend payments on the underlying securities. While dividends are usually paid initially to the custodian, there would be a valid trust over the debt in respect of them from the custodian to the depositary. However, there is probably no valid trust over unsegregated cash in the hands of the depositary.[4] Therefore warnings should be included in the terms and conditions in relation to the cash, so that investors appreciate that they take the credit risk of the depositary (although in practice this is not usually done). The exclusion of the cash from the trust should be raised with the Stock Exchange in a derogation letter.

(e) Terminology

(I) GLOBAL (OR MASTER) CERTIFICATES

Standard documentation refers to 'definitive' and 'global' (or 'master') certificates. Definitive certificates may be issued to DR holders; global or master certificates are immobilised with depositories acting for the clearing systems. This terminology is borrowed from the markets for bearer debt instruments, which may be issued in global or definitive form. However, the terminology is not, strictly, appropriate for registered securities such as DRs.[5]

---

[1] Whereby all DR holders co-own each of the underlying securities.
[2] *Barlow Clowes International Ltd (in liquidation) v Vaughan* [1992] 4 All ER 22.
[3] The Listing Rules, rule 3.35.
[4] Under English law, the creation of a valid trust requires the three certainties (intention, beneficiary and subject matter). A purported trust over unsegregated cash fails for want of certainty of subject matter (*Mac-Jordan Construction Ltd v Brookmount Erostin Ltd (in receivership)* [1992] BCLC 350). However, an equitable charge may arise. See chapter 5 above for a fuller discussion.
[5] Certificates issued in respect of registered securities do not constitute the securities but merely evidence them. Ownership is determined by reference to the register of the issuer. A certificate in favour of a depositary is as definitely evidentiary as a certificate in favour of a DR holder.

(II) BARE TRUST[1]

The depositary does not own the underlying securities beneficially but holds them on trust for DR holders. Standard documentation describes the depositary as a bare trustee. However, a bare trustee is one who has no active duties to perform.[2] The depositary has many active duties (including the exercise of powers and discretions) under the depositary agreement.[3] The reason for describing the depositary as a bare trustee may have been a desire to limit its duties. However, the need is to limit, not the *scope* of the trustee's duties (which cannot be done on the existing commercial basis) but the *level* of those duties (and hence liability for breach of duty). Recent case law indicates that the level of a fiduciary's liability can be effectively limited to negligence and wilful default.[4] Implied fiduciary duties should not distort a commercial relationship.[5] In conclusion, omission of the term 'bare trustee' should not increase the depositary's exposure, provided correct duty-defining language is included in the depositary agreement.

(f) Section 53(1)(c) of the Law of Property Act 1925

This section requires dispositions of equitable interests to be in writing. Secondary market transactions in DRs represented by global certificates are not made in writing. However, as the clearing systems through which global certificates are held are located outside England, it may be argued under private international law that section 53(1)(c) does not apply. However, this argument is not conclusive. The further argument may be available under English domestic law, that the nature of a secondary market transaction is not a disposition caught by the section.[6]

(g) Fraud risk

In respect of registered securities, there is a line of authority[7] that places the risk of fraudulent transfers on the issuer. This exposure is based partly

---

[1] The author is grateful to Madeleine Timms of Clifford Chance for this point.

[2] 'A simple trust is a trust in which the trustee is a mere repository of the trust property, with no active duties to perform. Such a trustee is called a passive or, more frequently, a bare trustee.' Underhill and Hayton, *Law Relating to Trusts and Trustees*, (15 edn 1991), Butterworths, London, p 44.

[3] On the basis of available case law, it is prudent to assume that these duties cannot be treated as merely contractual, and therefore are part of the terms of the trust. See the Law Commission Consultation Paper, *Fiduciary Duties and Regulatory Rules*, (1992), p 31.

[4] See chapter 8 for a full discussion.

[5] See in particular *Kelly v Cooper* [1993] AC 205. For a fuller discussion see chapter 8.

[6] Very broadly, it might be argued that because the trust operates in favour of holders from time to time, the interest of A is not transferred to B, but rather extinguished, and replaced by an interest in favour of B. In other words, the property does not move, but the persons do. For a full discussion of these issues, see chapter 3, section B.6, above.

[7] Eg *Davis v Bank of England* (1824) 2 Bing 393; *Sloman v Bank of England* (1845) 14 Sim 475; *Re Bahia and San Francisco Rly Co* (1868) LR 3 QB 584; *Re Ottos Kopje Diamond Mines Ltd* [1893] 1 Ch 618; *Oliver v Bank of England* [1901] 1 Ch D 652; on appeal, 86 LT 248, CA; *Bank of England v Cutler* [1908] 2 KB 208; *Welch v Bank of England* [1955] 1 All ER 811. See chapter 3, section C.3.f, above.

on the issue of certificates by the issuer.[1] The issue of definitive certificates may therefore expose the depositary to fraud risk, unless there is express wording on the certificate making it clear that no representation of title is given.

[1] A fraudulent transfer is no transfer, so the issuer must restore the defrauded true owner to the register. Moreover the issuer is estopped from denying the title of a bona fide purchaser from the registered fraudster, on the basis of the representation of the issuer that the fraudster had good title constituted by the registration of the fraudster, and the issue of a certificate to the fraudster. Accordingly the issuer must buy securities in from the market to make good the shortfall.

Chapter 10

Settlement: general principles

This chapter considers settlement risk in broad terms in the context of the major international clearing systems. After a discussion of the background to securities settlement in section A, below, section B considers delivery versus payment, and argues that the policy imperatives of insolvency and fiduciary law in many jurisdictions cuts across the objectives of the securities markets. Section C, below, suggests that infrastructural changes intended to reduce settlement risk may raise new and unintended legal risks ('hidden risk'). Section D considers systemic risk, while the collateralisation of settlement risk by custodians and settlement systems is discussed in section E. Later chapters will look at particular London settlement systems in detail.

A Background

The settlement of transfers of clients' securities is an important part of the service provided by the global custodian. Securities settlement is a major industry, and the risks associated with it have generated a wide-ranging debate. Some argue that settlement risk has been seriously underestimated (while market risk has been overestimated) in regulatory policy.[1]

1 History of debate

The discussion of settlement risk originally concerned payment systems,[2] and more recently turned to securities settlement systems. The terms of the debate about securities settlement and risk were set by a 1989 report of the Group of Thirty ('G30').[3] Its report, *Clearance and Settlement Systems in the World's Securities Markets* ('the *G30 Report*'), defines settlement as 'the completion of a transaction, wherein securities and corresponding funds are delivered

---

[1] In particular, in regulatory capital weighting following the Capital Adequacy Directive.
[2] See in particular the 1989 *Report on Netting Schemes* (Angell Report) and the 1990 *Report of the Committee on Interbank Netting Schemes of the Central Banks of the Group of Ten Countries* (Lamfalussy Report), both prepared by the Bank for International Settlements.
[3] G30 is a New York-based think-tank for the securities industry.

134

and credited to the appropriate accounts.'[1] Settlement concerns the interval of time which, in the securities markets, separates bargain and completion.

The impetus for the *G30 Report* was a settlement crisis that occurred with the worldwide collapse in equity prices in 1987, with unprecedented volumes of transactions leading to backlogs of unsettled trades. The *G30 Report* makes 9 recommendations for settlement; the text of these appears in Appendix 3. While the report itself indicated an unrealistic implementation timetable,[2] progress has been encouraging in some jurisdictions.

The debate has been taken forward by a number of important later studies.[3]

2 The settlement systems

The *G30 Report* called for the establishment of central securities depositories in each country, in which securities may be dematerialised or immobilised.[4] An example of such a CSD is the DTC in New York.[5] European settlement

---

[1] *G30 Report*, Glossary. Settlement must be distinguished from clearance, which the glossary to the *G30 Report* defines as 'The process of determining accountability for the exchange of money and securities between counterparties to a trade; clearance creates statements of obligation for securities and/or funds due'. In other words, clearance determines what is due between the parties; settlement delivers it.

[2] Calling for implementation of most of its recommendations by 1992, and for its trade comparison recommendation by 1990.

[3] These include Federation Internationale Des Bourses De Valuers, *Improving International Settlement*, (1989); International Organisation of Securities Commissions, *Report of the Technical Committee on Clearing and Settlement*, (1990); Bank for International Settlements, *Delivery Versus Payment in Securities Settlement Systems*, (1992) (the *DVP Report*); International Society of Securities Administrators, *Report on Cross-Border Settlement and Custody*, (1992); Morgan Guaranty Trust Company of New York, Brussels Office *Cross-border Clearance, Settlement and Custody: Beyond the G30 Recommendations*, (1993); Bank for International Settlements, *Central Bank Payment and Settlement Services with respect to Cross-Border and Multi-Currency Transactions*, (1993); Bank for International Settlements, *Cross-Border Securities Settlement*, March 1995 ('the *G10 1995 Report*'); and Randall Guynn, International Bar Association, *Modernizing Securities Ownership, Transfer and Pledging Laws*, (1996). Other reports are available, including specialist studies of settlement risk in the emerging markets and in the derivatives and foreign exchange markets. For a longer, US-centred list, see *Policy Perspectives on Revised UCC Article 8*, JS Rogers, UCLA Law Rev, June 1996, p 1413, p 1436, n 3.

[4] Recommendation 3: 'A Central Securities Depository's (CSD) principal function is to immobilise or dematerialise securities, thereby assuring that the bulk of securities transactions are processed in "book entry" form. The depository system provides the basis for achieving efficient and low-risk transaction settlement. ... Ideally, Central Securities Depositories should contain all fungible issues in its markets. Preferably, CSDs should accept as many domestically traded securities issues as possible, in bearer or registered form; be they equities, debt instruments, warrants, money markets or other types of instruments.' *G30 Report*, pp 7, 8.

[5] Under the New York Uniform Commercial Code ('NY UCC') shares in a New York corporation may be transferred (inter alia) by transfer within a central depository system. In such a case the shares are registered in the name of a clearing corporation and may under certain conditions be transferred by the making of appropriate entries to the accounts of the transferor and transferee in the books of the clearing corporation.

The Depository Trust Company ('DTC') was formed in 1973 as a successor to the New York Stock Exchange's Central Certificate Service. It is a limited purpose trust company organised under the Banking Law of the State of New York, a member of the Federal Reserve System and a clearing agency registered pursuant to the provisions of Section 17A of the Securities Exchange Act of 1934. It is a 'clearing corporation' within the meaning of Section 8–102(3) of the NY-UCC. It is owned by its participants, who are broker-dealers, banks and other financial institutions or their representatives.

is dominated by two great international central securities depositories (ICSDs), namely Euroclear[1] and Cedel.[2,3] Originally developed for settlement in the eurobond markets, the ICSDs now settle a wide range of securities. The two systems are linked by a bridge, and each has a network of links with local central securities depositories, providing a single gateway for settlement in multiple markets.

3   Legal issues

Two fundamental legal issues underlie the legal aspects of settlement risk, both of which have been discussed at length earlier in this book.

DTC is engaged in the business of a securities depository for corporate stocks and bonds traded by members of the New York Stock Exchange, the American Stock Exchange, and the National Association of Securities Dealers. It accepts securities for deposit from participants. Securities deposited with DTC are credited to the account of the depositing participant and are part of a fungible bulk of securities held in DTC's custody. Such securities may be transferred to other participants and re-transferred within the DTC system, or pledged as collateral for loans and released from pledge, by computerised book entries on DTC's books without physical delivery of the certificates representing such securities. It is possible for a transfer of securities between participants on DTC's books to be a transfer of a limited interest, including an interest by way of security.

When shares are deposited with DTC the certificates are returned to the company's transfer agent and cancelled. The shares are registered in the name of CEDE & CO ('CEDE'), a New York partnership which acts as nominee of DTC and the partners of which are officers of DTC. On the first occasion when shares in a company are deposited with DTC, a new certificate is issued in CEDE's name, but this is retained by the company's transfer agent. It does not record any specific number of shares but is expressed to be in respect of the shares from time to time shown on the company's transfer sheets as represented by the certificate. When further shares in the company are deposited, the certificate relating to such shares are cancelled and the transaction is recorded on the company's transfer sheets; but no new certificate is issued to CEDE.

DTC is not concerned with and is unaware of the beneficial owners of the securities within its system. It knows only the identities of its participants to whose accounts the securities are credited.' Unreported court transcript of *Macmillan v Bishopsgate*, pp 28, 29. (The case was subsequently reported as *Macmillan v Bishopsgate (No 3)* [1995] 3 All ER 747; the quoted passage does not appear in the case report.)

[1] 'Euroclear was founded in 1968 by the Brussels office of Morgan Guaranty Trust Company of New York (MGT). However, since then its organisational structure has changed in several ways, and it currently has a rather complex structure. The Euroclear system is owned by a UK company, the Euroclear Clearance System Public Limited Company, which, in turn, is owned by more than one hundred of its participants. Policies for the Euroclear system (including admission, pricing and rebates) are set by the board of directors of a Belgian cooperative, the Euroclear Clearance System Societe Cooperative, which is owned by the UK company and system participants. However, MGT continues to operate the system (through its Euroclear Operations Centre (EOC)) under the terms of a contract with the cooperative, and MGT maintains all securities and cash accounts for participants, provides banking services (eg funds and securities loans and foreign exchange transactions) and bears and manages the risks associated with providing those banking services. Admission to membership is for the most part limited to banks, broker-dealers and their affiliates.' The *G10 1995 Report*, p 16.

[2] 'The Centrale de Livraison de Valeurs Mobilieres (Cedel) was incorporated in 1970 as a limited company under Luxembourg law. Cedel is owned by more than one hundred financial institutions (banks and brokers). It is currently registered in Luxembourg as a bank. Participants hold their cash and securities accounts with Cedel. Cedel provides some banking services (eg intraday credit) but other services (eg securities lending) are provided by banking syndicates, which bear the risks of participants' financial difficulties. Participation is generally limited to banks, broker-dealers and their affiliates.' The *G10 1995 Report*, p 17.

[3] The ICSDs are also discussed in chapter 3, section A.1, above.

(a)   Personal and proprietary rights

The issue first is the difference between personal and proprietary rights. The distinction between the two is central to all systems of civil and common law. Personal rights are enforceable against persons and proprietary rights are enforceable against assets.[1] The difference between the two is the difference between *owning* and being *owed*; this is important on the insolvency of the obligor or custodian (together, the 'counterparty'). Very broadly, personal rights are vulnerable to the insolvency of the counterparty; proprietary rights are not.[2] When a bargain to buy or sell securities has been struck, the purchaser's rights are merely contractual (ie, it is owed securities). Upon delivery, its rights become proprietary (ie, it owns securities). If the vendor becomes insolvent after the end of the settlement interval, it generally does not matter to the purchaser. However, if the vendor becomes insolvent during the settlement interval, the purchaser may never receive the securities. It only has an unsecured contractual right against the vendor for their delivery, which may be defeated by the vendor's insolvency.[3] The position for the vendor and its claim to the purchase price is similar.

(b)   Conflict of laws

As a very general rule, under private international law, the system of law that governs personal contractual rights is that chosen by the parties. In contrast, proprietary rights are generally governed by the law of the jurisdiction where the assets are located, ie *lex situs*. For this reason, it is essential to identify the nature and location of the interests in securities in question. Because securities are increasingly dematerialised and held through cross-border intermediated electronic arrangements, this can be a difficult task. The important point is that the use of clearing systems can change the nature and location of interests in securities.

Also, the law that would govern the insolvency of the party delivering value in settlement is relevant for determining finality of delivery (see section B, below). Any analysis of settlement risk should go on to consider the jurisdictions of any intermediaries through whom settlement is effected, as local law may affect the proprietary rights of the parties.

The major difficulty in this area is lack of clarity as to which law will govern the cross-border arrangements which are characteristic of much securities settlement. Conflict of laws is probably the major source of legal risk in settlement and in the securities markets generally. Conflicts are discussed in some detail in chapters 6 and 7, above.

---

[1] See chapter 2, section 4, above.

[2] Subject to liquidator's remedies that may affect improper transactions entered into shortly before insolvency: see section B, below.

[3] '...counterparties to securities transactions are subject to replacement cost risk, that is, the risk that a counterparty may default prior to settlement, denying the non-defaulting party an unrealised gain on the unsettled contract. The resulting exposure equals the cost of replacing the original contract at current market prices.' *DVP Report*, p 3.

B   Delivery versus payment

G30 calls for delivery versus payment or DVP (in recommendation 5) to address the risk that one party to a transaction may perform while the other does not ('principal risk').[1] Although DVP is not a general panacea,[2] it is a central idea in the debate about settlement risk. The project of DVP accords with the call, in relation to the foreign exchange markets, for PVP or payment versus payment.[3] However, progress with both DVP and PVP have been disappointing.[4] The reasons for this are partly operational and partly legal. True DVP will always remain something of a holy grail, for the reasons discussed below.

DVP requires payments and deliveries that are not only simultaneous, but also irreversible.[5] Certain systems (identified as Model 3 systems in the *DVP Report*) provide that transfers of securities are not final until cash settlement at the end of the day or the next business day. Such systems are a major source of systemic risk, causing consequential failures where securities are on-transferred before reversal. However, even when the system provides contractually for finality of delivery, insolvency[6] or fraud[7] may cause transfers to be unwound. The commercial courts developed the concept of negotiability to protect the markets in bearer securities from the risk of tracing claims. However, chapter 3 has argued that computerised securities, such as securities immobilised in Euroclear and Cedel, cannot be negotiable instruments. While alternative legal bases for irreversibility may be available, the position is unclear. The loss of negotiable status is one of the hidden risks of the implementation of the G30 recommendations.

---

[1] 'Because principal risk involves the full value of the securities transferred, a default by a participant in a securities settlement system that permits such risk may well entail credit losses so sizable as to create systemic problems.' *DVP Report*, p 3.

Some argue that principal risk in relation to unsettled transactions should be treated the same for risk purposes as an unsecured loan.

[2] 'Even if principal risk is eliminated through the achievement of DVP, however, participants are still exposed to replacement cost risk and liquidity risk.' *DVP Report*, p 3. See also p 15.

However, DVP eases liquidity risk: '... by eliminating concerns about principal risk, DVP reduces the likelihood that participants will withhold deliveries or payments when financial markets arc under stress, thereby reducing liquidity risk.' *DVP Report*, p 15.

[3] See *Settlement Risk in Foreign Exchange Transactions*, (1996), Bank for International Settlements.

[4] In the UK, real time gross settlement on inter bank payments is an important precondition of true DVP and PVP; it has only recently been introduced in CHAPS.

[5] 'Only the final transfer of a security by the seller to the buyer constitutes delivery, while only final transfer of funds from the buyer to the seller constitutes payment.' *DVP Report*, p 12.

[6] In the UK, the transferor's liquidator may challenge the transaction depending on all the circumstances, for example as a preference (Insolvency Act 1986, section 175), a transaction at an undervalue (section 238), a preference (section 239) or a transaction defrauding creditors (section 423). Whatever the consideration, if the transaction was concluded after the presentation of a winding-up petition, the deal is void (section 127). If the transaction was entered into on a recognised investment exchange, Part VII of the Companies Act 1989 may provide protection. However, if it was an OTC contract, Part VII does not apply.

[7] Where an intermediary fraudulently disposes of assets held in a fiduciary capacity, the law seeks to protect beneficiaries by the principle that a fraudulent transfer is no transfer, so that the assets may be traced into the hands of third parties and restored to the true owners. On the other hand, the law also seeks to protect the integrity of the market by permitting bona fide purchasers to retain the assets they have bought from or through fraudsters. The litigation following the Maxwell scandal provides examples of the conflicting claims of defrauded true owners and third-party recipients.

Insolvency and fraud are inevitable aspects of financial life. Because the reversal of transfers following insolvency and fraud is based on a policy desire to protect general creditors and beneficiaries, it is often deeply engrained in legal systems and cannot be excluded by contractual provision within a settlement system. This is part of a wider point, that the objectives which are uncontroversial within the securities markets (such as irreversibility and netting) may be controversial within the wider community, because they tend to prefer market participants over third parties whose interests may conflict with theirs. Thus legal risk in settlement is partly due to the courts' insistence that the securities markets must accommodate those competing interests.

C Hidden risk

This section will suggest that the project of achieving DVP through the use of international clearing systems, dematerialisation and associated develop-ments introduces new risks which may not have been fully anticipated at the time of the *G30 Report*.

1 Intermediation

Participation in domestic or international clearers may be limited,[1] and the domination of certain markets by the clearers obliges many investors, who are themselves not participants to settle their trades (and therefore hold their securities) through global and other custodians. While intermediation may increase settlement efficiency, it also introduces the risk of intermediary insolvency, negligence and fraud. As the settlement systems do not in general 'look behind' the custodian participant to the beneficial owner, the benefits of DVP in the system may not be available to the investor, because they are in effect blocked by the credit risk of the custodian.[2]

2 Leap of faith

Conversely, risk within the global custodial network may be increased by the system's requirement that the participant should instruct the delivery out of cash or securities before confirmation that corresponding value will be received. The problems associated with this 'leap of faith' are discussed at

---

[1] In particular, the admission of corporates to the major international systems is a fairly recent development.

[2] 'Settlement mechanisms often look to the securities transferred as collateral securing the settlement obligations of the participant acting on the investor's behalf. If the participant fails to meet its settlement obligations, securities which are received on the investor's behalf may be sold to satisfy the participant's debt. This will be true even if the investor had adequate funds on deposit with the participant to cover the purchase of the securities. If the participant is also insolvent, the investor may find that it is a general creditor of the failed participant, rather than the owner of securities.' BIS *1995 Report*, p 48.

length in the BIS *1995 Report*.[1] It is notorious that large sums of money continued to be received on behalf of Barings well after its failure became public.

3 Dematerialisation

G30 calls for the use of central securities depositories[2] in which securities should be either immobilised or dematerialised;[3] dematerialisation is the ultimate goal.[4] It should be noted however that dematerialisation may have indirect legal consequences adversely affecting the securities markets. Under English law, three points arise, relating to transfers, collateral and intermediation respectively.

As discussed above, dematerialisation removes negotiability. The strong position of the holder in due course of a negotiable instrument is important for the integrity of the bond markets. But one cannot be a holder in due course if there is nothing to hold.

The simplest and traditionally most popular way of giving securities as collateral is to deliver physical possession of the certificates or documents of title by way of pledge. The pledge of securities has much to recommend it. Unlike the legal mortgage, it involves no transfer formalities. Unlike the charge, it is never registrable. Unlike the equitable mortgage, it takes priority over subsequent legal security interests.[5] Unlike the lien, it confers a power of sale. However, pledge is based on physical possession,[6] and one cannot pledge an intangible which is incapable of possession. A purported pledge of intangibles may take effect as a charge, which may in turn be registrable as a floating charge or a charge on book debts.[7]

Chapter 7, above, discussed intermediary risk, or the need for an investor to show that its rights against the intermediaries through whom its securities are held, are proprietary and not contractual. As indicated in chapter 4, above, under English law, there are only two ways of achieving this: bailment and trust. The intermediary cannot be a bailee if the investment is dematerialised, for bailment involves physical possession. The investor must therefore identify a trust. He may meet with some resistance from intermediaries, however, whose perception may be that trustee status necessarily involves higher fiduciary duties.[8]

---

[1] See p 23. The implications of the equivalent problem in the foreign exchange markets is considered in *Settlement Risk in Foreign Exchange Transactions*, (1996, BIS).

[2] Recommendation 3.

[3] See chapter 3, section A, above, for the definitions of these terms.

[4] Pp 8, 56 of the *G30 Report*.

[5] More accurately, because it is based on possession (ie control), it generally prevents the granting of subsequent security interests.

[6] It is a form of bailment.

[7] These issues arose when sterling instruments were dematerialised in the CMO. See chapter 12, below.

[8] These can, however, be addressed in the custody documentation: see chapter 8, above. For US custodians, trustee status may involve a regulatory capital burden.

4   Securities lending

A significant number of securities transactions fail to settle on the agreed date, particularly in cross-border trading. The *G30 Report* calls for securities lending to be encouraged[1] in order to address liquidity risk,[2] and the *DVP Report* acknowledges the importance of securities lending in achieving liquidity in some systems.[3] There has been a huge growth in the volume of securities lending in recent years, whether through the automatic centralised lending facilities of clearing systems or through independently negotiated contracts between participants. G30 cautions market practitioners in areas 'where the practice of securities lending and borrowing is new'.[4] However, it should be emphasised that there may be hidden risks even in areas where the practice is not new. This is because the involvement of foreign counterparties and foreign collateral raises conflicts of law issues.

The value of the collateral taken in connection with securities loans may not be determined by the law governing the securities loan agreement. If a security interest is taken over the collateral, this may require to be perfected *lex situs*.[5] If a set-off structure is adopted,[6] it is important to ensure that it will be recognised under the law that would govern the insolvency of the counterparty (and it may be necessary to go on to consider the law of the collateral securities as well). Local advice should be taken where possible; where this is not feasible, it would be prudent to assess the risk of the transaction as if it were uncollateralised.[7]

D   Systemic risk[8]

Systemic risk, or the domino effect,[9] has been much debated in recent years.[10] Some argue that systemic risk only arises when the payment systems are disrupted, and that the relative liquidity of the assets of securities firms (as opposed to those of banks) means that systemic risk belongs to the banking sector and is not significant in the securities markets. However, most commentators agree that systemic risk is present in the securities markets. Automated settlement systems brings market participants closer together, overcoming the inefficiencies associated with poor communications outside the system. However, if this proximity permits effective delivery of cash and

---

[1] In recommendation 8.
[2] Or the risk that a temporary inability to deliver will cause settlement to fail.
[3] P 18.   [4] P 16.
[5] See chapter 7, section C, above.
[6] This is customary in the London markets.
[7] This accords with the regulatory capital treatment of securities loans (and repos) under the Capital Adequacy Directive, whereby a net (as opposed to gross) weighting is dependent upon a legal opinion that insolvency set off is available.
[8] 'The objective of clearance and settlement reform initiatives is not to eliminate the possibility that major players in the securities markets may fail. To the contrary, recognition of the reality of that possibility is the starting point of all modern work on clearance and settlement.' Rogers, *Revised Article 8*, op cit, p 1437.
[9] The glossary of the *G10 1995* Report defines systemic risk as 'The risk that the inability of one institution to meet its obligations when due will cause other institutions to be unable to meet their obligations when due.'
[10] See the proposal for an EC directive on settlement finality and collateral security for payment systems (CO (96) 193 final). The failure of Barings re-focussed regulatory attention on systemic risk.

securities, it may also deliver illiquidity from one participant to another. The ring-fencing of illiquidity (and credit risk) within a settlement system is very difficult, and as bridges are formed between systems, the possibility of industry-wide systemic risk arises.

1   Concentration

The heart of settlement systemic risk is the concentration of cash balances. In many ways the ICSDs are akin to global custodians. As discussed in chapter 4, above, clients generally *own* securities in the hands of the global custodian, while they are merely *owed* cash balances. Equally, moneys held by participants in the clearers generally constitute unsecured debts in the hands of participants. The debt claims of participants are owed by the clearer itself, being a bank (in the case of Cedel), or by an associated bank (in the case of Euroclear), or by a group of settlement banks (in the case of systems such as the CGO and CREST) (together, 'settlement banks'). Although settlement banks routinely extend credit to participants in the course of settlement and otherwise, the converse is also true, and participants bear significant intra-day credit exposures to settlement banks, particularly with cross-border settlement where participants may be required to pre-position funds. Thus, the use of settlement systems may concentrate credit risk in a single or a few settlement banks. The failure of a settlement bank would be catastrophic for market liquidity and, possibly, for the solvency of market participants.

(More generally, cash credit risk is becoming concentrated among the bank intermediaries in the financial markets, who in effect guarantee the payment side of transactions, whether by acting as settlement banks or by providing formal and informal overdrafts to their clients as clearing systems and custodians. As many of the banks who fund the clearing systems also act as global custodians, credit risk is concentrated in the custody community. With increased competition among custodians, clients expect contractual settlement,[1] and it may be difficult for custodians to refuse to bear the associated credit risk.)

The insolvency, or even illiquidity, of a settlement bank would have major implications for the securities markets. The benefits of book entry transfer and DVP are clear, and these are the reasons for the use of electronic clearing systems. However, risks associated with the concentration of cash balances following such developments should not be underestimated.

2   Spread

However, if settlement systems tend to concentrate cash risk, they may conversely tend to spread risks associated with the securities side of a trade, by exposing a wide community of participants to shortfalls originally attributable to one participant.

This spread of risk is due to commingling, or the mixing together in one account of securities belonging to more than one investor. Commingling occurs

---

[1] Ie the crediting of an asset to a client's account on the contractual settlement day, whether or not it has actually arrived. For a discussion of contractual settlement, see chapter 7, section D.7, above. Custodians generally only accept contractual settlement in markets where they are fairly confident of timely settlement.

both within the accounts of participants in the clearing systems who act as custodians, and within the clearing systems themselves as securities held for different participants are pooled in the course of settlement or in the hands of local depositories.

The risk of bad deliveries cannot be excluded from any settlement system. Where securities are accepted into a system, the consequential credits to participants' accounts may need to be subsequently reversed if the inward delivery of securities either fails to complete or is reversed, whether due to insolvency, court orders, fraud or other reasons (a 'bad delivery').[1] Before the bad delivery is discovered, the participant to whose account the affected securities ('bad securities') were originally credited may have transferred the bad securities to one or more other participants; indeed, multiple onward deliveries may spread the bad securities widely across the entire system.[2]

Different settlement systems deal with this problem in different ways. In CREST, a tracing methodology is adopted whereby the system seeks notionally to trace the progress of bad securities through the system, allocating consequential shortfalls to 'innocent' participants who are unlucky enough to have received bad securities into their accounts. The Euroclear adopts an approach which, in the author's view, is better, reserving the right to allocate the burden of bad securities within the clearing system across all participants.[3] (This 'common misfortune' approach accords with recent English case law on tracing in the financial markets.[4])

Either way, when the system accepts bad securities into the pool, any or all participants may bear the consequent shortfall. While this may be onerous for participants affected in this way, it may be desirable for the market as it reduces overall the risk of participant insolvency.[5]

E   Collateral

Settlement risk is inevitable. Initiatives such as G30 have done much to address it, but it cannot be eliminated and recent developments have introduced some new types of settlement risk. A crucial trend, both for the settlement systems and for the global custodians and other intermediaries who use them, has been to seek to collateralise settlement risk, using the securities held by or through them.[6]

The use of international portfolios of securities as collateral is a vast subject. This section will discuss, in very general terms, some of the legal issues affecting

---

[1] The term 'bad delivery' is used in a wide sense here, for convenience.
[2] This phenomenon, of one party in effect bearing another's shortfall, can occur at any level in the securities markets where commingling occurs.
[3] Section 17 of the 'Terms and Conditions Governing Use of Euroclear'.
[4] *Barlow Clowes v Vaughan* [1992] 4 All ER 22.
[5] This ties in with a wider phenomenon of the capital markets serving to spread financial risk. This was well observed by Michael Foot, Executive Director of the Bank of England, in his keynote address, *Managing Systemic Risk*, delivered on 11 September 1996 at the IBC Conference, Risk in Clearing Houses and Futures and Options Exchanges: '... the growing interrelation of markets has allowed the laying-off and spreading of risk to quite an unprecedented extent. One has only to compare the much greater spread of Mexico's creditors in 1995 with that in 1980 to see the point. To my mind, the structural development of financial markets in recent years has increased the chances of ripple effects spreading from one market to another, but correspondingly reduced the risk of those being serious waves rather than ripples.'
[6] Collateral is particularly important for the margining of derivatives transactions.

the use of client securities as collateral, both for the clearing systems and for global custodians, before turning to some specific English law points for the global custodian seeking to collateralise its exposures.

1 Generally

As indicated above, the use of settlement systems introduces complex interdependences. Several studies have confirmed that this has the result that settlement exposures are inherently impossible to predict with accuracy, and hence the vital importance to custodians and clearers of having recourse to the securities held by or through them as collateral.

This book has argued at several points that the manner in which securities are held can alter their legal nature. Commingling, intermediation and computerisation may all have the result that the asset available to the client to give as collateral may not be bonds or shares (or otherwise, securities) but rather an interest (contractual or proprietary) *in* or *in respect of* securities. It is therefore vital to draft any security language sufficiently widely to catch the asset of the client, whatever it may be.

Multiple intermediation is an increasing trend in the securities markets, and on many occasions the direct client of the custodian or clearing system will not be the beneficial owner of the assets. The problem for the collateral taker, simply put, is that the collateral assets may not be the client's to give. A purported security interest given in breach of fiduciary duty may not be effective, unless the collateral taker can show bona fides and the absence of notice of the breach. For this reason warranties are often taken that, where the client is not beneficial owner, it is authorised by the beneficial owner to deal with the securities in the manner contemplated by the agreement. The risk for the collateral taker is that, where there is breach of fiduciary duty, it may be left with a mere action for breach of warranty, and not good collateral. Further, there may be regulatory restrictions on intermediaries encumbering client assets in favour of custodians and clearing systems. Cedel restricts its general pledge so that it does not apply to SFA or IMRO-regulated client assets.

Securities in the hands of custodians and clearing systems may be subject to multiple encumbrances. Settlement banks will routinely take security interests over assets in the settlement systems. The settlement system itself may take a charge in respect of its exposures to participants (contractually in the membership documentation, or by legislation as in the case of the statutory privilege in favour of Cedel[1]). The custodian with whom the client deals directly may also take a security interest. All of this is in addition to any security interests given by the client to third parties to which it wishes to offer its portfolio as collateral for its own business exposures. The economic importance of portfolios of securities as collateral for international finance cannot be overestimated. Priorities between these competing security interests is therefore a crucial issue.

The reason for a creditor to take security is to ensure that its claims rank in priority to those of unsecured creditors of the debtor. The multiplication of competing security interests over securities held in clearing systems weakens

---

[1] Luxembourg Law of June 1994 Relating to Pledging, Transfer and Loss of Securities, article 1 (creating a new article 11(1) in the Law of 1971).

the position of those having only contractual rights against participants. This brings us back to counterparty risk. Before settlement, the claims of purchasers of securities are merely contractual. The trends in the settlement industry following the *G30 Report* may have led to a shorter settlement interval, but the position of the counterparty during it may, in commercial reality, be becoming weaker. This is another hidden settlement risk.

Complex conflict of laws issues are involved in the use of international portfolios of securities as collateral, and these are discussed in chapter 7, section C, above.

2 English law

It has always been difficult to advise London-based global custodians on collateralising their settlement exposures to clients. This is because, while recent analysis has identified how vast and unpredictable these exposures may now be, in this service-orientated industry it has not become customary for custodians to formalise their collateral arrangements to the extent that may be commercially appropriate for them.

The use of client cash balances as collateral is easier than such use of securities balances, because of mandatory insolvency set-off under English law (in rule 4.90 of the Insolvency Rules 1986). Under rule 4.90, sums owed by the custodian to the client (in respect of custody cash balances) should generally[1] be available for set off against sums owed by the client to the custodian, provided there is mutuality (ie neither party is acting as agent, or if it is, it acts for only one principal).[2] It is customary contractually to extend cash set off in the global custody agreement (eg to sums owed to affiliates of the custodian and/or by affiliates of the client) but as such provisions exceed the scope of rule 4.90, it should be assumed that they would not be effective in the English law insolvency of a client.[3]

The use of client securities as collateral is less straightforward, as insolvency set off only applies to debts.[4] Historically, custodians have relied on liens over client securities. As bankers, custodian banks may enjoy implied liens over client securities in respect of sums owed. However, an implied lien does not confer a power of sale, and it is customary to include an express power of sale in the global custody contract. This may raise problems of its own, as a purported lien with a power of sale over a changing portfolio, in circumstances where the client retains freedom to dispose of the assets without the custodian's consent, may be vulnerable to recharacterisation (in the client's

---

[1] Set off is not available for a debt if its creditor had notice that a meeting of creditors had been summoned or a petition for winding up was pending at the time the debt became due: rule 4.90(3).

[2] Where the client holds cash balances as trustee (ie client money) there is doubt as to whether mutuality is present.

[3] This is because of the rule in *British Eagle International Airlines Ltd v Compagnie Nationale Air France* [1975] 2 All ER 390, very broadly that contractual provision purporting to alter the effect of statutory insolvency law will be ineffective. See also the unreported case of *BCCI v Prince Fahd* (1996).

[4] It is possible to extend set off to securities under 'outright transfer' arrangements modelled on stock lending, but this is not customary: see below.

insolvency) as a floating charge, void for want of registration.[1] A pledge of client securities in favour of the global custodian may be contained in the global custody contract. A pledge is not registrable, and does confer a power of sale. However, a pledge is based on possession, and cannot take effect over intangible property (such as shares[2] or interests in Euroclear accounts). A purported pledge over a changing pool of intangibles, where the client retains freedom to deal, may again be recharacterised as a floating charge, again void for want of registration.

Of course, if the client does not have freedom to deal in the charged portfolio,[3] no floating charge would be created. However, this is generally unacceptable to clients. Legally speaking, the ideal course for the custodian would be to register floating charges against its custody clients. Certain clearing systems (and settlement banks) regularly register charges. However, this may be commercially unacceptable for custody clients.[4] Finally, it should be remembered that a floating charge is a relatively weak form of security.[5]

Where client exposures are very significant, some custodians have considered 'title finance' or 'outright transfer' arrangements, whereby ownership of the securities is transferred by the client to the custodian, and the custodian's redelivery obligation is conditional on repayment of all sums owed. These arrangements owe something to modern stock lending collateralisation, as well as the 'flawed asset' arrangement familiar to bankers. However, many custodians will feel this is something of a sledge hammer to crack a walnut, as the transfer of property in securities to the custodian raises major taxation, balance sheet and risk issues (see chapter 5, section B.1, above).

Chapter 4, above, argued that in most cases, the global custodian is a trustee. A further alternative for the custodian, currently little exploited, is to collateralise its settlement exposures by developing the trustee's implied right on indemnity under the general law of equity. This enables the trustee to recover its expenses properly incurred in carrying out the business from the trust property. The right of indemnity is not subject to many of the difficulties surrounding security interests (registration, priorities and *lex situs*). However, a weakness is that it is not available where there has been a breach of trust. It would therefore not assist, for example, where the credit extended to the client by the custodian was not permitted by the terms of the custody agreement. Nevertheless, a contractual development of the implied right of indemnity may well prove to be valuable for the custodian.

There is some doubt under the general law of equity concerning the ability of the trustee to take a security interest over trust assets. However, as far as the author is aware, this point has never been taken in connection with a custodian's security interest over its client's portfolio.

[1] Under section 395 of the Companies Act 1985, a floating charge created by a company subject to the Act is void against a liquidator or other creditor if not registered at Companies House within 21 days of its creation.
[2] As opposed to share certificates.
[3] So that it cannot remove securities without the prior consent of the custodian.
[4] Clients may be unwilling to accept the publicity involved. They may be subject to negative pledges (particularly if they have issued debt securities). UK banks are not permitted by the Bank of England to give floating charges.
[5] Floating charges are frozen on administration, and rank in priority after fixed charges, together with other disadvantages.

F   Conclusions

A major part of settlement risk is legal risk, or legal uncertainty. A way forward has been suggested in a recent IBA report,[1] which calls on other jurisdictions to follow the lead of Luxembourg, Belgium and the US in passing local legislation to clarify the legal fallout of evolving settlement practice. Because business is cross-border and because conflict of laws rules make it impossible to ring-fence legal risk in the 'good' jurisdictions, this legislation needs to be supplemented by further cross-border co-operation.

In the meantime, custodians need to be alert in seeking to address the hidden risks, as well as the overt risks of securities settlement. Good communications between the back office and risk management personnel is essential.[2] At a practical level, global custodians seeking to manage settlement risk on a day-to-day basis may find useful the following checklist (prepared by KM Partnership):

- If a single payment needs to be stopped, can the system do so without stopping all payments?
- If an inward payment is missing, does the Risk Department get told immediately?
- Are late payments reflected in the limits?
- Do the limits reflect the different risk profiles of individual currencies/payment systems?

---

[1] Randall Guynn, *Modernising Securities Ownership Transfer and Pledging Laws*, (1996), IBA.
[2] Although the Barings episode demonstrated the need for the back office to be segregated from the trading desk for the purposes of supervision, it is also important that settlement should not be isolated for risk management purposes.

Chapter 11

The Central Gilts Office

A Introduction

The Central Gilts Office ('the CGO') is an electronic system for the paperless settlement of gilt-edged securities.[1]

1 The gilts market

Gilts are registered debt securities, denominated in sterling, issued by the Bank of England on behalf of the UK government. Market liquidity is provided by gilt-edged market-makers ('GEMMs') who continuously quote two-way prices for gilts. GEMMs deal with each other electronically on a no-names basis through inter-dealer brokers. For a discussion of stock lending and repos in the gilts market, see below.

2 The CGO

Ninety per cent of gilts are held through the CGO. The CGO is operated by the Central Gilts Office of the Bank of England ('the Bank').[2] The CGO offers dematerialisation, or the removal of stock certificates and stock transfer forms necessary to evidence and transfer gilts outside the CGO. An assured payments system provides for the payment of the cash consideration for transfers through settlement banks. Dividends are paid outside the CGO by the registrar to registered holders. Although all gilts are eligible for CGO settlement, investors may elect to hold their gilts in certificated form.[3]

---

[1] The UK registered securities of the European Bank for Reconstruction and Development can also be settled in the CGO (under SI 1991/340).
[2] It was established in 1986 as a joint initiative by the Bank and the London Stock Exchange.
[3] Certificated gilts may be dematerialised in the CGO, and CGO gilts may be recertificated.

B   Core legal structure

1   Dematerialisation

Outside the CGO written instruments are required for the transfer of government stock.[1] Dematerialisation is based on the Stock Transfer (Gilt-Edged Securities)(CGO Service) Regulations 1985 ('the 1985 Regulations') made under the Stock Transfer Act 1982.

2   Legal and equitable ownership

(a)   Legal title

Legal title to gilts is determined, both within and outwith the CGO, prima facie by registration in the register maintained by the Bank.[2]

In addition to entries in the register, CGO members have accounts at the CGO. CGO transfers are effected by debiting the CGO account of the transferor member and crediting that of the transferee member. Notification of CGO transfers is made electronically by the CGO to the Bank of England registrar.[3] Registration generally follows CGO transfer within two business days.[4]

(b)   Equitable interest

The CGO *Reference Manual* provides in effect that book entry transfer vests the equitable interest of the transferor in the stock in the transferee.[5] Stock can be on-transferred before the initial transfer is registered.[6]

Any CGO transfer may relate to a part only of the transferor's registered holding of stock. The question therefore arises, which stock within that registered holding is subject to the equitable interest in favour of the transferee?[7] The *Reference Manual* addresses this problem by identifying an equitable

---

[1] The Government Stock Regulations 1965 (SI 1965/1420) permit government stock to be transferred either by written instrument according to the Stock Transfer Act 1963, or through the CGO (regulation 4).

[2] The Government Stock Regulations 1965, regulation 1(2).

[3] Section 136 of the Law of Property Act 1925, which requires legal assignments of choses in action to be in writing, is disapplied by section 1(2) of the Stock Transfer Act 1982.

[4] However the Bank is only required to register transfers ten clear days after notification from the CGO: regulation 10 of the Government Stock Regulations 1965.

[5] Sections 8.2.4 and 8.2.8. See also section 4(1) of the membership agreement.

Section 53(1)(c) of the Law of Property Act 1925, which requires dispositions of equitable interests to be in writing, is disapplied by section 1(2) of the Stock Transfer Act 1982.

[6] If A transfers to B, and B transfers to C, and C transfers to D all before the transfer to B is registered, A will hold its interest in the stock on trust for B, who will hold its interest in the stock on sub-trust for C, who will hold its interest in the stock on sub-sub-trust for D.

[7] As a general rule of trust law, a valid trust requires certainty of subject matter. This issue is discussed at length in chapter 5, above.

tenancy in common over the whole of the registered holding, in which the account holder and any transferee hold proportionate interests.[1]

3   Payments

(a)   Assured payments system

As a precondition of membership, each member must appoint a settlement bank to provide assured payment facilities on its behalf.[2] Movements of stock between CGO accounts generate automatic payment instructions which place an obligation ('assured payment obligation') on the settlement bank of the buyer to pay to the settlement bank of the seller a sum equal to the consideration for the transfer[3] ('assured payment'). The creation of the Assured Payment obligation in respect of a transaction discharges the obligation of the transferee member to make a payment to the transferor member in respect of that transaction, to the extent of the Assured Payment obligation.[4]

The form of documentation governing the relationship between a settlement bank and the members for which it acts is a commercial matter to be settled by those parties. Usually an assured payment facility agreement and a deed of charge are executed.[5]

Inter-settlement bank payments are made through the CHAPS system outside the CGO. Payments between settlement banks and their CGO member clients are made outside the CGO as a commercial matter.

There are currently restrictions on CGO deliveries free of payment or at non-market prices, but these are proposed to be relaxed when the CGO is upgraded in 1997 (see below).

---

[1] Section 8.2.8.

[2] *Reference Manual*, section 2.3.2; membership agreement, recital A and section 3(11).

[3] See *Reference Manual*, section 12. The assured payment obligation is imposed by the settlement bank agreement made between each settlement bank and the Bank, and the multi-party assured payment agreement entered into by the Bank and each settlement bank.

   In particular see section 2(1) of the assured payment agreement and section 4(2) of the settlement bank agreement.

   The CGO calculates a daily reference price based on the mid-market price for stock. Transfers valued in excess of £3,000,000 for a price which is 10% or more discrepant from the reference price are rejected. With smaller transactions, a 10% or more discrepancy is tolerated only if the member confirms the input. Accordingly, in cases where consideration is widely discrepant from market value (eg stock returns at the redelivery date of a stock lending transaction) a balancing cash payment may be required outside the assured payments system. However, these arrangements will be revised when the CGO is upgraded in 1997: see below.

[4] Membership agreement, section 4(3); *Reference Manual*, section 12.2.2.

[5] CGO settlement bank charges are protected under Part VII of the Companies Act 1989 (as brought into effect by SI 1991/488 and SI 1991/878 and as modified by SI 1991/880 (the Financial Markets and Insolvency Regulations 1991)).

   Very broadly, this privileges such charges as 'market charges' by disapplying provisions of the Insolvency Act 1986 which would otherwise affect the effectiveness and enforceability of the charges in the administration or receivership of the chargor.

   By way of background, it is understood that when the CGO was being set up, the settlement banks were uneasy with the limited liability involved in the assured payments system, and that this unease grew when the Insolvency Act 1986 restricted the value of a floating charge where the chargor goes into administration. In the circumstances, the banks desired the support of Part VII as a quid pro quo for these exposures.

(b) Delivery versus payment

The assured payment obligation is synchronised with the transfer of the equitable interest in the CGO. However, neither of these events is final or irrevocable. The transferor may not receive actual payment if either its settlement bank or that of the transferee becomes insolvent. Further, a CGO transfer may not proceed to registration in certain circumstances (see below under bad deliveries).

4 Stamp duty and SDRT

Transfers of gilts (within and outwith the CGO) are exempt from stamp duty[1] and SDRT.[2]

C Custody accounts

Special considerations arise for the CGO member who is acting as custodian, holding stock in the CGO on behalf of its clients. Although the Bank makes special provision for custody stock, it cannot be obliged to recognise the interests of custody clients.[3]

1 Nominee accounts

In the late 1980s the standard CGO membership agreement was amended to permit CGO accounts to be opened in the name of persons other than the CGO member, in order to permit stock to be registered in nominee companies. The membership agreement imposes liability on the member for its nominees;[4] as the member is liable for breaches by its nominees of the CGO regime, it is important to ensure that satisfactory controls are in place to ensure compliance by nominees and their staff.

2 Client documentation

Where the CGO member acts as custodian, the membership agreement requires

---

[1] Stamp Act 1891, Schedule 1, General Exemption.
[2] Finance Act 1986, section 99(5)(a).
[3] Regulation 16 of the Stock Transfer (Gilt-Edged Securities) (CGO Service) Regulations 1985.
[4] Recital B and section 2(2).

it to obtain from its client an acknowledgement and authority in prescribed form.[1]

This language authorises the custodian member to hold client stock in accordance with the CGO regime in general terms. However, it would be prudent to go further in the custody documentation to draw the client's attention to the particular risks associated with the CGO discussed below, and obtain the client's consent to them.

3   Settlement bank charge

The settlement banks usually collateralise their exposures to their member clients by a charge over the assets of the client in the CGO (see above); this charge in its standard form contains a warranty of beneficial ownership. Clearly, a custodian member could not give such a warranty. Without the express consent of its custody clients, it cannot properly give such a charge. Even with the clients' consent, the following problems arise.

In many cases, the direct clients of the custodian will not be the beneficial owners of the gilts (for example where the custodian's clients are mutual or pension funds); the consent of the ultimate beneficial owners is needed to give an effective charge.[2]

---

[1] '3(16) If and whenever the CGO Member acts or proposes to act as nominee or agent for another person ("a principal") in relation to stock held or to be held on, or transactions over, CGO Accounts of the CGO Member, to obtain from that principal before beginning to act as nominee or agent for that principal:
(a) an acknowledgement that the holding of stock for the account of that principal on the CGO Accounts of the CGO Member and all transactions over those CGO Accounts or otherwise in relation to facilities relating to the CGO Member's membership of the CGO Service will be subject to all of the provisions of this Agreement and to the CGO Rules and in particular (but without limiting the generality of the foregoing):
   (i)   that the stock is to be introduced into the CGO only if it has been purchased or is held on terms authorising the holder to deal with it free from any proprietary or equitable interest of any other person and in particular free from any unpaid vendor's lien; and
   (ii) that the Bank of England and its servant, and agents, with certain limited exceptions expressly provided for in this Agreement, are exempt from liability caused directly by or indirectly by the provision or operation of the CGO Service or any part thereof, or by any loss, interruption or failure in the provision or operation of the CGO Service or any part thereof, and entitling the Bank of England without liability to act without further enquiry on instructions or information or purported instructions or information received through the CGO Service or otherwise in accordance with the CGO Manual; and
(b) an authority for the CGO Member on behalf of that principal to do all such acts and things and execute all such documents as may be required to enable the CGO Member fully to observe and perform its obligations under this Agreement and the CGO Rules, and enter into any arrangement which the CGO Member considers proper for the purpose of facilitating clearance of or settlement of transactions effected on behalf of the principal through the CGO.'
The terms of 3(16)(a)(i) are compatible with custody arrangements, as they provide, not that the stock *is* free from third party equities, but that it may be *dealt* free from such equities.

[2] Under the rule, *nemo dat quod non habet*, or, none can give that which it does not own, where a security interest is purportedly given without the consent of the beneficial owner of the charged assets, the chargee may have a valid security interest if it can show that it acted as bona fide purchaser of the legal estate for value without notice of the lack of consent. A chargee can be treated as a purchaser for this purpose, but only if it takes a legal security interest. A charge is always equitable, so that the settlement banks cannot be protected by this doctrine, and will always be vulnerable if the true owners did not consent to the charge.

Further, where the securities of more than one client are commingled in one CGO account, the settlement bank charge will be given in respect of all those securities without distinction. Thus, the assets of one client will in effect serve as collateral for obligations referable to the business of another client. A well-advised client will not consent to these arrangements, which may amount to breach of fiduciary duty by the custodian.

4 Pooling

While separate CGO accounts may be opened for individual custody clients, such arrangements are expensive, and the pooling of client stock is customary.[1] One problem with such an arrangement relates to the settlement bank charge, and is discussed above. Another problem relates to bad deliveries. In certain circumstances (discussed below) a CGO transfer may fail to proceed to registration, causing a shortfall to arise. Where client securities are commingled, a shortfall attributable to the business of one client may be borne by other clients whose securities are held in the same account.

5 Proposals for sponsored membership

It is proposed that when the CGO is upgraded in 1997, sponsored membership will be permitted. These arrangements are currently available in CREST, and permit investors to have securities registered directly in their names, through an account operated by a sponsor on their behalf. CREST sponsors require authorisation under the Financial Services Act 1986, and such authorisation may also be required for CGO sponsors.

D Risk

The CGO has operated successfully for over a decade. Nevertheless, certain risks are inherent in the system. The success of the CGO depends to a large extent on the cooperation of participants; the Bank does not stand behind either the cash side, or the securities side, of CGO settlement.[2]

1 Credit

The assured payment system was introduced because '... it was judged essential to have a payments system that would provide assurance of payment. ...'[3] However, the system does not eliminate credit risk for the seller of stock.

---

[1] On the other hand, it would be possible for the custodian to open a segregated account for a particular client, identified on the register by a special alpha-numeric, or even expressly to register the custodian as trustee: regulation 12(1) of the Government Stock Regulations 1965.

[2] The bank has no duty to monitor or enforce compliance of any member or settlement bank with the CGO regime: membership agreement, section 7(1).

[3] *Gilt edged settlement. Phase 2 of the CGO Service*, Bank of England Quarterly Bulletin, February 1987.

It merely replaces the credit risk of the buyer of stock with that of both the settlement bank of the buyer and the settlement bank of the seller.[1]

Where large volumes of gilts are sold, the credit risk of the member to its own settlement bank should be assessed. There is provision in the assured payment facility agreement to limit the exposure of the settlement bank to the member by limiting the daily aggregate of assured payment obligations that the member may cause the settlement bank to incur. The only way for a member to achieve equivalent protection for itself is in practice to limit the daily volumes of stock sold through the CGO. This presents a problem for custodian members, as the volumes of stock sold through their CGO account will depend upon their clients' instructions. Custodians may therefore consider including provision in their custody agreements to limit the daily volume of CGO transfers that they may be required to effect.

Finally, it should be noted that the assured payments system does not extend to all payments that may be associated with the CGO. Return payments associated with bad deliveries are not covered.[2] Also, balancing payments required to be made for free deliveries and transactions not at market value, must be made outside the system.[3]

2　Bad deliveries[4]

In certain circumstances, CGO transfers may not proceed to registration. Where the transferor is insolvent, the transfer may be avoided in section 280 of the Insolvency Act 1986. The stock may be frozen by a court order,[5] or affected by fraud.[6] In no sense can the Bank be said to stand behind the CGO transferee's rights in respect of such stock.[7]

Where stock is brought into the CGO system, it is credited to the taker's

---

[1] The arrangement is for the buyer's settlement bank to pay the seller's settlement bank, and for the seller's settlement bank in turn to pay the seller. If any link in this chain fails, the seller will not be paid. The seller's settlement bank's duty to pay is limited to sums it actually receives (assured payment facility agreement, Schedule 3, final paragraph). The Bank has no obligation to stand behind a defaulting settlement bank. Indeed, it is expressly stated that the Bank is under no obligation to monitor or enforce the compliance of settlement banks under the CGO regime (settlement bank agreement, section 5(1)(i)).

　　Moreover, if a settlement bank itself suffers loss due to the failure of another settlement bank, the member may be liable under an indemnity given by the member in the assured payment facility agreement (section 4(1) and Schedule 3, paragraph b).

[2] *Reference Manual*, section 10.3.6.

[3] The CGO currently restricts the transfer of stock otherwise than for cash consideration at market value (see the *Reference Manual*, section 6.3). Members are obliged in effect to conclude free deliveries and non-market value deliveries by making balancing cash payments outside the CGO. When the CGO is upgraded in 1997, these restrictions will drop away.

[4] 'A bad delivery is a transfer of stock which has been rejected by the Registrar' *Reference Manual* section 10.3.1.

[5] Ie a charging order, stop order or stop notice.

[6] In such circumstances the Bank is protected from liability by provision in regulation 3 of the Stock Transfer (Gilt-Edged Securities) (CGO Service) Regulations 1985, that a CGO credit is not a representation that the member has title to the securities.

[7] 'Information concerning the movement of fully paid stock within the CGO system is passed to the Registrar but the CGO service gives no guarantee of subsequent registration of such movements' *Reference Manual*, section 8.1.5.

CGO account upon receipt by the CGO of the relevant documentation.[1] The credit entry will be reversed if the stock is rejected by the registrar (for example because the transferor is not registered with sufficient stock, or because the certificate has been reported stolen).[2] These arrangements, combined with the practice of multiple book entry transfers between register updates, presents systemic risk, as one failed inward delivery may lead to a series of intra-CGO delivery failures. However, since most gilts are not dematerialised, this source of risk may be smaller than in the past.

If there is a bad delivery of stock to A which is not detected until after the stock has been on-transferred within the CGO to B, the account of A will go into overdraft and A will be contractually obliged immediately to bring in new stock to eliminate the shortfall.[3] This raises special concerns for custodians. It should take express indemnities from its clients in respect of this personal obligation to eliminate shortfalls, and may wish to consider collateralising the exposure. Its commingled clients will be concerned that their securities may be automatically applied by the CGO in making good bad deliveries which are attributable to the business of other clients.

Systemic risk raises further concerns. The obligation of A to make good the shortfall is merely contractual, and A may default. In such a case, the CGO will allocate the shortfall to other CGO members in accordance with its own tracing methodology.[4] Thus, members' accounts may be debited in respect of bad stock introduced into the system by third parties. This risk should be expressly disclosed to clients.

In view of the relatively long registration cycle in the CGO[5] it will be impracticable for custodians to refuse to settle client sales before their purchases are registered. However, it is important that they should reserve the right to reverse stock credits in respect of bad deliveries. Custodians should also consider how to collateralise their exposures where client bad deliveries cause shortfalls to arise.

3 Custody documentation

Special risk concerns arise for the custodian holding client securities through the CGO, and these should be addressed in client custody documentation. In order to ensure that the risks relating to credit and bad deliveries discussed above are borne by their clients and not by themselves, custodians should expressly disclose them to their clients in their custody documentation, and carefully limit their liability.[6] As all members (including custodians) are obliged to indemnify the Bank in respect (broadly) of the member's CGO business,[7]

---

[1] Ie the stock transfer form and certificate or enfacement: *Reference Manual*, section 8.6.6. Only in the case of inward deliveries of over £5m in value is there a special checking procedure.

When the CGO is upgraded in 1997, this may change, so that stock will not be available to members until after registration of the deposit.

[2] The Bank of England as registrar has the right to reject any transfer unless it is furnished with such evidence as it may require of the transferor's right to make the transfer: Government Stock Regulations 1965, regulation 5.

[3] *Reference Manual*, section 10.3.5 and section 3(9) of the membership agreement.

[4] See the *Reference Manual*, sections 8.2.6 and 10.3.4.

[5] Currently three days.

[6] Particularly in view of the severe limitations on the liability of the Bank in the membership agreement (section 9(1) and 9(3)).

[7] Membership agreement, section 9(2).

a corresponding indemnity should be taken by the custodian from the client. This should also expressly cover the liability of the custodian member to make good any shortfalls in CGO accounts[1] and the potential liability of the custodian associated with its warranty that all CGO transfers it settles will be genuine.[2] In addition, custodians should consider whether their collateral arrangements are sufficient in view of the personal liabilities they may bear as CGO members. Where custodians access the CGO through nominees, care should be taken to ensure that any indemnities and collateral arrangements extend to liabilities of the nominee.

E Collateral, stock lending and repos

An important use of gilts is as collateral for borrowings, or in stock lending and repo (or repurchase) transactions.

1 Collateral

CGO gilts may be used as collateral either through CGO collateral facilities, or alternatively through arrangements effected by the parties to the arrangement independently of the CGO.

(a) Independently of the CGO

A CGO member may wish to confer a legal mortgage in its gilts, transferring them to the CGO account of the mortgagee. However, CGO contractual documentation contains 'absolute transfer' provisions,[3] cutting across the retention by the mortgagor of any proprietary interest in the gilts such as the usual equity of redemption. If they are effective, a purported legal mortgage would be re-characterised as an outright security transfer, leaving the collateral giver exposed to the credit risk of the collateral taker for any excess in the value of the gilts over the collateralised exposures. A further difficulty is that, until the upgrade of the CGO in 1997, the transfer of gilts by way of security will have to be matched by the payment of cash consideration through the assured payments system. Such payment will be inappropriate in some cases (for example where the collateral is required for variation margin in respect of derivatives exposures) and will require a balancing payment to be made outside the CGO.

It might be sought to confer an equitable mortgage or charge over stock remaining in the collateral giver's account. However, any such security interest may contravene the negative pledge routinely given to settlement banks in support of their settlement charges.

There are three CGO facilities for the use of gilts as collateral, namely delivery-by-value, long-term collateral certificates and overnight collateral chits. Delivery-by-value involves the transfer of collateral between CGO

---

[1] Membership agreement, section 3(9).
[2] Membership agreement, section 5(2). See also section 5(3) and 5(4).
[3] *Reference Manual*, section 8.2.4; membership agreement, section 4.1.

accounts. Long-term and overnight collateral chits involve the issue of physical certificates and the freezing of stock in the collateral giver's account.

However, these arrangements are also subject to 'outright transfer' provisions,[1] cutting across any equity of redemption in favour of the collateral giver.

(b) Delivery-by-value

Collateral may be provided on an overnight basis through the delivery-by-value mechanism. The collateral giver specifies the aggregate value of securities to be delivered from its account to that of the collateral taker, but not the types of securities to be so delivered.[2] The CGO system selects the stock to be delivered, and as usual an automatic payment instruction arises in respect of the transfer. Both the payments and the stock movements are reversed automatically the following morning ('returning equivalent securities to those delivered . . .'[3]). The movements of stock do not proceed to registration.

The recipient of delivery-by-value collateral may use it for 'on-pledging';[4] however it cannot be transferred otherwise than as CGO collateral within or out of the CGO.[5]

The legal status of these arrangements is unclear. The interest of the DBV taker can only be equitable, as (in the absence of registration) legal title remains with the DBV giver. However, the freedom to on-pledge and the equivalent return provisions seem to suggest outright transfer. It is important that documentation between the collateral giver and taker clarifies the nature of the collateral taker's interest.

In practice DBV is used for stocklending and repos (see below).

(c) Long-term collateral certificates

These are a form of physical collateral that the CGO system will issue to members in respect of stock held by them in the CGO. The issue of the certificate freezes the stock to which it relates in the account of the member.[6] While long-term collateral certificates may be convenient as a form of collateral that can be physically delivered, they do not protect that collateral taker from risks affecting the collateral giver's title, discussed above (bad deliveries).[7]

---

[1] *Reference Manual*, section 9.1.2.

[2] Although the member giving collateral may specify whether British government stocks alone, or non-British Government stocks alone or any stocks are to be used: *Reference Manual*, section 9.3.6.

[3] *Reference Manual*, section 9.3.17.

[4] 'Once stock is credited to a taker's CGO Accounts, it may be used either for onward Deliveries-by-Value or, in circumstances which the CGO considers to be exceptional, for the issue of Overnight Collateral Chits . . .' *Reference Manual*, section 9.3.15.

[5] Section 9.3.15. These restrictions on the use of collateral by the collateral taker do not accord with the legal analysis suggested by section 9.1.2, ie that the giver of collateral retains no property in it.

[6] The certificate confirms on its face that the named member's account is credited with a specified amount of a certain stock, and that no instructions involving the release of that sum of the stock will be accepted unless the certificate has been surrendered.

[7] Note (4) on the certificate states 'In accordance with Regulation 3 of the Stock Transfer (Gilt-edged Securities) (CGO Service) Regulations 1985 this certificate is represented by the Bank to a person acting on the faith of it that prima facie evidence of title in the member to the stock to which it relates have been produced to the Bank but is not to be taken as a representation that the member has any title to such stock.'

A further risk is that these arrangements fail to confer a property interest in the gilts on the collateral taker; this would mean that enforcement might be avoided in the collateral giver's insolvency.[1] Again, it is essential clearly to document such arrangements, confirming that a property interest is conferred under an equitable mortgage or fixed charge.

(d) Overnight collateral chits

Overnight collateral chits are akin to long-term collateral chits, but are more short-term.[2] They are issued to market makers and money brokers only.

2 Gilt title finance (stock lending and repos)

(a) Restricted and free market

Until January 1996 the rules of the London Stock Exchange[3] prohibited gilt repos and restricted gilt stock lending to GEMMs[4] and Stock Exchange Money Brokers (SEMBs) serving GEMMs.[5] The purpose of permitted borrowing was limited to the filling of a short position. The restrictions on gilt stock lending were mirrored in taxation legislation.[6]

In January 1994 the Bank developed arrangements for supplying liquidity in the banking system through the use of gilt repos between the Bank and market counterparties.[7]

On 2 January 1996 an open gilt stock lending and repo market was introduced by changes in the Stock Exchange rules.[8] GEMMs continue to be obliged to quote continuous two-way prices on gilts, but now any market participant is free to engage in stock lending or repos of gilts with any counterparty for any purpose.

(b) Stock lending

The former restriction of gilt stock lending to GEMMs and SEMBs has now been relaxed, and the role of SEMBs has dropped away.[9] However, GEMMs continue to dominate gilt stock lending.

---

[1] Under section 127 of the Insolvency Act 1986.
[2] They expire at noon on the business day following their day of issue.
[3] Chapter 11.
[4] And discount houses for stock up to seven years' maturity.
[5] GEMMs incur short positions in the course of their market making. To cover these short positions, they must borrow stock. Until January 1996, they were only permitted to borrow from SEMBs who in turn borrow stock from Inland Revenue approved institutional lenders.
  The restrictions meant in effect that only GEMMs could go short in gilts, and that therefore only they could make a market in gilts.
[6] Regulation 5 of the Stock Lending Regulations (SI 1989/1299) (made under section 129 of the ICTA 1988). The restrictions did not operate as absolute prohibitions, but as conditions for the favourable tax regime available for 'approved' stock lending (ie relief from corporation tax and capital gains tax: ICTA 1988, section 129(3) and TCGA 1992, section 271(9)).
[7] Back-to-back repos between the Bank's counterparties and other gilt holders were also permitted.
[8] The ability to borrow gilts ceased to be confined to GEMMs; the permitted purpose of borrowing ceased to be limited to covering a short position and gilt repo transactions were permitted.
[9] The Stock Exchange Rules and the CGO *Reference Manual* no longer refer to this category. The firms that used to make it up are seeking a wider intermediary role, while many participants in gilt stock lending enter into their transactions direct, without using intermediaries.

The borrowed stock is transferred in each case through the CGO; the assured payment for the transfer serves as cash collateral for the loan. Certain institutional lenders may prefer to hold securities to cash for investment and risk management reasons.[1] They therefore often require alternative collateral in the form of DBVs. In addition, GEMMs may have surplus gilts but not surplus cash, preferring to 'borrow back' the cash collateral and substitute gilts through the DBV system. The assured payment for the DBV serves as the return of the cash collateral.

As DBVs are automatically returned on the next business day, it is necessary to 'roll over' or redeliver DBVs on a daily basis during the currency of the loan.

(c) Repos

Tax reforms were introduced at the same time as the creation of a free market in gilt repos.[2] Those wishing to take advantage of the new ability to receive interest on gilts free of withholding tax must hold their gilts in special 'STAR' accounts.[3] Certain enhancements to the CGO system were introduced to assist the new repo market.[4] The Bank issued a gilt repo code of best practice for use by market participants.

F CGO 2

In November 1995 the Bank announced proposals to upgrade the CGO on the basis of the software used in CREST, the settlement system for corporate registered securities. The upgraded system ('CGO 2') is expected to be operational in early 1997. The upgrade will keep open the option of merging the CGO and CREST in the future. CGO 2 will offer many of the facilities currently available or proposed in CREST. These are proposed to include free deliveries; debit caps; 2-hour registration; sponsored membership; escrow balances; enhanced gilt repos (automatic payment of interest); enhanced stock lending (automatic returns, revaluation and margining) and enhanced DBVs (optional concentration limits; the return of DBVs will depend on available headroom under the assured payments system).

---

[1] In the past, certain institutional lenders faced tax problems with cash collateral, but these are largely historic.

[2] Taxation provisions for withholding tax on interest and manufactured interest were reformed under ICTA 1988, sections 51A and 737(1B) respectively. 'From 2 January 1996, UK and overseas companies and certain other investors will be able to receive gross dividends. The effect is that withholding tax should not be applied to dividend payments on most gilt holdings. Manufactured dividends will be payable gross in all circumstances. This means that *all* counterparties to a gilt repo or stock loan will be able to manufacture gross dividend payments; most will also receive gross real dividends,' *The Gilt Repo Market*, Bank of England Quarterly Bulletin, November 1995, p 4.

[3] 'If that were the extent of the reforms, the Exchequer would suffer a one-off cash-flow loss. In order to offset this, UK-taxable investors who enter the new gross-paying arrangements will be subject to quarterly accounting to the UK tax authorities for tax on gilt interest. Investors wishing to take advantage of this gross payment regime will need to hold their gilts in special accounts (known as 'STAR' accounts) in the Central Gilts Office (CGO),' ibid.

[4] Including introducing new hardware, extending the normal CGO daily timetable, and relaxing the usual limits on free deliveries (ie deliveries free of payments) within the CGO.

Chapter 12

The Central Moneymarkets Office

A Introduction

The Central Moneymarkets Office ('the CMO') is a depositary and electronic settlement system for sterling money market bearer securities such as bills and certificates of deposit.[1] It is operated by the Bank of England ('the Bank').[2] Securities held in the CMO are immobilised in a vault at the Bank.[3]

As with the CGO, securities are transferred between CMO members electronically by debiting the account of the transferor and crediting the account of the transferee.[4] Associated payment instructions are notified daily to members' settlement banks for payment. Unlike the CGO, the CMO does not operated an assured payments system.

Whereas securities in the CGO are in registered form, securities in the CMO are in bearer form.[5]

---

[1] The CMO will accept the following types of sterling-denominated bearer securities: treasury bills, local authority bills, eligible bank bills (defined in Appendix 2 of the CMO *Reference Manual* as 'A bank bill accepted by a bank whose acceptances are eligible for discount at the Bank of England.'), ineligible bank bills, trade bills, bank certificates of deposit (provided the issuing bank is authorised under the Banking Act 1987), building society certificates of deposit and commercial paper (including short-term certificates, defined in Appendix 2 of the *Reference Manual* as 'An undertaking given by the London Stock Exchange STC Office to transfer securities and/or pay cash secured against securities held by a member or participant of the STC service in his TALISMAN trading account'): *Reference Manual*, section F.1.2.

All instruments held in the CMO must be payable at maturity by a CMO member or at the office of a CMO member (section 7(8) of the membership agreement) and where the liability arises under an acceptance, the acceptance must be generally in accordance with section 19 of the Bills of Exchange Act 1882 (*Reference Manual*, section F.1.2).

[2] The CMO was launched by the Bank in 1990 following a failure by market participants to establish their own system.

[3] Except in the case of dematerialised securities in respect of which there are no instruments: see below.

[4] A transfer between CMO members operates in the following broad stages:

(a) *Transfer instructions*. The transferor gives instructions for the transfer via its CMO terminal.

(b) *Transferee acceptance*. The transferee gives instructions for acceptance of the transfer via its CMO terminal.

(c) *Book entry*. The securities are debited from the transferor's CMO account and credited to the transferee's CMO account.

(These stages correspond with the first three stages of a transfer within the CGO. However, unlike the CMO transfer, a CGO transfer involves two further stages, namely notification to the registrar and registration. There is no equivalent to these in the CMO, as CMO securities are bearer and not registered.)

[5] But see the discussion of dematerialised CMO securities below.

The CMO has facilities for the automatic presentation of matured securities to CMO member issuers.[1] CMO securities may be withdrawn from the CMO and subsequently relodged.[2]

Certain securities are dematerialised within the CMO (see below).

B Core legal structure

1 Possession

While the operational provisions of the CMO and the CGO are similar, their legal structures are fundamentally different. In contrast with the CGO, the proprietary aspects of the CMO have no statutory basis and rest on general law concepts derived from common law possession. This reflects the fact that the securities represented in CMO accounts are tangible instruments.[3]

These concepts are bailment[4] and attornment.[5] The Bank holds the instruments in the CMO as bailee for the participants to whose accounts they are credited.[6] The effect of a book entry transfer within the CMO is an attornment by the Bank to the transferee.[7]

There are provisions for the use of CMO securities as collateral,[8] and these are referred to in the CMO *Reference Manual* as involving a pledge. Pledge is the common law method of giving security by transfer of possession.

Dematerialisation affects the availability of these possession-based concepts (see below).

2 Negotiability

The secondary markets in bearer securities have traditionally benefited from the doctrine of negotiability. A negotiable instrument has two attractive features. Firstly, it is transferable without formalities. Secondly, honest acquisition confers good title (even if the transferor did not have good title), ie the holder in due course takes free from prior equities and defects in the title of the transferor.

Instruments held within the CMO are intended to be negotiable.[9] There is no legal difficulty in characterising CMO transfers of physical securities as negotiations.[10]

---

[1] See *Reference Manual*, section L.1.

[2] *Reference Manual*, sections J.1 and J.1.13.

[3] Except, of course, in the case of dematerialised securities (see below). CGO securities are registered and therefore intangible.

[4] Bailment is a common law relationship of safekeeping based on the transfer of physical possession of a tangible asset.

[5] Attornment is an undertaking whereby a bailee acknowledges that it holds property for a third party.

[6] *Reference Manual*, section J.2.5. See also section 4(1)(a) of the CMO membership agreement.

[7] Section 4(1)(f) of the CMO membership agreement.

[8] See below.

[9] The CMO membership agreement defines 'CMO Instrument' as '... a negotiable bearer instrument of a description for the time being specified in the CMO Manual as capable of being held within the CMO Service'.

[10] Negotiation involves the delivery of an instrument by transfer of possession. The fact that CMO instruments are immobilised is not problematic, as possession for this purpose includes constructive possession; attornment is the transfer of constructive possession.

However dematerialisation affects the negotiable status of CMO instruments (see below).

3   Payments

As with the CGO, each CMO member is required to appoint a settlement bank as a condition of membership.[1] Electronic transfers of securities within the CMO automatically generate payment instructions to the settlement bank of the transferee member to make a payment to the tranferor's settlement bank equal to the purchase price. These payment instructions are synchronised with the change of ownership of the securities on book entry transfer. Payments are made between the settlement banks at the end of the day through the CHAPS system.[2]

In contrast to the assured payments system of the CGO, payments in the CMO are not assured, and settlement banks can reverse payments.[3] In the event that payment is reversed, the associated transfer is not affected and the Bank will not assist the transferor in recovering payment.[4]

C   Custody accounts

1   Nominee accounts

CMO accounts may be opened by a member in nominee names. The membership agreement imposes liability on the member for its nominees.[5]

2   Client documentation

Where the CMO member acts as custodian, the membership agreement requires it to obtain from its client an acknowledgement and authority in prescribed form.[6] Because of the special risks discussed below, additional risk disclosure wording should be included; risks to the custodian should be addressed with an express indemnity and possibly collateral arrangements.

---

[1] *Reference Manual*, section N.1.1 and membership agreement, recital B and section 7(11).
[2] See *Reference Manual*, section N.2 and section 4(1) of the CMO settlement bank agreement.
[3] See section N.1.6 of the *Reference Manual*.
[4] *Reference Manual*, section N.1.6.
　　'In the exceptional event of a settlement bank deciding to refuse to meet a payment instruction, the associated transfer of instruments will not be reversed by the CMO and the CMO will have no role in any subsequent negotiations between the parties to the transaction.' *Summary of the CMO Service*, p 9.
[5] Recital D and section 2(3).
[6] '7 The CMO Member undertakes to the Bank ... (16) whenever the CMO member acts or proposes to act as nominee or agent for another person (a "principal") in relation to CMO Instruments held or to be held on, or transactions over, CMO Instruments Accounts of the CMO member, to obtain from that principal before beginning to act as nominee or agent for that principal–
(a) an acknowledgement (expressed to be in favour of the Bank and its servants and agents) that the holding of CMO Instruments for the account of that principal on a CMO Instruments Account of the CMO member and all transactions over such a CMO Instruments Account or otherwise in relation to facilities relating to the CMO Member's membership of the CMO Service will be subject to all of the provisions of this Agreement and to the CMO Rules and in particular (but without limiting the generality of the foregoing) –
　　(i)　that instruments are to be lodged with the CMO Service only if they have been purchased or are held on terms authorising the holder to deal with them free from any proprietary or equitable interest of any other person;

3 Segregation

While separate CMO accounts may be opened for individual custody clients, such arrangements are expensive. Moreover they may be unnecessary. This is because the CMO operates on an allocated basis. When instruments are lodged at the CMO, each is mechanically stamped with a distinctive number, which is quoted in every subsequent transfer and withdrawal of the instrument.[1] The segregation of the assets of one client from another may be achieved without separate CMO accounts, provided the records of the custodian allocate particular securities to particular clients.

4 Recognition by the Bank

The Bank does not recognise any trusts,[2] even in the case of designated nominee accounts.[3]

    (ii)   that except as required by law the Bank is not bound by or compelled to recognise any proprietary or equitable interest in or any other right in respect of any CMO Instrument other than an absolute right to the entirety of that CMO Instrument in the CMO member to whose CMO Instruments Account that CMO Instrument is for the time being credited or for whose account that CMO Instrument is otherwise held for the time being, and that the principal will not assert or permit any person claiming under or through him to assert any such proprietary or equitable interest or other right against the Bank;

    (iii)   that the Bank and its servants and agents, with the limited exceptions expressly provided in this Agreement, are exempt from liability caused directly by or indirectly by the operation of the CMO Service and entitling the Bank without liability to act without further enquiry on instructions or information or purported instructions or information received through the CMO Service or otherwise in accordance with the CMO Manual; and

  (b) an authority for the CMO Member on behalf of that principal to do all such acts and things and execute all such documents as may be required to enable the CMO Member fully to observe and perform its obligations under this Agreement and the CMO Rules, and enter into any arrangement which the CMO member considers proper for the purpose of facilitating clearance of or settlement of transactions effected on behalf of the principal through the CMO Service.'

All of these provisions are also required in respect of the CGO except (ii) which is unique to the CMO and reflects the lack of statutory basis for the Bank's exclusion of notice of trusts.

    In addition, the dematerialisation agreement (see below) requires custodian members, in section 4(1) '... to obtain from [the custody client], before beginning to act as nominee or agent ... an acknowledgement (expressed to be in favour of the Bank and its servants and agents and of every CMO member for the time being) that the holding of Dematerialised Instruments for the account of that principal on a CMO Instruments Account of the CMO Member and all transactions over such a CMO Instruments Account or otherwise in relation to facilities relating to the CMO Member's membership of the CMO Service affecting Dematerialised Instruments will be subject to all the provisions of this Agreement, the CMO Membership Agreement and the CMO Rules.'

[1] Equivalent procedures are in place to allocate distinctive numbers to dematerialised securities.
[2] CMO membership agreement, section 4(1)(c). See also section F.1.5 of the *Reference Manual*.
[3] See section 4(1)(d) of the CMO membership agreement. However, where the Bank has actual notice of trusts (for example where a trust is indicated in an account title) there must be doubt as to the effectiveness of contractual provisions in the membership agreement in defeating the proprietary claims of third party beneficiaries. Some of this doubt may be addressed by the requirement in section 7(16)(a)(ii) of the CMO membership agreement, which overcomes the problem of privity by requiring the CMO custodian member to include in its custody agreement with clients an acknowledgment from the client that the Bank does not generally recognise trusts; however this would not of course address the risk of claims of beneficial owners other than the direct clients of the custodian.

    Similar concerns do not arise in the CGO as the exclusion of notice of trusts has statutory backing.

D   Risk

1   Credit

There is no assured payment system in the CMO. Because settlement banks are able to revoke payment instructions (see above), the system does not offer true delivery versus payment.

2   Defects in title to securities

A major legal issue is the risk that securities held in the CMO may be forged, stolen or otherwise subject to adverse claims from third parties. A credit entry in a CMO account does not mean that the account holder has title to the relevant securities. Rather, it indicates that, whatever interest the Bank has in the securities by virtue of possession, it holds as bailee for the account holder.[1] In other words, CMO members and not the Bank bear the risk of defects in title.[2]

Certain provisions are included in the CMO documentation to reduce the risk of defects in title. If the Bank receives notice of adverse claims in respect of CMO securities it may freeze or withdraw those securities[3] and if a member receives such notice it must inform the CMO system.[4] Further, there are restrictions on lodgement. Whereas any CGO member may bring stock into the system, securities may be lodged in the CMO only by the issuer (or acceptor) or their agent[5] because only they can guarantee the validity of the instruments.[6] (Accordingly, custodians wishing to settle transfers into the CMO will have to act as agent of the issuer or acceptor. This will in turn entail entering into a lodging agency agreement with the issuer, and executing a lodging agents undertaking in favour of the Bank.)[7]

However, some aspects of the system increase risk. Securities are credited to CMO accounts before they are lodged and checked,[8] and there is provision for the lodging of non-security printed instruments.[9]

---

[1] Membership agreement, section 4(1)(b).

A credit entry in a CMO account indicates a bailment (ie the relationship between the Bank and the member) but does not indicate title (ie the relationship between the member and the issuer of the securities).

In this respect the position of a CMO member is weaker than that of a CGO member; a credit balance in a CGO account constitutes a representation by the Bank that prima facie evidence of title in the member has been produced.

[2] See *Reference Manual*, section H.2.3.

[3] CMO membership agreement, section 4(4)(a).

[4] CMO membership agreement, section 4(4)(b).

[5] *Reference Manual*, section H.2.2.

[6] Lodging members must replace any defective instruments lodged by them: membership agreement, section 7(10). See *Reference Manual*, section H.2.8 and membership agreement, section 5(2).

[7] *Reference Manual*, sections H.2.5 and H.2.6.

[8] *Reference Manual*, sections F.1.7, H.2.18, H.2.20 and H.2.31.

[9] Such instruments must carry a statement in bold capitals on their face that 'This Certificate is valid only when stamped by CMO with an identifier number' *Reference Manual*, section H.4.2.

Exposure to adverse claims is possibly increased by the non-negotiable status of dematerialised securities (see below).

3 Liability of custodians[1]

As indicated above, there may be significant risks associated with defects in title to securities within the CMO. The liability of the Bank for such risks is extremely limited.[2]

In contrast, the liabilities of CMO members in relation to fraudulent securities are onerous. Lodging members[3] are obliged to make good any shortfall arising on the discovery of bad stock.[4] Moreover any member (whether it introduces stock or not) must indemnify the Bank in respect of any adverse claims to any CMO securities.[5] Custody members are required to indemnify the Bank and all other CMO members against adverse claims from their clients in respect of dematerialised securities.[6]

Thus where the CMO member is a custodian, it must (in effect) guarantee the validity of its customer's securities (and those of its nominees' customers).[7] This may be a very significant exposure.

E Dematerialisation

1 Generally

Since September 1994 it has been possible for sterling certificates of deposit to be issued into the CMO system in dematerialised form.[8] Dematerialised securities[9] may be withdrawn from the CMO; on withdrawal of a dematerialised security, the original lodging member is required to make available a security printed instrument at the CMO counter.[10]

---

[1] This section considers the liability of members acting as custodians. Significant liabilities are also imposed on members who act as lodging agents, including liability for fraud by or through customers. Both the lodging agent and the custodian are required to assume risks that they are unable to control. While it might be argued that the lodging agent who introduces bad paper into the system should properly bear the cost of it, it is less clear why a custodian should be exposed if its clients buy bad paper through it.

[2] The Bank excludes liability as a result of defective instruments in section 8(4) of the CMO membership agreement. See also *Reference Manual*, sections H.2.3, H.2.16, H.2.28, and J.1.6.

[3] Ie members introducing stock into the CMO, such as custodians settling client transfers into the system. If defects in title cause loss to another CMO member, it may sue the Bank. The Bank's liability is contractually extremely limited (see above). However, there may be some risk that the limitation provisions are ineffective. If so and if the Bank suffers substantial liabilities, the indemnity in favour of the Bank may represent an important exposure.

[4] *Reference Manual*, section H.2.9.

[5] Membership agreement, section 4(2). See also section 8(2). If defects in title cause loss to another CMO member, it may sue the Banker.

[6] Section 4(2) of the dematerialisation agreement.

[7] Because a member is liable for its nominees (see above).

[8] Ie without any paper instrument. See section H.4.6 of the *Reference Manual*.

[9] The CMO uses the term 'dematerialised instrument'; however an instrument is necessary physical.

[10] *Reference Manual*, section J.2.3 and section 4 of the deed of covenant (see below).

2   Documentation

As a precondition of CMO membership, all members must enter into a dematerialisation agreement.[1] In addition, a precondition of issuing dematerialised CMO securities is the execution by the issuing member of the CMO deed of covenant.[2] These documents ('the dematerialisation documentation') are drafted to provide that the dematerialisation does not affect the rights of CMO members to whose accounts dematerialised securities are credited ('holders').[3] However, it is not clear that this objective is achieved for the following reasons.

3   Negotiability

Physical instruments held in the CMO are regarded as negotiable instruments,[4] and the dematerialisation documentation is drafted with a view to replicating contractually the benefits of negotiability. In the deed of covenant, issuers agree and acknowledge that holders shall have the same rights as against them (the issuers) in respect of dematerialised securities as if the holders held the security in physical form.[5] Dematerialised securities cannot be negotiable.[6] The chief benefit of negotiable status under the law merchant is (broadly) that the holder in due course of a negotiable instrument takes it free of adverse claims from the issuer[7] or third parties.[8]

Holders of dematerialised securities are contractually protected against claims from issuers (by the deed of covenant) and from other CMO members.[9] However, not all third party claims are excluded. For example, if CMO custodian A fraudulently sells securities belonging to its clients to CMO member B, B might be sued by A's clients.[10] Because the basis of the CMO is merely contractual and not statutory it cannot affect the rights of third parties who are not contractually bound. For this reason, the full benefits of negotiability cannot be replicated.[11]

---

[1] An agreement for the dematerialisation of CMO instruments between the Bank and CMO members was executed in 1994. Persons becoming CMO members after that date are bound by the terms of the dematerialisation agreement by an agreement of adherence, a form of which is given in Schedule 3 of the agreement. The requirement to enter into the dematerialisation agreement as a condition of membership is referred to in section B.1.4 of the *Reference Manual* and section 6 of the dematerialisation agreement.

[2] Section 2(a) of the dematerialisation agreement and *Reference Manual*, section H.4.6. This is a deed of covenant made in favour of the members for the time being of the CMO. The purpose of the deed of covenant is to evidence the rights of members to whose accounts dematerialised securities are credited (recital (E)).

[3] Recital (C) of the dematerialisation agreement and recital 3 of the deed of covenant.

[4] See above.

[5] Section 1.

[6] Negotiability is based on the physical possession of a tangible instrument.

[7] Eg in respect of sums owed to the issuer by previous holders.

[8] Eg previous holders claiming to be the true owners because an earlier transfer was fraudulent.

[9] By section 3(3) of the dematerialisation agreement.

[10] In such circumstances A would be contractually bound to indemnify B under section 4(2) of the dematerialisation agreement.

[11] Section 3(1)(d) of the dematerialisation agreement provides that the CMO Rules may make provision that a holder of dematerialised securities 'may have rights equivalent to those of a holder in due course of an Equivalent Paper Instrument and shall accordingly acquire a title to that Dematerialised Instrument which is free of equities'. However, this can only take effect in respect of persons bound by the CMO Rules.

In some circumstances protection from such claims may be available from the rules of equity if not under the doctrine of negotiability.[1] However, it is important for the CMO custodian to appreciate that, to the extent that there are increased risks of adverse claims from its custody clients, it bears them personally under an indemnity it is required to give to the Bank and other CMO members.

4 Formalities of transfer

As indicated above, the CMO documentation provides that the legal basis of CMO transfers is attornment by the Bank as bailee. The provision that the Bank holds CMO instruments as bailee cannot apply to dematerialised securities, for two reasons. Firstly, bailment requires a tangible subject matter.[2] Secondly, it is not clear that the Bank *holds* the intangible securities at all, for they are issued straight on to the screen.[3] Whereas, in the case of physical securities, the CMO involves intermediation (by the Bank) there is no intermediation in the case of dematerialised securities.

Section 136 of the Law of Property Act 1925, which requires legal assignments of choses in action to be (inter alia) in writing,[4] does not apply to physical instruments in the CMO as these are deemed by the law merchant to be documentary intangibles and choses in possession, requiring no formalities for their transfer. However, this is not true of dematerialised securities. It is therefore arguable that these are subject to the restrictions in section 136. Because the requirement for a written assignment is not satisfied by book entry transfers in the CMO, it may be that CMO transfers of dematerialised securities cannot be effective in law and can only take effect in equity.

Section 53(1)(c) of the Law of Property Act 1925 requires dispositions of equitable interests to be in writing; purported dispositions subject to but not complying with the section can take effect only in contract. The CMO does not benefit from statutory disapplications of these provisions.[5] There may therefore be some risk that transfers of dematerialised securities within the CMO may be unwound in the insolvency of a transferor.

F Collateral, repos and securities lending

1 Collateral

Investors may wish to use CMO securities as collateral. Special facilities are available within the CMO for this purpose (the pledged-out memorandum

---

[1] A CMO transferee may have a defence against adverse claims as a bona fide purchaser of the legal estate without notice of the adverse claim. However, the availability of this defence depends on all the circumstances.
[2] The express provision that the Bank holds securities as bailee in section 4(1)(a) and 4(1)(b) of the membership agreement only relates to physical instruments.
[3] The Bank maintains the database whereby ownership of the securities is recorded, but this role is akin to registrar and not custodian.
[4] More accurately, it exempts such assignments complying with its terms from the general common law prohibition of the assignment of claims.
[5] Unlike the CGO.

account). Alternatively, CMO securities may be put up as collateral independently of the CMO.

(a) Pledged-out memorandum account

Collateral may be delivered within the CMO using the CMO pledged-out memorandum account. Collateral securities appear as pledged out in the account of the collateral giver and as collateral in the account of the collateral taker.[1] The collateral giver cannot use the securities for any purpose; the collateral taker is free to 'on-pledge' the securities[2] but is not generally otherwise free to deal with them.[3] There is no automatic return of collateral.[4] Exchanges of collateral require positive acceptance by the collateral taker.[5]

Although the *Reference Manual* describes these arrangements as a pledge, it goes on to provide that the status of collateral delivered in this way depends entirely upon the arrangements between the parties, which do not necessarily constitute a pledge.[6] However, the *Reference Manual* indicates that, as far as the Bank is concerned, all CMO collateral pledges constitute outright transfers as the Bank will not recognise any residual right (or equity of redemption) in the collateral taker.[7]

Irrespective of what the Bank will or will not recognise, it is not clear that, as a matter of law, these arrangements can constitute outright transfers. The restrictions on the freedom of the collateral taker to deal with the collateral securities may be incompatible with full title.

When collateral is delivered using this facility, it is crucial to establish that the interest of the collateral taker over the securities would be enforceable in the insolvency of the collateral taker. Broadly, it should be enforceable if it is proprietary, and will not if it is merely contractual.[8] Although the position taken by the Bank (ie the outright transfer provisions) may assist in showing that property has passed, this will not be conclusive. Therefore it is important carefully to document any security interest using the pledged-out account to ensure that a proprietary security interest is conferred.

(b) Independently of the CMO

For instruments outside the CMO, a legal security interest may be created under a legal mortgage or pledge, by transferring (respectively) legal title or possession by way of security. As legal title in bearer instruments passes by

---

[1] *Reference Manual*, section K.1.6.
[2] *Reference Manual*, section K.1.8.
[3] *Reference Manual*, section K.1.9.
[4] *Reference Manual*, section K.2.
[5] *Reference Manual*, section K.3.
[6] *Reference Manual*, section K.1.2.
[7] '... the Bank acts upon instructions in relation to a CMO instrument only from the CMO member to whose account it is credited and does not recognise any proprietary or equitable interest or other right in respect of the instrument other than an absolute right in that CMO member to the entirety of the instrument.' *Reference Manual*, section K.1.4. Similar provisions are contained in section F.1.5.

As indicated above, pledged-out securities are credited to both the account of the collateral giver and that of the collateral taker; however, since the Bank accepts the instructions only of the collateral taker in relation to such securities, the above provisions should presumably be taken to mean that only the interest of the collateral taker will be recognised.

[8] This is because of the restriction in section 127 of the Insolvency Act 1986 on dispositions of a company's property after the commencement of winding up.

possession, both a legal mortgage and a pledge may be created by transfer of possession; the intention of the parties (recorded in security documentation) determines which type of legal security interest was created.

Because CMO securities are immobilised or dematerialised within the CMO, the CMO member cannot pledge them to a third party independently of the CMO; it may be able to do so through a CMO transfer, but the position is highly uncertain. However, where the CMO member is a custodian, the beneficial owner may pledge CMO securities (other than dematerialised securities) to the custodian.

It might be possible for a CMO member to create a legal mortgage in favour of a third party through a CMO transfer; however, there may be some danger that the outright transfer provisions contained in the CMO documentation[1] may cut across the equity of redemption of the chargor.

It is not clear that an equitable mortgage can be created in CMO securities as this form of security interest traditionally involves the delivery of physical documentation. Possibly, the only type of equitable security interest that can be created in CMO securities is an equitable charge, which may be registrable.[2]

Thus, the placing of instruments in the CMO may reduce the options for their use as collateral.

(c) Dematerialisation

The dematerialisation of securities in the CMO renders them ineligible to be pledged, as a pledge can only relate to a tangible subject matter. Purported pledges will probably take effect as charges. Care should be taken to ensure the registration provisions of the Companies Act 1985 are complied with. Where a custodian or other intermediary takes a security interest from investors, it may be necessary to place restrictions on the investors' freedom to deal in the securities in order to avoid the creation of a registrable floating charge.

2 Repos

CMO securities can be delivered under repurchase transactions through the CMO. However, there are no special facilities for automatic returns or in relation to collateral margining. Both the initial delivery of the securities, and the redelivery of equivalent securities, must be input by the parties as separate outright transfers.[3]

3 Securities lending

It is not customary for CMO instruments to be loaned under securities lending arrangements. However, such instruments are used as collateral for securities

---

[1] *Reference Manual*, section F.1.5.

[2] Pledges are not registrable. Charges created by UK corporates may be registrable under section 395 of the Companies Act 1985 if, inter alia, they are charges over book debts or floating charges. Charges over CMO instruments should not constitute charges over book debts, as CMO instruments would be recorded in the books of the chargor as securities and not as book debts. Very broadly speaking, the defining characteristic of a floating charge is that the chargor retains the freedom to deal in the charged assets. This may well be the case with CMO securities, unless they are removed from the account of the chargor.

[3] *Reference Manual*, section I.2.2.

loans. Standard securities lending documentation[1] provides for the outright transfer of collateral. It is customary for this collateral to be delivered through the pledged-out account.

G   Tax

The withholding tax position on interest paid by an issuer of securities held in the CMO follows general principles. There may be additional considerations where the security is a certificate of deposit, the interest on which is beneficially owned by an individual but these are not addressed in this discussion.

If the interest on the CMO security has a UK source and is short interest (broadly speaking, payable on a security with a term of 364 days or less) the interest will be payable gross. In other circumstances, the interest will be paid under deduction of tax[2] at the lower rate (currently 20%) unless a specific exemption is available, for example if the interest is paid by a bank in the ordinary course of its business.[3]

To the extent that the issuer of a security held in the CMO is not resident in the UK, for example, the UK branch of a non-resident issuer, the interest will constitute a 'foreign dividend' for the purposes of the collecting agent rules, under which a UK custodian may be required to withhold tax on interest payments received.[4] However, the Inland Revenue have confirmed that where foreign dividends have a UK source so that section 349 of the Income and Corporation Taxes Act 1988 applies to them (or would but for an exemption in that section) they are not also treated as falling within the collecting agent rules.

No stamp duty will be payable on the transfer of securities within the CMO. First, it is likely that the DMO security will constitute loan capital, the transfer of which is exempt from stamp duty. The transfer across CMO accounts by book entry of bearer securities, the transfer of which would be exempt if physically delivered, will also not attract stamp duty. Finally, if the CMO securities have been dematerialised, there will be no instrument of transfer or documentary evidence thereof. Stamp duty reserve tax will likewise not be payable on an agreement to transfer CMO securities, the transfer of which is exempt from stamp duty.

---

[1] Ie the ISLA documentation.
[2] Section 349(2) of the Income and Corporation Taxes Act 1988.
[3] Ibid, section 349(3)(b).
[4] Ibid, section 118A–K.

Chapter 13

CREST[1]

A Introduction

CREST[2] is an electronic system for the paperless settlement[3] of transactions[4] in corporate registered[5] securities in London.[6] CREST offers dematerialisation,[7] an assured payments system, and can handle corporate actions.

CREST is optional both for issuers and investors.[8] CREST is owned and operated by CRESTCo, which in turn is owned by members of the securities industry. CREST follows previous failures in London to dematerialise equity settlement.[9]

---

[1] The author is grateful to Mark Kirby of CRESTCo for his help in preparing this chapter.
[2] The name is not an acronym.
[3] Trade confirmation takes place outside CREST, although pre-settlement matching occurs within CREST.
[4] Such as transfers, securities loans and corporate actions.
[5] Bearer securities are ineligible. However, securities which are bearer in paper form such as allotment letters may be dematerialised if a register is created: see *CREST: The Business Description*, Bank of England, December 1994, p 14.
[6] Foreign securities may be brought into CREST through depositary receipt schemes.
[7] Ie the removal of the certificates and instruments of transfer which are otherwise generally necessary to permit UK registered securities to be evidenced and transferred. *The Group of Thirty Securities Clearance and Settlement Study of 1989* ('the *G30 Report*') defines dematerialisation as 'The elimination of physical certificates or documents of title which represent ownership of securities so that securities exist only as computer records'.
[8] Issuing companies may elect whether to make their securities eligible for CREST. In addition, investors in CREST-eligible securities may elect whether their securities should be held in uncertificated form in CREST, or in certificated form outside it. Certificated securities may be brought into CREST, and uncertificated securities may be recertificated.
[9] In 1979 the Stock Exchange introduced Talisman, an electronic system providing for automated settlement between stock jobbers (today's market makers). In Talisman, SEPON, the Stock Exchange Pool Nominee, acts as nominee custodian during settlement on behalf of member firms and their clients, who maintain SEPON accounts. Shares are registered in the name of SEPON, to whom certificates are not issued. Beneficial ownership of stock passes within Talisman by book entry.
    In 1981 the Exchange proposed to extend the system to the market as a whole, using a centralised database to maintain records of all shareholdings. The proposal was defeated by commercial registrars, who would have been put out of business.
    The privatisation programme of the eighties led to a settlement crisis in 1987, and brokers' back offices were unable to cope with the unprecedented volumes of trades. The October crash and ensuing market chaos provided the impetus for change.

B Core legal structure

1 Dematerialisation

Outside CREST, UK company legislation generally requires companies to issue share certificates[1] and to register transfers only on receipt of instruments of transfer.[2] Dematerialisation is based on the Uncertificated Securities Regulations 1995[3] ('the Regulations').

2 Legal and equitable ownership

The legal structure of CREST is closely modelled on that of the CGO. As with the CGO, legal title to CREST securities is prima facie determined, both within and outwith the system, by registration.[4] Notification of CREST transfers is made electronically by the CREST system to the registrar of the issuer. In addition to entries in the register of the issuer, CREST participants have accounts at CREST.[5] The usual statutory requirements for written transfers are expressly disapplied.[6]

Registrars are normally required to register CREST transfers within two

---

In 1989 the Group of Thirty, a New York-based think tank for the securities industry, published its report, *Clearance and Settlement Systems in the World's Securities Markets*. Recommendations included delivery versus payment, three-day rolling settlement and dematerialisation.

CREST was built by the Bank of England out of the ashes of Taurus, the proposed electronic settlement system that failed in 1993.

In 1989, the same year as the *G30 Report*, the Exchange appointed the Securities Industry Steering Committee for Taurus ('SISCOT') with a brief to find a compromise solution that would prejudice no interest group. Registrars (again fearing redundancy) insisted that a central database be rejected in favour of a distributed system. Private client stockbrokers (fearing loss of shareholder entitlements) rejected SEPON-style pooling and insisted on direct ownership (investors names on registers). Plcs supported direct registration but, with a distributed network, feared that delay in identifying investors would increase vulnerability to takeovers. They were given a complex system-wide search facility.

The result prejudiced none and failed all. Taurus collapsed under its own weight in March 1993 because it was over-complex. It would have cost too much, and taken too long to complete. Consequential losses were variously estimated as between £200 and £500 million.

The Bank of England stepped into the breach and set up a broadly-based task force which proposed CREST in June 1993.

[1] Section 185 of the Companies Act 1985.
[2] Ibid, s 183.
[3] SI 1995/3272, made under section 207 of the Companies Act 1989, which '... enable title to units of a security to be evidenced otherwise than by a certificate and transferred otherwise than by a written instrument ...' (regulation 2(1)). Regulation 14 expressly permits the electronic transfer of title. This is broadly comparable to statutory provision permitting the dematerialisation of gilts within the CGO.
Interestingly, the Regulations are not limited to CREST and do not mention it by name. Accordingly, competing systems (including the continental clearers) are in theory free to apply for recognition under Regulations to settle UK equities. The view has been expressed that the need to handle the complex corporate actions associated with UK equities may keep such competition at bay; another factor is the continuing applicability of stamp duty.
For the sake of convenience, this chapter will refer to the system contemplated by the Regulations as CREST.
[4] See section 361 of the Companies Act 1985 and regulation 20.
[5] CREST securities accounts are regularly reconciled to the issuer's register: see the CREST *Reference Manual*, section 5.
[6] Sections 53(1)(c) and 136 of the Law of Property Act 1925 are disapplied by regulation 32(5).

hours. In order to protect the transferee from the credit risk of the transferor during this short interval, it was considered necessary to ensure that book entry transfer confers on the transferee equitable ownership of the securities.[1] Securities in the course of settlement are pooled without allocation to particular purchasers. As discussed at length in chapter 5, there is doubt at general law as to the validity of purported trusts over unascertained property ('the allocation problem'). In order to address the allocation problem in CREST, it was considered necessary to make express statutory provision.[2]

The allocation problem was addressed in the CGO and Talisman by expressly providing for a tenancy in common.[3] However, the Treasury took a different approach with CREST. Instead of actual allocation through co-ownership,[4] regulation 25 provides for notional allocation where there is no actual allocation.[5]

3 Payments

(a) Assured payments system

CREST offers an assured payment system[6] through the use of settlement banks. Every CREST participant is required to have appointed a settlement bank as a condition of admission into CREST.[7] When book entry settlement takes place within CREST, the settlement bank of the transferee becomes irrevocably obliged to pay the purchase price to the settlement bank of the transferor.[8]

---

[1] 'The Government considers that this provision will provide the best possible level of protection for the transferee in the event of insolvency of the transferor after settlement but before registration.' (HM Treasury *Consultation Document on the Draft Uncertificated Securities Regulations*, January 1995, p 71.)

[2] 'In the absence of statutory intervention, due to the unascertainability of the units, it is possible that if the transferor's name were not on the register, the buyer would not obtain a proprietary interest' (ibid, pp 93, 94).

[3] This reflects the solution probably implied by general law: see chapter 5.

[4] Whereby all the securities in the pool are allocated to all the participants in the pool under a global trust.

[5] Regulation 25 provides that, at the time when the CREST system instructs the registrar of the issuer to register a transfer:

'(1) ... (a) the transferee shall acquire an equitable interest in the requisite number of uncertificated units of the security of the kind specified in the Operator-instruction in which the transferor has an equitable interest by virtue of this regulation, or in relation to which the transferor is recorded on the relevant register of securities as having title ...

(6) This regulation has effect notwithstanding that the units to which the Operator-instruction relates, or in which an interest arises by virtue of paragraph (1) ... may be unascertained.'

[6] Modelled on the CGO assured payments system.

[7] CREST Rules, chapter 2, rule 1.2.1.

[8] The assured payments obligation is contained in section 4.2.1 of the settlement bank agreement entered into bilaterally by each settlement bank and CRESTCo and also in section 2.1 of the assured payments agreement entered into multilaterally by CRESTCo and all the settlement banks. New settlement banks are bound by the terms of the assured payments agreement under a deed of adherence.

The assured payment obligation of the settlement bank is calculated by reference to the cash memorandum account of the member for which it acts, in which the payment obligations referable to the member's purchases are recorded. 'Each member will have a Cash Memorandum Account (CMA) which records all his payment obligations arising from receipts and sales. The CMA balance will also reflect cash movements not directly related to the transfer of securities, for example receipts of dividends paid through CREST. The balance (if negative) shows his use of intra-day credit ... Each member will have one (or more) "real" bank accounts outside CREST to which the bank will post the member's final end of day cash position in CREST (ie the balance on his CMA) ...' *Intra-day Credit and Caps in CREST*, April 1995.

This assured payment obligation discharges any payment obligation of the transferee. Inter-settlement bank payments are made through the CHAPS system outside CREST.[1] Payments between settlement banks and the CREST participants for whom they act are settled outside CREST as a commercial matter.

Settlement banks may take charges over clients' assets within CREST: see section D, below.

Unlike the CGO, there is no restriction on deliveries free of payment or for non-market prices.[2]

Under the assured payments system, settlement banks are exposed to each other's credit risk intra-day. This exposure will be addressed when CREST permits real time gross settlement.[3]

(b) Delivery versus payment

It is claimed that CREST offers delivery versus payment or DVP.[4] It is true that a settlement event (the passing of an equitable interest in securities on book entry transfer) is synchronised[5] with a payment event (the arising of the assured payment obligation). However, neither of these events is final. Settlement may not proceed to registration in certain circumstances including transferor insolvency (see section D.2, below). The transferor may not receive payment if either the settlement bank of the transferee or its own settlement bank becomes insolvent.

Assured payments are in one of a range of currencies: 'CREST is being built with the capacity to settle in multiple currencies, though initially the strongest demand will be for sterling.' *CREST, The Business Description*, Bank of England, December 1994, p 5. It is understood that sterling and Irish pounds will be offered initially, with other currencies proposed to follow. A separate cash memorandum account will be required for each currency, so that multi-currency settlement will limit netting efficiencies between client sales and purchases.

[1] Inter-settlement bank obligations are discharged by net payments across accounts at the Bank of England: see *CREST: The Business Description* (above), p 49.

While in practice settlement is on a multilateral net basis, the arrangements escape the rule in *British Eagle* [1975] 2 All ER 390 (broadly that contractual netting arrangements that purported to vary statutory insolvency netting are not effective) because the contractual payment obligations are calculated on a bilateral net basis, in accordance with rule 4.90 of the Insolvency Rules 1986. See section 2.2.2 of the assured payments agreement.

These arrangements are akin to those in the CGO and the CMO.

[2] In the proposed upgrade of the CGO using CREST software, 'CGO 2', free deliveries will be permitted.

[3] CREST proposes to take advantage of real time gross settlement ('RTGS') as early as possible (at least for larger transactions); see *CREST: The Business Description*, Bank of England, December 1994, pp 10, 53. Alternative assurance is provided by an assured payments system. In the absence of RTGS, settlement banks can limit their exposures to their client members (under debit caps: see below) but not to each other. It is understood that the banks demanded a link to RTGS as a condition of acting as CREST settlement banks; in view of operational difficulties of providing this from the outset, CREST offered RTGS as soon as practicable.

[4] In its 1989 report on securities settlement, the Group of Thirty called for DVP, or the simultaneous exchange of securities and cash to settle a transaction, as a key element in addressing counterparty risk.

[5] 'The CREST model of assured payment for a delivery involves the simultaneous creation of:
   (a) a credit to one CREST stock account;
   (b) the debit of another;
   (c) the creation of a register update request;
   (d) the creation of an unconditional obligation of one bank (the buyer's) to pay another (the seller's).' *CREST: The Business Description*, Bank of England, December 1994, p 48.

(c)   Real time gross settlement

CREST proposes to take advantage of RTGS as soon as possible (at least for larger transactions).[1]

4   Regulation

(a)   The CREST system

CRESTCo is regulated as a recognised clearing house ('RCH'[2]) by the Securities and Investments Board.[3] In addition CRESTCo has been approved and is subject to supervision by the SIB as operator of CREST in accordance with the Regulations[4] and, in respect of any non-clearing activities, is an exempt person for the purposes of the Financial Services Act 1986 ('FSA').[5]

CREST will not assist with the observance of US regulatory holding restrictions.[6]

However, in a discussion paper[7] it is indicated that CREST should monitor and enforce discipline in matters such as bad deliveries and maintenance of adequate debit caps. Delays in matching and settlement might attract fines and other sanctions. Non-performing custodians should not be excused if their failures are caused by customer default.[8] Custodians should monitor this exposure and ensure they have adequate indemnities in their customer documentation.

(b)   CREST members

In general, participation in CREST does not of itself entail authorisation under the FSA. However, CREST members may require authorisation, as follows.

(I)   SPONSORS

Persons acting as CREST sponsors (see the sections on custody accounts below) require authorisation under the FSA.[9]

(II)   CUSTODY

Irrespective of CREST, CREST members acting as custodians will require authorisation under proposals to render custody authorisable.[10]

---

[1] See *CREST: The Business Description* (above), pp 10, 53.
[2] For the purposes of section 38 of the Financial Services Act 1986 ('FSA').
[3] Such recognition was necessary in order to settle Stock Exchange transactions. As a recognised investment exchange for the purposes of section 36 of the FSA, the Stock Exchange is required under paragraph 2(4) of Schedule 4 to the FSA to clear transactions either itself or through a RCH.
[4] Under Part II.
[5] Under the Financial Services Act 1986 (Exemption) Order 1996 (SI 1996/1587).
[6] For a discussion of these, see chapter 9, above.
[7] *Settlement Discipline*, CRESTCo, April 1996.
[8] Ibid, p 9.
[9] By virtue of the Financial Services Act 1986 (Uncertificated Securities) (Extension of Scope of Act) Order 1996 (SI 1996/1322).
[10] See the Treasury consultation document, *Custody*, June 1996.

5 SDRT

Stamp duty reserve tax and not stamp duty is payable on uncertificated transfers of chargeable securities within CREST.[1]

C Custody accounts

Three options are available to custodians. The custodian's name (or that of its nominee) may appear on the issuer's register without any particular client designation (pooled accounts), or with a particular client designation (designated accounts). Alternatively, the client's name (or that of its nominee) may appear on the register (sponsored membership).

1 Pooled accounts

In many cases, the securities of more than one client will be pooled in a single account maintained by a custodian CREST member. A single debit cap will permit efficiencies in the use of credit.[2] In the absence of effective trust arrangements between the custodian and its client, pooling may pose certain risks concerning the beneficial title of clients. A further risk is that a shortfall attributable to the business of client 1 may be borne by client 2.

2 Designated accounts

Individual designation may be desired by clients to avoid the above risks, or by the custodian for tax planning.[3] This is permitted within the holding of a CREST member by the use of separate accounts. CREST notes these different accounts against the name of the member in the register of the issuer.[4,5]

---

[1] 'CREST collects ... SDRT on behalf of the UK authorities ... from the purchaser on all transfers in CREST at the standard percentage rates of the stampable consideration. ... Certain securities (principally fixed-interest securities) are exempt from stamp duty. CREST will recognise these by means of exempt flags linked to their ISIN codes.' *Reference Manual*, p 112. 'UK-registered securities held on behalf of exempt bodies such as charities should be held in one or more member accounts with an exempt member account tax status. Transfers into such accounts will be automatically exempted from duty. The Inland Revenue have stipulated the inclusion of charity reference numbers on the associated legs of transfers destined for charities in particular where custodians acquire securities on behalf of charities.' *Reference Manual*, p 112.

[2] So that clients who are net sellers of securities on any day can fund clients who are net purchasers.

[3] Eg to segregate different securities attracting different rates of SDRT.

[4] 'A designation may be an alphanumeric but should not give any indication of the identity of any beneficial owner ... Where a member ... has more than one member account, each member account is reflected on the register. Member accounts can therefore be used to segregate one type of holding from another ...' *Reference Manual*, p 22.

[5] It is unclear how such designations in the register of UK shares accord with section 360 of the Companies Act 1985, which provides that 'No notice of any trust ... shall be entered on the register.' Related provisions are included in rule 19.14. The correct view may be that such designations are ineffective against the issuer (so that it is not fixed with notice of custody trusts) but are effective against the liquidator of the custodian (so that it cannot make the custody assets available to creditors of the custodian on the basis that any custody trust fails for want of certainty of subject matter). Independently of CREST, it has long been customary for company registrars to note special designations on the register beside members' names.

Also, it is possible for one person to have more than one CREST membership.

Such designation is considerably less expensive to the member than equivalent designation in the CGO or the CMO, and accordingly clients may expect it. Greater levels of designation may also make corporate actions easier to handle, reducing the incidence of fractional entitlements.

However, even where a custodial trust is effective as against the custodian member and its liquidator, it will not be effective against CRESTCo, which will not assist any custody client in claims against a custodian member.[1]

3   Sponsored membership[2]

Certain custody clients may wish to have their names on the register of the issuer in place of the custodian, and may therefore wish to be sponsored members of CREST.[3] Sponsored members have CREST accounts in their own names[4] and are therefore the registered holders of CREST securities. However, their sponsor (the custodian) will maintain the electronic links with CREST and operate their CREST accounts on their behalf.[5] The arrangement is comparable to the administration by a custodian of certificated securities registered in the client's name through the use of a power of attorney. It protects the client from the custodian's insolvency but not from its fraud. Fraud risk may be reduced by specifying daily withdrawal limits.[6]

Sponsored members must appoint their own settlement banks,[7] and custodians may be expected to arrange for this banking facility and prepare the documentation as part of the custody package. With separate settlement bank arrangements, sponsored members have separate debit caps.[8] The use

[1] Regulation 33(3) provides that 'The Operator shall not be bound by or compelled to recognise any express, implied or constructive trust or other interest in respect of uncertificated units of a security, even if he has actual or constructive notice of the said trust or interest.'

[2] See *Reference Manual*, chapter 4, section 11.

[3] This may be particularly attractive to pension funds.

[4] Sponsored members must enter into a sponsored membership agreement with CRESTCo (as well as a settlement bank agreement, and a commercial agreement with the sponsor). Where the sponsored member is a nominee, it may instead enter into a sponsored membership (nominee) agreement which differs from the sponsored membership agreement principally in that the undertakings and warranties are given by the nominee's parent instead of by the nominee.

[5] In CREST terminology, the sponsored member is a *participant* and the sponsor is a *user*.

[6] The sponsored membership agreement, section 7.2.

[7] *CREST: The Business Description* Bank of England, December 1994, indicates (at p 31) that 'A sponsored member will often be able to grant a charge over his assets in CREST for the benefit of the [settlement] bank, which should ensure that he will normally have no difficulty in obtaining an adequate amount of intra-day credit for his account to be operated within CREST.' However, it may not be able to give such a charge if it is itself subject to fiduciary or regulatory restrictions (eg if it is a pension trustee or insurance company).

[8] In the case of private investors becoming sponsored members of CREST through their brokers, a debit cap set at zero is envisaged, on the basis that purchases are settled initially into the broker's CREST account, and then (after the client has put the broker in funds outside CREST) transferred free into the client's CREST account. See *Sponsored Membership of Crest for the Private Investor*, Bank of England, April 1995, pp 9, 10.

This approach may also be adopted by custodians, who may operate a settlement account with an adequate debit cap for the initial settlement of client trades, and then (following payment outside CREST) transfer securities nil paid to clients' sponsored member's accounts. This enables the custodian to concentrate credit in one account and keep control of the banking side of settlement.

of different debit caps for different custody clients may have the benefit of shielding one client from settlement gridlock attributable to excess purchases by another client; a disadvantage is that netting between one client's purchases and another's sales will not be available for the purposes of calculating headroom.

Sponsored members may not wish to handle their own corporate actions. Even though the client's name is on the register, the issuer could be instructed to direct any mailings to the address of the custodian on the client's behalf. However, this may be inconvenient for the custodian, who will be required to respond to any election separately for each sponsored member, and not once for a global holding.[1]

The role of sponsor involves certain risks for the custodian. It is obliged[2] to notify CREST immediately of the occurrence of events affecting the sponsored member's ability to transfer title to CREST securities, although it is not clear that it would know of such an event.[3] In addition, similar concerns about confidentiality and risk arise for the sponsor as for the custodian member (see section D, below). The drafting of the commercial agreement between the sponsor and its sponsored member (the terms of which are left to the parties to decide) will be of great importance in limiting the risk of the custodian sponsor.

4   Visibility

Concern has been expressed[4] at the prospect of more intermediation of the holdings of private investors and the consequent loss of 'shareholder visibility', ie the ability of issuers readily to identify investors in their shares.[5]

It may not be feasible for custodians to take the alternative approach of deferring the settlement of the initial purchase until they are put in funds by clients, for the following reason. In settlement, the giver of both cash and securities can specify the priority of the trade and this will determine the order in which it is settled. A zero priority on securities will in effect freeze the transfer of securities until the priority is lifted. However, on the cash side of any transaction, at the end of the settlement day a zero priority is automatically raised. Thus, the securities side of a transaction can be frozen, but the cash side cannot. Therefore a custodian wishing to defer a purchase until it is put in funds by its client faces the problem that it is committed to the purchase as soon as the trade is matched. (The automatic raising of zero priorities on cash transfers was introduced in response to market consultation.)

Custodians may even be willing to transfer free to a sponsored member's account in advance of payment outside CREST, as they may be in a position to freeze securities in that account in exercise of any lien taken in their commercial documentation with the sponsored member. The Sponsor's Agreement does not require the sponsor to agree with CRESTCo that it will obey all instructions from the sponsor.

[1] The same may be true for designated accounts.
[2] Under section 8 of the sponsor's agreement.
[3] The provision is included on the basis that it might. 'The obligations placed on the sponsored member to notify the Operator of anything which might give rise to a risk of a bad delivery or of any insolvency, is repeated in the Sponsor's Agreement, given that the sponsor may often be the first to learn of his client's situation.' *CREST Membership Agreements*, Bank of England, July 1995, p 7.
[4] By, among others, ProShare, a lobby group for small investors.
[5] The development of CREST prompted a much-aired concern about loss of shareholder visibility, or the ability of issuers to identify investors by reference to the register. While investigation of beneficial ownership is possible under section 212 of the Companies Act 1985, this procedure is cumbersome. Ready identification of investors is more important to issuers in the UK than on the continent, because of the higher UK incidence of hostile takeovers.

While the move to rapid rolling settlement may increase the use of nominees, it has been argued that sponsored membership will offset this, and '... any net losses of visibility will be small.'[1] The effort to protect visibility has been influenced by the CBI; some clients of custodians may have legitimate and compelling reasons to wish to be invisible.[2]

D   Risk

1   Credit

Credit may be the major risk issue for the custodian in CREST, both in terms of the need to ensure sufficient credit or headroom is available promptly to settle clients' trades, and the need to control credit exposures to clients.

As a general point, if the settlement bank of a purchaser defaults, neither CRESTCo nor the vendor's settlement bank is obliged to make good the loss to the vendor.[3] Custodians should make it clear in the client documentation that, in the event of settlement bank default, they are not obliged to make good any shortfall, and that their only obligation is to account for sums actually received.[4]

(a)   Headroom

Through the assured payment system, the settlement bank of a purchaser of securities will assume personal liability for the payment of the purchase price. The CGO settlement banks are generally collateralised (where the participant owns the securities in its account) by taking security over the assets within the CGO system. Generally, CREST securities can be charged in the same way,[5] permitting collateralised capped assured payments ('CCAP').[6] However, in CREST as in the CGO, significant legal difficulties arise where

---

[1] *CREST: The Business Description*, Bank of England, December 1994, p 93.
[2] Eg the desire of high net worth individuals to keep the extent of their wealth confidential for security reasons.
[3] Clause 3.3.4 of the Membership Agreement in effect excludes any duty on CRESTCo in relation to the risk of the default of other CREST members or settlement banks.
[4] Because inter-settlement bank payments are made on a net basis, allocating cash shortfalls to particular clients may be a complex matter.
[5] CREST provides facilities for the maintenance of margin, ie the monitoring of the value of securities charged as collateral in relation to a settlement bank's exposures.
[6] See chapter 6, section 3, of the *Reference Manual*.
    Charges in favour of CREST settlement banks are protected as 'system charges' by the Financial Markets and Insolvency Regulations 1996 (SI 1996/1469). Protections include (broadly) disapplications of the restrictions on enforcement of a security interest in the chargor's administration, the power of an administrator to deal with charged property and avoidance of property dispositions.
    Equivalent provisions (using the term 'market charge') protect CGO settlement bank charges by virtue of section 173(1)(c) of the Companies Act 1989 and the Financial Markets and Insolvency Regulations 1991 (SI 1991/880). (In the early days of the CGO, unease among settlement banks about their exposures increased when the Insolvency Act 1986 greatly reduced the value of floating charges as security. As a quid pro quo of their continuing involvement, it is understood that they were promised some statutory concession, which eventually took the form of the 'market charge' provisions of Part VII of the Companies Act 1989.)

custodian participants seek to charge assets beneficially owned by their clients, and therefore CCAP may not be available to custodians.[1]

Unlike in the CGO, settlement banks may control their CREST exposures by imposing debit caps, ie limits on the volumes of net purchases they will permit a participant to settle on any day.[2,3] Such caps are not the norm in settlement systems, and raise certain concerns.[4] A member is in practice free to delay the settlement of a purchase by ensuring that it has insufficient headroom to settle it. Moreover, the possibility of gridlock must be present. At times of volume surge (following privatisations or in market crashes) such caps might lead to the very settlement backlogs that, in the mid-80s, prompted the search for a better settlement system.[5] CREST does not monitor the exhaustion or withdrawal of credit caps; where headroom is exhausted, back-ups will simply occur, prompting members to seek to resolve the problem amongst themselves (although its document *Settlement Discipline* indicates that CRESTCo may monitor timely settlement). Because of the inter-dependencies of settlement credit and the omission of CRESTCo to regulate the matter, the ability of the system to function will depend on each member taking a responsible approach.

Custodians must also consider the risk that heavy buying by one client may affect its ability to settle purchases for another client.[6]

---

[1] Briefly, the custodian is not empowered to charge the assets without the consent of the client. The client may not be free to give such authority because of fiduciary, regulatory or constitutional restraints on it, particularly if it is an insurance company or a pension fund.

Where the assets of more than one client are held together in one CREST account, the granting of a charge would result in one client's assets being used to secure exposures referable to the business of another client. It is hard to envisage authority properly being given for a charge to be granted in such circumstances.

[2] 'The cap allows a payment bank to control the amount of intra-day credit available to a member. The cap represents the maximum cumulative net debit position on its CMA(s) that a member can run during the settlement day. A zero cap is possible.' *Reference Manual*, p 90.

'Transactions which would cause a member's total net payments to exceed his cap (credit limit) will be queued until sufficient sales have settled to create headroom under the limit. "Circles" processing will help to resolve potential gridlock.' *The Business Description*, p 17. For a discussion of circles, see section 6 of the *Reference Manual*.

'CREST will ensure that the cap is not breached. Banks may be willing to provide more credit if the customer can provide more collateral. ... Those with inadequate credit will be more likely to have settlement delays and fails ...' *Intra-day Credit and Caps in CREST*, April 1995.

[3] The ability to alter debit caps is frozen while the circles process is operating, *Reference Manual* pp 27, 28.

[4] See *Cross-Border Securities Settlement*, Bank for International Settlement, Basle, March 1995, pp 18, 19.

[5] On the other hand, it might be argued that the problem is not peculiar to CREST, as insufficient credit within a market will always impede settlement in practice.

A CREST publication, *Intra-day Credit and Caps in CREST*, April 1995, takes a positive view, indicating that 'The normal cap does not have to be large enough to cope with an exceptional intra-day credit need. A member and his bank can agree and rapidly implement a temporary increase in the cap, in advance or during the day, to allow an exceptional trade to settle. The "circles" process will settle dependent deliveries. This may reduce the need for intra-day credit for CREST members who aim to end each day more or less flat.'

[6] Unless the custodian opens separate designated client accounts and negotiates separate debit caps for them, all clients will share the same cap (see the *Reference Manual*, p 91). Custodians may wish to address this in the custody agreement by imposing volume limits on clients, and making express disclosures about the possibility of delays.

(b) Credit exposures to clients

Outside CREST credit arrangements with clients may be undocumented, with informal overdrafts arising in the course of settlement[1] and credit limits being unadvised to clients. However, the involvement of settlement banks and debit caps in CREST precludes such an informal approach. Where custodians operate pooled accounts, they cannot rely on the debit cap effectively to control credit exposures to *particular* clients.[2] Internal credit controls, based on the custodian's own books and not merely on the pooled accounts of CREST, will be necessary.

However, provided custody documentation grants custodians effective security interests over their clients' securities, these exposures may be effectively collateralised by virtue of the approximation to 'DVP' within CREST.

2 Bad deliveries and fraudulent transfers

It is not suggested that dematerialisation increases fraud or bad deliveries. Paper based fraud is endemic in the City, and CREST may even provide a more secure environment. However, the custodian and its clients should note both the types of CREST transfers that are permitted to fail by the CREST system, and those that are allowed to proceed.

(a) Bad deliveries

The major protection against bad deliveries in CREST is the fact that the interval during which they can occur is (generally) only two hours long.[3] A further protection is that incoming securities will not be credited to a member account until registered.[4] However, the risk cannot be excluded that some CREST settled trades will not proceed to registration, for example where the securities in question are affected by a court order or insolvency.[5] Regulation

---

[1] The custodian might simply pay the purchase price on behalf of its clients and then seek to be put in funds to the extent of any overdraft.

[2] This is because where client A is a net buyer and other clients are net sellers, an overall debit cap will not prevent client A in effect buying securities with the proceeds of the other clients' sales, nor relieve the custodian from the obligation of repaying to the other clients those proceeds of sale.

[3] CREST also seeks to reduce the risk of bad deliveries by providing (in rule 19.14) that the constitutional documents of issuers of CREST securities must not permit notice of trusts to be entered on the register. This is presumably intended to reduce tracing claims by reducing notice of beneficial interests.

[4] *The Business Description* p 61.

[5] Regulation 25(8) states that the transfer provisions of regulation 25 do not take effect in relation to transfers which 'would otherwise be void by or under an enactment or rule of law'.

   (Arguably, this was necessary because section 207(4) of the Companies Act 1989 provides (broadly) that regulations to be made under section 207 shall leave unchanged 'so far as practicable' rights and obligations in relation to uncertificated securities.)

   No direct financial criteria are imposed on CREST members in order to reduce the risk of member insolvency. 'In principle, anyone can be a member of CREST. ... CREST will not itself impose a criterion of, or tests for, financial soundness on potential members.' (*The Business Description*, pp 8, 14.) It may be that the obligation to appoint a settlement bank will operate indirectly to exclude bad credit risks from membership. In any case 'CRESTCo does not owe the Member any duty in relation to the admission of any person as a system-member ...' (Membership Agreement section 3.3.8).

23 contemplates and permits bad deliveries, in the sense that the general requirement of participating issuers to register book entry transfers is disapplied in certain circumstances.

Where custody client A purchases securities, it may expect to be able to sell them immediately they are credited to the custodian's CREST account, in advance of registration. The risk is therefore present that if the first transfer fails after A has on-sold the securities, a shortfall will arise.[1] If the account also contains the securities of clients B, C and D, these clients bear A's shortfall (in effect, the custodian has lent the securities of B, C and D to A). In order to avoid breach of duty to its clients, the custodian should disclose these risks to B, C and D.[2] It should also consider collateralising the exposure to A.

Custodians face further risk (in relation to bad stock held for their clients) by the Membership Agreement, which provides[3] in effect that CREST may take action to seek to avert a bad delivery at the risk of the member and with the benefit of an indemnity from the member.

(b)   Fraudulent transfers

The dematerialisation of forged securities should not give rise to bad deliveries because securities are not credited to CREST accounts until registered in the name of the CREST transferee.[4]

While the circumstances in which the Regulations permit issuers to omit to register CREST transfers include (very broadly) notice of fraud against a participant or a sponsored member,[5] they do not include notice of fraud against an indirect beneficial owner of CREST securities. There is no protection for frauds outside the system. The difficulty with this is that the system reduces the issuer's ability to respond to fraud. Even if an issuer's registrar had actual notice of such a fraud against a custody client, it would apparently have

---

A potential source of bad deliveries is the indication in the note to rule 19.9 that securities which are not freely transferable may be admitted to CREST in exceptional circumstances. 'In such cases CRESTCo does not supervise compliance with the limitations', so non-compliant transfers (possibly subject to reversal by court order or even ineffective under the articles of the issuer) will be permitted.

The Membership Agreement seeks to limit risk by requiring the member to warrant, represent and undertake that it will not bring into CREST any securities if it is aware of any defect in its title (section 3.2.6). If the member becomes aware of a stop notice or court order, or if other circumstances occur that might affect the member's ability to transfer securities through CREST (whether it is aware of them or not!) it is required immediately to notify CREST under section 9.1.

[1] There will be a shortfall if A's account does not contain additional securities sufficient to absorb the debit.

[2] In practice, the custodian would look to A immediately to eliminate the shortfall and, if A failed to do so, would buy securities in the market to make good the account, looking to A to repay the purchase price.

[3] In section 9.2.

[4] *Reference Manual*, p 29, et seq.

[5] Under regulations 23(3)(d) and 29(5)(a)(i) to (iii).

to register the fraudulent transfer under regulation 23.[1] Clients may therefore be particularly exposed to custodian fraud in CREST.[2] Equally, custodians bear the risk of fraudulent transfers affecting their client securities.[3]

(c) Unscrambling bad deliveries

Rule 18 makes provision for the unscrambling of bad deliveries.[4] Depending on the circumstances, bad deliveries will be reversed, replaced or addressed by tracing.

(I) REVERSALS

Broadly speaking, where sufficient securities remain in the account of the transferee, CREST will reverse the bad delivery at the price for which it was made.[5] Reversals raise the following exposures in relation to the return of the purchase price. Reversal is dependent on the availability of sufficient 'headroom' in the cash memorandum account of the original transferor, which is placed under an absolute obligation to increase this if necessary.[6] This raises concerns for the custodian. If CREST transfers *from* the custodian's clients fail, it may be absolutely required to obtain additional credit and therefore unable to resist commercially unreasonable terms from its settlement bank. Even where the custodian acts as its own settlement bank, the CREST Rules may require it to return the purchase price even if its clients have spent it, exposing it to their credit. If CREST transfers *to* its clients fail, its ability

---

[1] While issuers can in effect escape liability for complying with their registration requirements in respect of instructions affected by fraud against the operator, a participant or a sponsored member (regulations 29(4) and 29(7)), the limitation of liability does not extend to circumstances where indirect beneficial owners are defrauded.

This may leave issuers exposed to claims from defrauded custody clients, where the issuer knowingly registered a fraudulent transfer because it was required to do so under the Regulations.

Where an issuer has actual notice of such a fraud, it may decide to seek a court order against itself forbidding registration; omission to register in breach of a court order is permitted under regulation 23(1)(a)(i).

Rectification of registers in relation to uncertificated securities are only permitted, under regulation 21(1) pursuant to a court order or with the consent of CRESTCo. Rule 17.6 indicates that consent will not be given where, after consultation, any affected member objects to the proposed rectification. This consultation process can take 5 business days in accordance with rule 17.8.

Regulation 30 imposes certain compensation obligations on the operator of CREST for losses in certain circumstances, but these are limited to £50,000 per applicant (regulation 30(5)) and do not affect the liability of any other person for losses associated with CREST (regulation 30(8)).

[2] Where they become aware of such a fraud, their only option may be to seek a court order to prevent registration; this may be difficult in view of the short (2-hour) settlement interval.

No assistance may be available from the CREST operator, as it is not bound by notice of any trusts and need therefore not recognise the rights of custody clients: regulation 33(3).

[3] Section 3.2.5 of the Membership Agreement requires the member to represent (broadly) that any form of transfer presented by it bringing stock into and out of CREST will be validly executed. Where such transfers are executed by clients or third parties, the custodian may not be in a position to confirm this.

[4] Bad deliveries are CREST transfers that do not proceed to registration: rule 18.1.1.

[5] Rule 18.3.

[6] Under rule 18.9.2.1.

to recover the purchase price for its clients will depend on the debit caps of the transferor.[1]

In cases where the original purchase price cannot be determined[2] CRESTCo seeks to unscramble the securities side of the transaction without assisting the transferee in getting its money back.[3] This may expose the custodian to other CREST members, unless this credit risk can be transferred to the custodian's clients by provision in the custody agreement.

(II) REPLACEMENT

In cases where insufficient securities remain in the transferee's account to reverse the book entry, 'The Original Transferor shall procure the free delivery (if necessary from a third party) to the Original Transferee of the relevant amount of registrable securities within two hours of being notified by CRESTCo of the bad delivery.'[4] Custodians may need to consider their operational ability to comply with the strict time limits, and may wish to take express indemnities from their clients in respect of this exposure.

(III) TRACING

The above techniques depend in some measure on participant co-operation and therefore may fail to resolve the bad delivery.[5] In these cases, tracing may be necessary for the following reasons. Where A transfers securities to B through CREST, B may also transfer those securities to C before the first transfer is registered (or rejected by the registrar) and hence the potential for the 'domino effect', considered in rule 18.7.[6] CREST securities are fungible[7] and there is therefore a need for rules for allocating bad deliveries across accounts, akin to the equitable tracing rules. Rule 18.7.1.1 specifies a tracing methodology.[8]

A member who was not the source of the bad stock may be required to make good the shortfall, if the burden is allocated to it. While this measure of systemic risk may be inevitable in any clearing system, custodians may wish to ensure that it is borne, not by them, but by their clients, through adequate disclosure in the custody agreement.[9]

---

[1] Custodians should consider expressly disclosing this risk to clients.

[2] The original price would only be undeterminable in rare cases involving 'complex deliveries' eg corporate actions involving the transfer of more than one parcel of stock against a cash payment. In such cases, it may not be possible to determine how much of the cash was attributable to a particular parcel of stock.

[3] Rules 18.4.1 and 18.6.1.

[4] Rules 18.5.2 and 18.6.2.

[5] For example, rules 18.5.2 and 18.6.2 contractually require the original bad transferor to provide replacement stock. As the major source of bad deliveries may be transferor insolvency, new securities may not be forthcoming under these Rules when they are needed.

[6] Entitled 'Consequent bad deliveries'.

[7] See rules 19.12: 'All units of the securities must be in all respects identical ...' and 19.13: 'The units of the security must not be numbered or otherwise identifiable individually'.

[8] Based on transaction order and size. It represents a departure from normal equitable tracing Rules.

[9] Rule 18.7.2 requires CRESTCo, if new securities are not forthcoming from the original 'bad transferor' within 2 hours, to notify subsequent 'transferees' of the bad stock 'so as to enable them to make such applications (whether to the court or otherwise) as they think fit.'

3 Custody agreements

Should custodians going into CREST include new drafting in their custody agreements? Because of the operational difficulty in obtaining the positive consent of existing clients to new terms, it might be hoped that new provision could be avoided for existing customers.[1] It may be possible effectively to bind existing customers with new provision concerning CREST by unilateral notice.[2]

In any case, new drafting is recommended for custodians for a number of reasons. Firstly, the custodian owes duties of confidentiality to its clients both as banker and as fiduciary. General law relieves these duties of confidentiality where there is a legal duty of disclosure. However, many of the disclosure provisions in the CREST agreements binding the custodian member are wider than this. Therefore, in order for the custodian not to be in breach of its duties of confidentiality to its clients, its disclosure obligations under the CREST agreements should be drawn to clients' attention, and their consent obtained in the custody agreement.

Secondly, special risks associated with CREST (and discussed in this section) should be disclosed to clients, and their consent to them obtained, in order to protect the custodian from liability for client losses attributable to such risks. While the Regulations relieve trustee participants from liability associated with the absence of DVP within CREST,[3] other CREST risks may involve the custodian in liability to clients suffering loss in consequence of them. Custodians' ability to recover any damages from CRESTCo is extremely limited by provision in the Membership Agreement.[4] Special provision in the custody agreement would be appropriate to protect the custodian from liability to its clients in connection with the use of CREST.

In addition, new drafting is considered necessary in order to discharge their contractual obligations to CRESTCo. The Membership Agreement requires[5] the custodian member (broadly) to obtain the consent of clients to aspects of CREST that may affect them.[6] This should be interpreted to mean express disclosure of relevant risks and, possibly, a signed acknowledgment and consent to such risks. In addition, the Membership Agreement obliges the custodian 'so far as it is able' to prevent clients making adverse claims against

---

[1] The original draft Membership Agreement (July 1995) prescribed specific wording which custodian members were to be required to include in their custody agreements (adopting the approach of the CGO and the CMO). Custodian institutions resisted this obligation and wished to be able to confine themselves to writing to clients in relation to CREST without obtaining client responses. Also, it might be hoped to rely on clients' general consent in existing documentation to the custodian using clearing systems on the terms of those systems. However, this approach is not recommended for the reasons discussed below.

[2] On the basis that CREST is a new development not envisaged in existing documentation, and that the client, by permitting the custodian to use CREST on the disclosed basis, has accepted the new CREST terms by conduct. However, this question must be considered on a case by case basis.

[3] In regulation 33.

[4] See sections 1.11, 3.3.5, 3.3.8, 3.3.9, 3.3.14, 5.3, 5.5, 6.1, 6.2, 6.4.3, 6.5, 6.6, 6.7, 7.1, 7.2, 7.4, 7.6, 7.7, 7.9, 9.2, 10.3, 11.5. As indicated above, regulation 30 provides for compensation orders to be made against CRESTCo in relation to (broadly) fraudulent CREST instructions, but limitations on the quantum of compensation (£50,000 maximum) and the circumstances in which it is available reduce the value of this provision.

[5] Section 3.3.16.

[6] Enforcing the commercial argument that such provision is necessary to protect the custodian.

transferred securities so as to prevent registration.[1] It is not clear how this can be achieved otherwise than by express contractual provision binding clients.

E   Cross-border issues

It is a general rule of private international law that formalities necessary for the transfer of property are determined by the law of the place where the property is situated, or *lex situs*. *Lex situs* of registered securities is generally the jurisdiction in which the [principal] register is located.[2] Because a UK statutory instrument cannot alter foreign law, the Regulations cannot dematerialise foreign securities.

One method of bringing foreign securities into CREST is to seek local legislation achieving the same result as the Regulations, and this approach has been taken in Ireland.[3] A pragmatic alternative is to turn foreign securities into UK securities, by repackaging them under English law depositary receipt ('DR') programs.[4] The need for such programs will be an opportunity for the London custodians able to offer them. The taxation of DRs in CREST is an important issue.[5]

F   Collateral and securities lending

An important use of UK equities is to serve as collateral, whether for securities lending or for other exposures. The changes to collateral practice introduced by CREST are of relevance to custodians, who are routinely involved in arrangements whereby their clients' securities are put up as collateral to third parties, and who may wish to collateralise their own exposures to clients.

CREST securities may serve as collateral in a variety of ways, both under arrangements within and outwith the CREST system. However, in all cases it is important to appreciate that CREST does not create security interests;

---

[1] Section 8.1.2. Since this may be clients' only effective recourse in the case of fraud, it may be hard to obtain their consent to such provision in the custody documentation. The custodian's obligation to CREST is not limited by reasonableness, and (where custody clients have suffered fraud) may cut across the custodian's commercial relationship with its clients.

[2] See Dicey and Morris, *The Conflict of Laws,* (12 edn, 1993), Sweet & Maxwell, London, p 931.

[3] The Irish Uncertificated Securities Regulations 1996 are made under section 239 of the Irish Companies Act 1990. The Channel Islands and the Isle of Man are considering taking the same approach, and South African companies are urging the authorities to make local dematerialisation legislation compatible with CREST.

[4] Special provisions relating to DRs are included in the rules 7.15 to 7.17. requiring inter alia the maintenance of a UK register.

[5] Normally, a triple charge of 1.5% is made on the entry of underlying securities into a DR program, and transfers of DRs thereafter are not subject to stamp duty or SDRT. Although there may of course be many more than 3 transfers of DRs during the life of a program, the triple charge is a disincentive as it is borne all at once by the same person. CRESTCo has been in discussion with the Inland Revenue with a view to disapplying the triple charge to CREST DRs on the basis that SDRT on subsequent transfers of DRs may be collectable though CREST. (The policy justification of the triple charge is the inability in practice to collect transfer tax on DRs transferred through offshore clearing systems.)

it merely facilitates them. Any security interest in CREST securities must be created by documentation[1] between the parties.

1 Security interests

A wide range of security interests is available under English law, varying in the degrees of formality involved and the robustness of the protection given to the security holder.

(a) Legal mortgages (CREST transfers)

Under a legal mortgage, legal title to assets is transferred by way of security, with the mortgagor retaining only the equity of redemption (ie the right to have the assets back free from the security interest upon the discharge of the secured obligations).

However, no SDRT duty relief is available for legal mortgages executed through CREST.[2]

(b) Equitable mortgage (escrow balance)

Outside CREST, much of the security given over English equities is by way of an equitable charge, which arises upon the deposit with the chargee of share certificates and blank transfer forms. With dematerialisation in CREST, this is not possible, and a need arises for the functional equivalent of an equitable mortgage of shares, ie a rapid and informal method of using shares as security which does not involve re-registering them.

This is offered by the escrow balance, an arrangement which involves blocking securities in a sub-account of the security giver's account, where they are subject to the order of the security taker.[3] Mortgagors are subject to the fraud risk of mortgagees who improperly dispose of the mortgaged securities, within CREST as outside it. The movement of securities to an escrow balance does not appear on the register of the issuer.

The crucial question is whether the interest of the security taker over securities in the escrow balance would be enforceable in the insolvency of the security giver. Broadly speaking, it will if the interest is proprietary, and will not if it is merely contractual.[4] Placing of securities in the escrow balance of itself probably does not confer a property interest in the escrow agent.[5] It is therefore important carefully to document any security interest using the escrow balance carefully, to ensure that a proprietary security interest is conferred.

The Membership Agreement places responsibility on the custodian member for the suitability and adequate use of the escrow balance. In practice, this may mean ensuring that no client fails to take effective security through the

---

[1] Or, in some circumstances, by operation of law.
[2] 'In the case of the transfer of shares as security for a loan, subject to stamp duty at 50 pence, the Inland Revenue have advised that to obtain relief for any such transfer the shares should be rematerialised, a transfer executed, and, if appropriate subsequently dematerialised in the name of the transferee.' *Reference Manual*, chapter 8, p 111.
[3] See *The Business Description*, p 87. See also chapter 7, section 1, of the *Reference Manual*. CREST refers to the mortgagee as 'escrow agent'.
[4] Because of the restriction in section 127 of the Insolvency Act 1986 on dispositions of a company's property after the commencement of winding up.
[5] The escrow balance is also used for corporate actions, in which case no property is conferred.

escrow balance. This is a very wide responsibility, in view of the possibility that the collateral agent's interest may be merely contractual.

An obvious limitation of the escrow balance is that CREST securities can only be encumbered in this way in favour of CREST participants. The corollary is an opportunity for CREST participants to act as security agent for non-CREST lenders who wish to take security over dematerialised securities.

(c) Charges

CREST members (and their clients) are free to charge their interests in CREST members' accounts in the ordinary way (subject to any negative pledge given to a settlement bank to support a settlement bank charge). If charged securities remain in the chargor's account, a floating charge may be created; floating charges created by UK corporates are registrable.[1]

(d) Pledges

A pledge involves the transfer of possession of a tangible asset, and therefore cannot be given in respect of shares, which are intangible. While share certificates were capable of pledge, with dematerialisation, the pledge becomes irrelevant for corporate securities.

2 Securities lending[2]

Provisions are available in CREST to facilitate the use of dematerialised securities in securities lending as loaned securities or securities collateral.[3] However, these are only available in transactions involving market makers.[4]

(a) Cash collateral

Where securities are transferred within CREST by way of a securities loan, the assured payment obligation constitutes the cash collateral.

Where CREST transfers are identified as securities loans, special facilities

---

[1] Under section 395 of the Companies Act 1985.
[2] CREST has no dedicated functionality for sale and repurchase agreements, although this is proposed to be developed in the future. However, participants are free to settle repos through CREST by settling two matched trades. Of course, no automatic margining will be available.
[3] 'While CRESTCo believes that the functionality has been designed to be consistent with the principles of the Equity and Fixed Interest Stock Lending Agreement (1994), CREST does not monitor or enforce compliance with the terms of that or any other agreement or with any other applicable regulatory or other requirement.' *Reference Manual*, chapter 7, section 1.

CREST facilitates the *settlement* of bilateral securities lending arrangements entered into (independently of CREST) between participants. This contrasts with securities lending arrangements in Euroclear and Cedel, where the clearers are involved in *arranging* securities lending programs between participants.
[4] 'Provided that the stock loan is to a Stock Exchange market maker to enable it to fulfil a contract, the transfer within CREST of stock back up the chain to the ultimate lender will be exempt from SDRT ... In addition, there will be statutory relief available in CREST from duty for the transfer and return of stock collateral associated with deliveries by value (DBVs), by market maker to intermediary, by the intermediary to the ultimate lender and back again, provided that the latter is a market maker. CREST will inhibit stock loan and DBV instructions which do not involve a market maker.' *Reference Manual*, p 120.

are available to handle automatic redeliveries[1] and the margining of cash collateral.[2]

(b) Securities collateral: delivery by value (DBV)

Where CREST securities are used as collateral,[3] automatic collateral selection is available through the delivery by value (DBV) system.[4] A member may instruct CREST to transfer securities from its account by way of collateral to another member's account; the value of the collateral, but not the individual securities, are specified.[5] In contrast to the CGO, DBVs in CREST are registered in the name of the collateral taker.[6]

DBV securities are automatically 'redelivered'[7] in the next business day.[8] New DBV collateral must be put up by the borrower daily; the amount of daily DBV collateral will need to be adjusted to reflect the margining requirements of the securities lending arrangement.

It may be operationally convenient to have a separate DBV account, although this is not necessary.[9]

---

[1] While there is no need for the lender to give instructions for the return, the automatic return instruction is given zero priority so that the borrower will need to intervene to lift the priority to permit settlement. See the *Reference Manual*, chapter 7, section 1.

[2] *Reference Manual*, chapter 7, p 100. In CREST (unlike in the CGO) these margin adjustments are automatically made through the assured payments system.

[3] In practice, a sequential combination of cash and securities collateral may be used, as follows. Following a request from a market maker for securities, a money broker will obtain the securities from a lending institution. The securities will be transferred from the account of the lender to that of the money broker, and then on into the account of the market maker. In respect of each of these transfers, the assured payment obligation of the transferee will serve as cash collateral. During the currency of the loan, the market maker may wish to use the cash that has been provided by way of collateral to the money broker. The money brokers are willing to release this money against the provision of further collateral. Outside CREST, this further collateral is provided in the form of Stock Exchange short-term certificates or other securities. Within CREST, it may be provided by DBV (the assured payment for the DBV constituting the return of the cash).

    DBV is only provided once daily towards the end of the settlement process. Intra-day, market makers may rely on cash collateral. Towards the end of the day, the market maker recovers the cash by substituting securities through DBV.

[4] This is modelled on a similar system in the CGO.

[5] Although securities will be ranked by quality into three categories, and each DBV will exclusively relate to one quality category; also, DBVs may optionally be subject to a 10% concentration restriction and DBV takers may exclude certain securities which they are prevented from holding. See the *Reference Manual*, chapter 7, section 2.

[6] CREST's 2-hour registration time frame (as opposed to the 3-day cycle in the CGO) makes this feasible. Moreover, whereas transfer of title in CGO is based on contract (*Reference Manual*, sections 4.2.4 and 4.2.8), the basis of transfer of title in CREST is statutory (regulation 25) and (unlike in the CGO) linked to registration.

    The collateral taker is exempted from the requirements of the Companies Act 1985 relating to the disclosure of interests in shares by the Disclosure of Interests in Shares (Amendment) Regulations 1996.

[7] Strictly, the 'redelivery' is not of the same securities but of equivalent securities; DBV securities are delivered outright and not by way of security.

[8] Unless countermanding instructions are given by the collateral taker wishing to enforce the collateral.

[9] It might be argued that the placing of DBV securities in a special account exposes the arrangement to the risk of recharacterisation as a charge (which might in turn be void for want of registration) as opposed to an outright transfer. However, provided there is no obligation on the DBV recipient to use a special account, and no restriction on its freedom to take the securities out of that account or to block their 'redelivery', this should not be a problem, as it does not imply any retained property in the DBV securities by their provider by way of a charge.

DBV is only available to CREST members who are market makers, and is therefore in practice confined to securities lending.[1]

G   Stock events[2]

CREST may be used to execute corporate actions.[3] Whether or not to use this functionality is the choice of the issuer and its agent. Corporate action details are held in the CREST system and special transaction types are designed for use in corporate actions.[4] However, compliance with the terms of event is not the responsibility of CREST.

H   Conclusions

The legal aspects of CREST have been drafted with a light hand. A consultative paper states, 'the government wishes to rely as far as practicable on the existing legal framework affecting shareholdings'. The deliverable was not law reform, but an effective settlement system. The result of this approach is that key legal aspects of the system are left to the contractual provisions to be developed between different players involved in CREST. For custodians, the negotiation of sponsorship and custody agreements, together with the terms of settlement bank facilities, will be of primary importance.

[1] While DBV may have been useful for repos, the Inland Revenue vetoed this option because of the collection of stamp duty on repos.
[2] See *Reference Manual*, Chapter 7, pp 107–109.
[3] It was here that TAURUS came to grief, and it has been argued that the need to handle complex stock events (together with stamp duty) has deterred the continental European clearers from competing for the settlement of UK equities.
[4] These are: complex deliveries, unmatched stock events, registrar's adjustment, transfers to escrow and transfers from escrow.

Chapter 14

Conclusions

1 Legal certainty

For all those involved in the global custody industry, the chief objective of legal analysis is certainty. It is of great importance to be able to determine, with as much certainty as possible, the rights, duties and liabilities of global custodians, their clients, the settlement systems, and all those dealing with any of them. Beginning with the position under English domestic and private international law, this book has sought to make some progress towards that objective.

Two challenges in particular have been encountered. Firstly, practice has moved ahead of the law, with the computerisation of the securities markets. This has cut across traditional legal analysis. Computerised securities cannot be negotiable instruments (chapter 3). The lack of a tangible subject matter takes custody beyond the scope of bailment (chapter 4). Secondly, international portfolios of securities raise complex conflict of laws issues. These are discussed in detail in chapters 6 and 7.

2 Intermediate securities

This book has indicated that the way ahead lies in focusing on the fact that the client's interest in the securities is characteristically fungible and indirect. Rather than owning particular securities, the client has commingled rights in a fungible bulk, often held through an international clearing system. It cannot enforce these rights directly against the clearer or other sub-custodian, but only through the intermediary global custodian. However, its rights are protected in the insolvency of the global custodian, and in this sense they are proprietary. Technically, these rights may be referred to as rights under equitable tenancies in common. However they are categorised, the main point it that they are commingled and indirect. These features unite interests under global custody with depositary receipts (chapter 9) and also with the interests of investors in computerised securities generally; all such interests have been categorised in this book as intermediate securities (chapter 3).

The same features also unite the position under English law with that under the laws of other jurisdictions, for these arrangements characterise the international securities markets. In particular, the analysis of intermediate securities under English law in this book accords in key respects with the concept of securities entitlements, introduced in the US by the revised article 8 of the Uniform Commercial Code.[1] With both, the interest of the investor is enforceable only through the intermediary, ring-fenced in the intermediary's insolvency and located, for conflict of laws purposes, in the jurisdiction of the intermediary. The advantages of this approach are clear. While the investor is protected from custodian credit risk, the location of the investor's interest with the intermediary settlement system provides a pragmatic solution to questions of ease and integrity of transfer (chapter 6). It also simplifies the use of custody securities as collateral (chapter 7), thereby in turn helping to address settlement risk (enabling settlement systems effectively to collateralise their exposures to participants). It is argued in this book that the position achieved by statute in the US is available under the general principles of English law.

3   Equity

As part of the intermediate securities approach, this book has suggested that the law of equity has an important role in global custody. Equity succeeds (where the common law and the law merchant fail) in meeting many challenges posed by computerised custody. These include the achievement of divided ownership without possession (chapter 4) and without individual allocation[2] (chapter 5). The enormous commercial value of the law of trusts rests partly on its synergy with the rules of private international law: the latter's emphasis on *lex situs* and the former's ability (with the intermediate securities approach) to place the situs of certain trusts with the trustee (chapter 7).

The importance of equity in solving the legal problems of global custody accords with the argument that, through electronic custody, bearer securities have become registered securities which, traditionally, are equitable (chapter 3). Both developments reflect the historic role of equity in permitting commercial law to adapt to developments in commercial practice where the common law is too inflexible (chapter 3).

It is appropriate that the computerisation (and therefore the dematerialisation) of custody securities should take us into the realms of equity, for equitable property has been described as if it were itself a species of dematerialisation.[3]

It is also appropriate that equity should support the modern global custodian, because of the obstinacy of equity in resisting the distinction between personal and proprietary rights. This distinction has been fundamental in Western

---

[1] See the discussion in JS Rogers, *Policy Perspectives on Revised UCC Article 8*, UCLA Law Rev, June 1996, p 1431. Revised Article 8 concerns custody: '... the indirect holding system rules in Revised Article 8 come into play only with respect to the custodial function', p 1495.

[2] Although recent caselaw indicates that common law may now also permit bailment without allocation: see chapter 4, section 3.b.

[3] Maitland, *Selected Essays*, (1936), *Trust and Corporation*, Cambridge University Press, pp 164, 165. Equally the doctrine of equitable tracing 'converted the "trust fund" into an incorporeal thing, capable of being "invested" in different ways.' p 172.

property law since Justinian.[1] However, an interest under a trust resists it (chapter 7).[2]

In an electronic environment, where rights in securities are held through multi-tiered, fungible and intangible arrangements, the assertion of a right *in rem* is almost fanciful.[3] In this context, the chief functional importance of the concept of property is avoidance of intermediary insolvency risk, and the trust achieves this. In its failure to take the ancient point that personal and proprietary rights are fundamentally different, equity anticipated computers.

4 Pragmatism

Equity, then, provides the appropriate jurisprudential base for global custody. However, the day-to-day legal needs of global custodians and their clients are more practical than theoretical. A pragmatic approach to the enforcement of security interests in custody investments is essential (chapter 7). Above all, the drafting of the global custody contract is the most important factor in defining the duties and liabilities of the custodian (chapter 8) and in avoiding commingling risk (chapter 5). Thus, this book has indicated that risks arising under domestic law may be addressed in the drafting of the global custody contract. As for international risks, some doubt always surrounds the legal aspects of international portfolios of securities, as domestic law may not govern any particular dispute. Thus the risk must always be considered that the courts of a country whose laws are unhelpful may assume jurisdiction. In many cases, a number of courts having different approaches to the same question may potentially have jurisdiction. Legal risk of this kind calls for a pragmatic approach. Enforcement is the key issue, and the systems of law that concerns the global custodian may be those where assets (of the clients or of the custodian itself) may be realistically attached, rather than those having a jurisprudential claim to jurisdiction (chapters 6 and 7).

More generally, the friction caused in the minds of lawyers between the traditional principles of commercial law and modern global custodial practice should not cause undue concern. Although expressed in terms of abstract principles, commercial law is not a theoretical discipline, and an abstract approach will not take one far (chapter 2). Commercial law is a pragmatic technique for resolving concrete disputes. It follows events, in two senses. Firstly, legal theory is derived from the facts of the cases that make up commercial law. It is not an *a priori* discipline, and the correct direction

---

[1] The distinction organises the layout of Justinian's *Institutes*, Blackstone's *Commentaries* and Dicey and Morris's *The Conflict of Laws* alike.

[2] '[The trust] was made by men who had no Roman law as explained by medieval commentators in the innermost fibres of their minds.' Maitland, *Selected Essays*, (1936), *The Unincorporated Body*, Cambridge University Press, p 130.

[3] '... the fact remains that modern securities markets have moved so far beyond the movement of pieces of negotiable paper that the property law construct is inadequate and unworkable.' CW Mooney, *Beyond Negotiability*, [1990] Cardozo Law Review, Vol 12, 305 at 303. In this article, which informed the revised draft 8 of the UCC, Professor Mooney suggests a securities law based not on property but on priority.

for legal reasoning is 'bottom up' rather than 'top down'.[1] It follows, secondly, that commercial law adapts well to changes in commercial practice.

Moreover, the commercial and financial markets have always been able to tolerate a large measure of legal uncertainty. Just as the commercial revolution of the late middle ages was able to take place without a common law concept of assignable debt, and the industrial revolution took place without developed company law (chapter 3), so the computer revolution of the late 20th century has not been, and did not need to be, preceded by a full legal account of itself. The complete legal account of computerisation in general, and of global custody in particular, will follow financial practice. This work has suggested a direction in which, in this jurisdiction, it may develop.

---

[1] 'Also it is to be remembered that the making of grand theories is not and never has been our strong point.' Maitland, *Selected Essays*, (1936), *Trust and Corporation*, Cambridge University Press, pp 218, 219.

Appendix 1

Legal nature of intermediate securities

(Chapter 3, section B.4(b))

What is the legal nature of intermediate securities?

The important point is that the way in which securities are held determines their legal nature. Intermediate securities are indirect and unallocated.

1 Indirect

It was shown above that the investor does not in general have directly enforceable rights against the issuer. Its rights in respect of the issuer can only be exercised through the intermediary.

In the case of immobilised securities, underlying physical securities are held through Euroclear or Cedel. Each of these clearing systems operates a system akin to global custody,[1] in that the physical safekeeping of physical securities is delegated by the clearer to depositories, which are generally located in the same jurisdiction of the issuer. Thus, there are two levels of intermediation. The investor has rights which are enforceable only through Euroclear or Cedel; the clearer has rights which are enforceable only through its depository; the depository, as holder of the physical securities, is their legal holder and therefore has directly enforceable rights against the issuer.

The position with global securities is similar, but more complex. We saw that a physical global bond in temporary or permanent form is issued directly to a common depository, which holds it for Euroclear and Cedel; they in turn hold their interest in it for participants who are investors. Thus, as with immobilised securities, there are two levels of intermediation.[2] Thus, in each

---

[1] In its legal structure; the clearers do not in general offer the value-added information-based services characteristic of the global custody product.

[2] Broadly speaking, the underlying property is the global note. However the position is less simple than that with immobilised securities because the rights represented by the global may in certain circumstances be replaced by rights under other documents, namely definitives and the deed of covenant. Together, the global, the definitives (if any are in issue) and the deed of covenant create a network of contingent and mutually dependent rights.

In the case of permanent global bonds, the underlying property comprises the covenant of the issuer to pay principal and interest to the holder of the global, together with the right of the holder of the global to exchange the global for definitives upon the default of the issuer. In the case of temporary global bonds, the underlying property comprises the right of the holder to exchange the global for definitives, together with the right to receive principal and interest if the issuer defaults in its obligation to issue definitives. (In cases where a deed of covenant is executed, the disappearing global provision, described above, does not affect the analysis of the underlying property as it is merely a contingency, occurring only on default.)

case, the underlying property is held for investors through two intermediaries.[1] In each case the underlying property is legally owned by the first intermediary (ie the intermediary having a direct link with the issuer, at one remove from the investor).[2]

As legal title is with the first intermediary, the investor's interest cannot also be in the nature of legal title. The only form of ownership that English law can confer on a person who does not have legal title to assets is equitable title. As a matter of English law, if the investor has a proprietary interest in the underlying property, it can only be equitable, because it is indirect. The separation of equitable and legal title creates a trust,[3] of which the first intermediary is the trustee. The beneficiary is the person for whom the first intermediary directly holds the underlying property, ie the second intermediary. If the interest of the second intermediary is an equitable interest under a trust, the only manner in which a proprietary interest can be conferred on the investor is under a sub-trust.[4]

This is the position under English law. Of course, the relationship between the second intermediary and the investor is not governed by English law, but by the governing law of the general terms and conditions of the clearers.[5] These jurisdictions do not recognise trusts in their domestic law. However, as chapter 7 discusses, these jurisdictions have passed legislation[6] in support of their clearing system which has the result of protecting the interests of investors under an arrangement akin to a trust. Under English conflicts rules they would be recognised *as if they were* trusts. The analysis under English private international law is to recognise these arrangements as if they were trusts, because of the wide terms of the Recognition of Trusts Act 1987 which implements the Hague Convention.

2 Unallocated

Intermediate securities are generally unallocated.[7]

---

[1] In the case of immobilised securities, these are the clearer and its depository. In the case of global securities, they are the clearer and its common depository.

[2] This is because in each case the underlying property consists of bearer securities, so that legal title is with the holder.

[3] An alternative view, namely that arrangements of this type give rise to bailment, is discussed in chapter 4.

[4] Under *Grainge v Wilberforce* (1889) 5 TLR 436, the law 'looks through' bare sub-trusts, so that where A holds property on trust for B, who holds the property on bare sub-trust for C, A is deemed to hold the property directly for C and B drops out of the picture. However, this principle will not apply here as the second Intermediary (the clearer) is not a bare sub-trustee as it has active duties under its general terms and conditions in relation to the administration of the assets.

[5] Belgian law for Euroclear and Luxembourg law for Cedel.

[6] Belgian Royal Decree No 62 of November 1967 and Luxembourg Grand Ducal Decree of February 1971.

[7] In the case of immobilised securities, the underlying property comprises definitive bonds that are issued with distinctive numbers. (In the case of bonds which are London listed the rules of the London Stock Exchange require definitive bonds to be issued with serial numbers: section 13.22.e of the Stock Exchange's Listing Rules.) Therefore particular physical securities forming part of the underlying property could in theory be allocated to particular immobilised securities. In practice however particular underlying bonds are not in general earmarked for particular accounts at Euroclear or Cedel. All securities accounts at Euroclear are fungible. While Cedel offers both fungible and non-fungible accounts, only a very small minority of securities are held on a non-fungible basis. Thus, the interest of the investor is pooled with the interests

The legal consequences of commingling the assets of different persons is a complex subject, which chapter 5 examines in detail. If the investor's right is unallocated, the only way that it can be a proprietary right attaching to the underlying property is by way of co-ownership with all the other investors in the same issue. Because the underlying property is unallocated, it is co-owned.

English law recognises two forms of co-ownership: joint tenancy and tenancy in common. Both terms derive originally from land law but can apply equally to the co-ownership of personal property. The difference between joint tenancy and tenancy in common lies in the four unities.[1]

In other words, in order for a joint tenancy to be established, each co-owner must be entitled to possession of the whole of the co-owned property, have the same quantum of interest in it, have title by the same instrument and have the interest for the same interval of time. The unities will in practice not be present in intermediate securities, which are therefore co-owned by investors under a tenancy in common.

Intermediate securities are therefore interests under equitable tenancies in common. In their legal nature, intermediate securities are akin to unit trusts.[2]

---

of all other investors in immobilised securities of the same issue, at the level of the second intermediary (the clearer). (There is no pooling at the level of the first intermediary, the local depository, because all the underlying property is held for the second intermediary, and there is therefore no pooling of the second intermediary's interest with the interests of third parties.)

In the case of global securities, the position is slightly different because the investor's interest is not merely unallocated, but also incapable of allocation, for the simple reason that there are no underlying definitives that could be earmarked for particular investors. The underlying property consists of a global note representing the entire issue of bonds. The fractional parts of the global equating to individual definitives do not have distinctive numbers and are not otherwise distinguishable one from the other.

The first intermediary holds the global for the two second intermediaries, Euroclear and Cedel. Thus, in the absence of allocation, the interests of the two second intermediaries are pooled with each other at the level of the first intermediary. As with immobilised securities, the interests of investors are also pooled at the level of the second intermediaries.

Thus, in the case of immobilised securities, there will be commingling in the jurisdiction of the second intermediaries (Belgium and Luxembourg); in the case of global securities, there will be commingling in the jurisdiction of the first intermediary (England in the case of an English global) and also in those of the second intermediaries (Belgium and Luxembourg).

[1] 'The four unities of joint tenancy which must exist, or the tenancy will be in common, are:
(1) Possession ...
(2) Interest ...
(3) Title ...
(4) Time ...'
Osborne's Concise Law Dictionary. See also Megarry & Wade, *The Law of Real Property*, (1984), Stevens & Sons, London, pp 419–422.

[2] The capital value of a unit trust is variable because units are redeemable as well as transferable. Immobilised securities and temporary global securities are comparable because the investor can remove his interest from the arrangement (by requiring physical delivery in the case of immobilised securities, or by calling for definitives in the case of temporary globals). Permanent global securities differ in that the interest of the investor can be transferred to another investor, but cannot be removed from the equitable tenancy in common.

The adverse tax consequences of unit trust status are avoided for the reasons discussed in chapter 3, section B.9, above.

Appendix 2

Depositary receipts

(Chapter 9)

Part a

Registration requirements for a public offer of securities by a foreign private issuer in the US

Section B.1

1 General requirements

The issuer must file a registration statement containing a prospectus and detailed disclosures concerning itself and the offered securities. After a public offering under the Securities Act, issuers become subject to the annual and periodic disclosure requirements of the Securities Exchange Act. Secondary trading of registered securities, private offerings and certain small issues are normally exempted. A public offering registration is made on Form F-1 (Form F-1 is available to private foreign issuers making an initial public offering of their securities). This imposes a significant disclosure burden. Incorporation by reference of filings under the Securities Exchange Act containing financial statements is not permitted. Financial statements conforming to US GAAP (generally accepted accounting practices) must be filed with the registration statement.

2 Short form registration

Short form registration statements in Forms F-2 and F-3 (with much less detailed reporting) are permitted in certain circumstances when the issuer already reports to the SEC. F-2 may incorporate Securities Exchange Act filings containing financial statements by reference, but the issuer must deliver the incorporated reports to potential investors with the prospectus. In the case of F-3, the issuer's most recent and subsequently filed Securities Exchange Act filings containing financial statements are deemed incorporated by reference, and there is no requirement to deliver copies of the financial statements. To be eligible to use Form F-2 or F-3, a foreign private issuer must be qualified to use Form 20-F to report under the Exchange Act: see below. A further short form of registration, in F-4, is available to foreign private issuers in certain reclassification, statutory mergers or consolidations, exchange offers and transfers of assets. The disclosure requirements for foreign private issuers using Forms F-2, F-3 and F-4 are similar to those for US issuers.

F-2 can be filed for equities if the aggregate market value worldwide of the issuer's voting stock held by non-affiliates is $300 million or more; or for debt if at least one nationally recognised rating organisation has rated the debt securities as investment grade.

F-3 can be filed if F-2 criteria are met and the issuer has been subject to the periodic reporting requirements of the Exchange Act for at least 36 calendar months. Issuers eligible to use Form F-3 may also be able to file a 'shelf' registration statement under rule 415. This may be prepared more than 30 days in advance of the offer to the public. Once a shelf registration statement has been declared effective, an offering may be made without further SEC review, subject only to providing the SEC details of the particular offering. Shelf registration statements are usually only used for debt and not equity, as the existence of registered but unsold securities, which might potentially dilute issued equities, might depress market prices. Since April 1994 it has been possible to make universal shelf registration statements, which may be used for either debt or equity without advance election between debt or equity.

3 DR requirements

In the case of programs opened in the US without the benefit of regulatory exemptions, SEC registration requirements apply. The form of registration and the level of detail involved varies depending on whether new capital is being raised. Where new capital is raised (Level III), full disclosure (without incorporation by reference) is required in Form F-1 for first-time registrants. Where no new capital is raised (Levels I and II), less disclosure (without incorporation by reference) is required in Form F-6.

Part b

Periodic reporting requirements under the Exchange Act

Section B.1

1 Applicability

Annual and periodic reporting requirements apply to foreign private issuers: (i) effecting a public offering under the Securities Act; (ii) listing securities (such as ADRs) on a national securities exchange, such as NYSE, or on the NASDAQ system; or (iii) possessing a class of equity securities with 300 or more holders resident in the US. The periodic disclosure requirements are similar to those in registration statements filed under the Securities Act for public offers; separate filings are required under both Acts, but in practice the Exchange Act filing incorporates information in such registration statement by reference.

A foreign private issuer is exempt if on the last day of its most recent financial year, the issuer has a class of equity securities held by fewer than

300 holders resident in the US and the securities are not listed on a national securities exchange or quoted on the NASDAQ system.

The ADRs representing the underlying deposited securities registered on Form F-6 (as opposed to the underlying securities) are exempt from the regular (annual and periodic) reporting requirements of the Securities Exchange Act.

2   Disclosure requirements

Form 20-F is the SEC's Exchange Act registration statement and annual report form for foreign private issuers. The requirements of Form 20-F are modelled on the requirements of annual reports of US corporations in Form 10-K. Issuers must generally include two years' audited balance sheets and three years' audited statements of income and cash flow. The requirements of Form 20-F include descriptions of exchange controls, taxes imposed by the foreign issuer's jurisdiction of incorporation, information concerning the deposit arrangement, rights of ADR holders and fees payable by ADR holders. If Securities Act registration is made in Form F-1, abbreviated filing in Form 8-A may be possible instead of under Form 20-F. Annual reports must be filed on Form 20-F and periodic reports must be filed on Form 6-K. Form 6-K requires information similar to that required by rule 12g3–2(b): see below.

3   Rule 12g3–2(b)

Issuers of unlisted ADRs can obtain exemption from reporting requirements under rule 12g3–2(b) ('home country disclosure'). The requirements for this exemption include the following:

(1) The issuer must supply all information that the issuer has or is required to make public by local law, has or is required to file with a stock exchange and which the exchange has made public and has or is required to distribute to its security holders. This information must be kept up to date.

(2) In connection with the initial filing, the issuer must inform the SEC of the number of holders of each class of equity securities resident in the United States, the circumstances in which such securities were acquired and the date and circumstances of the most recent public distribution of securities by the issuer or an affiliate. (If an issuer is neither a reporting company under the Securities Exchange Act 1934 nor has obtained a rule 12g3–2(b) exemption, a depositary cannot create an unsponsored ADR facility.

A disadvantage for the issuer in obtaining a rule 12g3–2(b) exemption is that unsponsored ADR facilities may become a possible obstacle to creating sponsored facilities. Where unsponsored programs exist, the establishment of a sponsored program would involve cancellation of the unsponsored facilities, and the payment of significant cancellation fees to the unsponsored depositaries by the issuer or the sponsored depositary. On the other hand, a rule 12g3–2(b) exemption facilitates 144(A) placements. See Part C below.

4 Additional requirements

In addition to annual reports in Form 20-F and periodic reports in Form 6-K, certain reports are required to be filed by beneficial owners of more than 5% of any class of voting equity securities which are registered under the Exchange Act. Registrants are obliged to maintain records and internal controls in accordance with the Act. Registrants will also become subject to certain US laws regarding foreign corrupt practices. Certain requirements will be imposed on third party tender offers for the registrant's securities, and registrants will be subject to disclosure requirements regarding self-tenders and 'going private' transactions.

Beneficial owners of more than 5% of any class of voting equity securities which are registered under Securities Exchange Act must make returns under that Act (unless the securities are exempt from the Securities Exchange Act reporting requirements pursuant to the exemptions for securities of foreign private issuers with 300 or fewer US holders or those permitted to furnish home-country disclosure documents pursuant to rule 12(g)3–2(b)). Issuers of registered securities and their subsidiaries are obliged to maintain records and internal controls in accordance with the Act.

Part c

Restricted securities (rule 144A)

Section B.2.a

1 Advantages

Rule 144A greatly increases the attractiveness of DR programs because it removes the need for lengthy SEC registrations and conforming to US GAAP. Avoidance of Securities Act registration offers reduced time and costs. The rule is often used in connection with privatisations, where timetables are tight. However, in 1994 it was stated that 'Currently there is a clear trend away from 144A issues towards full registration with the Securities and Exchange Commission'.

2 Formalities

Securities offered in rule 144A do not have to be registered under the Securities Act. Technically no prospectus or offering circular is required, but in practice investors require sufficient information to enable them to make an informed decision. Therefore an information memorandum or offering circular is usually provided. It is usual to give the information that would be provided on full registration, and QIBs now expect this. Where a rule 144A offering is combined with an international offering involving a prospectus, usually the same document is used. Issuers do not have to file periodic reports under the Securities Exchange Act. However, if the issuer is not subject to reporting requirements of the Securities Exchange Act or, in the case of foreign private issuer, does not furnish information under rule 12g3–2(b), the issuer must agree to provide information to investors on request. This is a brief description of its business and products and services, most recent balance sheet and profit and loss and retained earnings statements and similar financial statements for two preceding financial years.

3   Structure of the offer

The issuer sells unregistered securities to offerees in a private placement. The restricted DRs are then resold among QIBs in reliance on rule 144A. The 144A offer usually constitutes the US part of global offering.

4   Continuing restrictions

144A DRs may not be sold to US public investors for at least two years, when QIBs may sell small amounts. After three years the 144A DRs generally become completely unrestricted. However, the three-year restriction operates on a rolling basis and will begin again if more restricted ADRs are created.

5   Trading and settlement

Restricted DRs trade among QIBs through PORTAL, the NASD's trading system for rule 144A securities (offering five-day settlement). '... liquidity is often not very good on the Portal secondary market trading system, so even the QIBs feel more comfortable buying public stock offerings.' Settlement is through the DTC.

Part d

Regulation S

Section B.2.b

1   The regulation

The following conditions are imposed:

(i) the sale must be an 'offshore transaction'
   – ie the offer must be made outside the US; and
   – the buyer must be or be reasonably believed to be outside the US; and
   – (broadly) the transaction must be executed on established foreign securities exchange or designated offshore securities market; and
(ii) there must be no 'directed selling efforts' into the US,
   – including telephone calls, mail circulars and adverts in newspapers having more than a minimal circulation in the US.

2 Continuing restrictions

Regulation S securities may not be resold to US public investors for at least 40 days, or one year if the offeror is a US company or an unregistered non-US company with significant US market interest in its securities.

GDRs sold under regulation S may be subject to a restricted period during which they may not be resold in the US or to or for the account for benefit of a US person. The length of this restricted period varies. Usually there is a 40-day restricted period (from closing) but in some jurisdictions it is longer (in India it is 45 days). The regulation S restricted period, however, will not apply to a non-US issuer issuing GDRs which represent securities of a class for which there is no 'substantial US market interest'.

Part e

Level I DRs

Section B.3.1

A level I DR program converts exiting shares publicly traded in the issuer's home market into dollar-denominated ADRs. The DRs are unlisted. They trade OTC on NASD's OTC Bulletin Board.

A registration statement in Form F-6 must be filed, which requires information concerning depositary arrangements. Levels of disclosure are not onerous; the deposit agreement and master certificate are annexed. In order to register in Form F-6, the issuer must be either a reporting company under the Securities Exchange Act or exempt under rule 12g3–2(b). (Levels II and III require greater degree of SEC registration, and reporting and reconciliation of issuer's financial statements under GAAP.)

Registration with the SEC in Form 20-F is not required. (Form 20-F is the SEC's Exchange Act registration statement and annual report form for foreign private issuers.) Exemption from the reporting requirement of the Securities Exchange Act pursuant to rule 12g3–2(b) is available. Issuers must provide SEC with English translations or summaries of information sent to shareholders or made public in the home market, and keep the SEC on their mailing list. Compliance with US generally accepted accounting principles (GAAP) is not necessary. However, a SEC proposal for amendment to NASDAQ is of concern. ('The one recent SEC initiative that has gone counter to the trend towards more accessible, open markets is a proposed amendment to NASDAQ rules governing the Over-the-Counter Bulletin Board System (OTC BBS). When the OTC BBS service was established in 1990 as an inter-dealer information system, non-US companies that were either 12g3–2(b) exempt or fully registered under the 1934 Exchange Act were eligible for inclusion. Over the years, many level I ADRs joined the OTC BBS and the system contributed to a more active, liquid OTC market. The proposed amendment would limit access to the OTC BBS to only those 12g3–2(g) companies admitted before 7/94, otherwise full registration would be required.

Not surprisingly, many level I ADR companies, their depositaries and securities lawyers are expressing their opposition in comment letters to the SEC, which is now re-evaluating its position.' Paper 4.95, Bank of New York Depository Receipts Divisions.)

A restricted offer may be followed, after a 40-day seasoning period, by a level I facility, making the same class of shares in DR form available to retail investors in US. ('With a side-by-side receipt facility, the issuer first places its securities with qualified institutional buyers (QIBs) under a rule 144A offering. Forty days later, the issuer establishes a publicly traded ADR program on the OTC market, making the securities available to retail investors and institutions which do not qualify as QIBs.' Euroweek, December 1992.)

Level I DRs trade side by side with restricted DRs. ('144A DRs carry resale restrictions for two years to US public investors whereas regulation S DRs carry shorter restrictions. After a compulsory 40-day period following the completion of the global offering, most companies that offer restricted DRs set up level I DR programs, creating US public market demand which may counter post offering flow back of securities to the home market.' World Equity, October 1994.)

Part f

Level II DRs

Section B.3.1

A level II program, like a level I program, converts existing shares into dollar-denominated ADRs. Unlike level-I ADRs, level II ADRs trade on a recognised US exchange: NYSE, Amex (defined in the Citibank Guide as 'American Stock Exchange (Amex). An organised exchange in New York City that is considered one of the national exchanges') or Nasdaq (defined in the Citibank Guide as 'National Association of Securities Dealers Automated Quotation System (Nasdaq). A screen-based computerised system for storing and displaying current price quotations. Dealers making markets in Nasdaq-listed stocks constantly monitor and update their own quotations on the System'). Preparing a level II program is a major exercise because of listing and regulatory requirements: SEC registration in form F-6 is required.

The issuer must file with the SEC a registration statement on Form F-20 and, thereafter, annual reports on Form F-20 and other reports on Form 6-K. The financial statements of the issuer must be prepared in accordance with or reconciled to GAAP.

The listing requirements of NASDAQ or a US securities exchange must also be met.

Part g

Principles governing concurrent restricted and unrestricted DR programs (SEC letter of 14 April 1993)

Section C.2.b

1. Non-fungibility. ('DRs that are permanently subject to resale restrictions (eg rule 144A DRs) must be distinguished from regulation S or unrestricted DRs by a different name, a different CUSIP number and, if applicable, a different ISIN number.')
2. Certification upon additional deposits of underlying securities. ('Following establishment of a restricted DR facility, additional deposits of underlying securities into that facility may be made (subject to paragraph 4 below) by any person willing to agree to observe the resale restrictions applicable to the DRs and underlying securities. The depositary must receive a written agreement on behalf of the beneficial owner of the DRs to be issued to observe the applicable restrictions.')
3. Certification upon withdrawal. ('Upon withdrawal of underlying securities from a restricted DR facility, the depositary must receive written certification establishing whether the withdrawn securities will be unrestricted or restricted in the hands of the beneficial owner thereof. In the latter case, the depositary must receive a written agreement on behalf of the beneficial owner of the withdrawn securities that, so long as the withdrawn securities are restricted, it will comply with applicable resale restrictions and will not deposit such securities into an unrestricted DR facility (including a regulation S DR facility under which the issuance and sale of additional DRs may be registered with the Commission). By the terms of the deposit agreement, restricted DRs and underlying securities may only be transferred in accordance with regulation S, rule 144A or, if available, rule 144.')
4. Restrictions prior to F-6 registration. ('Until such time as a registration statement of Form F-6, if any, is effective with respect to a particular DR facility, the depositary must be satisfied that any issuance to additional DRs thereunder under deposit of underlying securities will be exempt from, or will not be subject to, the registration requirements of the Securities Act. In the case of a regulation S DR facility, prior to effectiveness of a registration statement on Form F-6 the depositary must also receive a written certification on behalf of the beneficial owner of the underlying securities to be deposited to establish that (i) such beneficial owner is not an affiliate of the issuer of the underlying securities or a person acting on behalf of such an affiliate, and (ii) the securities to be deposited are not restricted securities within the meaning of rule 144(a)(3).')
5. 40-day restriction. ('It is the position of the staff of the Division that a registration statement on Form F-6 with respect to a new unrestricted DR facility or with respect to DRs to be issued from an existing regulation S DR facility following termination of the applicable restricted period and effectiveness of the registration statement should not be filed with the Commission until 40 days after a regulation S offering involving

regulation S DRs or underlying securities of the same class as the securities underlying the DRs to be registered.')

6.   Status of F-6 registration statement. ('The Commission, by declaring effective a registration statement of Form F-6 with respect to an existing regulation S DR facility, is not thereby taking any position on whether the regulation S DRs or underlying securities in that facility may be resold into the United States or to a US person without registration under the Securities Act in reliance upon section 4(1) or 4(3) or otherwise; and such action by the Commission does not relieve any party to any transaction of any responsibility that such party may have under the US securities laws.')

Appendix 3

Group of Thirty recommendations regarding securities clearance and settlement

(Chapter 10)

1 Trade comparison

By 1990, all comparisons of trades between direct market participants (brokers/dealers) should be accomplished by trade date plus one day (T + 1).

2 Trade confirmation/affirmation

By 1992, indirect market participants (institutional investors) should be members of a trade comparison system that achieves positive affirmation of trade details.

3 Central security depository

By 1992, a central securities depository should be in place, and the broadest possible industry participation should be encouraged.

4 Trade netting

By 1992, the potential benefits of a trade netting system should be studied and, if appropriate, implemented.

5 Delivery versus payment (DVP)

By 1992, DVP should be employed as the method for settling all securities transactions.

6 Same-day funds

Payments associated with securities transactions should be made in same-day funds.

7   T + 3 settlement

By 1992, final settlement should occur on T + 3.

8   Securities lending

Securities lending and borrowing should be encouraged as a method of expediting the settlement of securities transactions.

9   Common message standard

By 1992, the standard for securities messages and the ISIN numbering system developed by the International Organisation for Standardisation should be adopted.

Bibliography

Atiyah, PS, *The Rise and Fall of Freedom of Contract* (1979) Clarendon Press, Oxford

Bank for International Settlements, *Central Bank Payment and Settlement Services with respect to Cross-border and Multi-currency Transactions* (1993)

Bank for International Settlements, *Cross-Border Securities Settlement* (March 1995) pp 15, 18, 19, 46; (May 1995) pp 20, 22, 52, Basle

Bank for International Settlements, *Report of the Committee on Interbank Netting Schemes of the Central Banks of the Group of Ten Countries* (Lamfalussy Report) (1990)

Bank for International Settlements, *Report on Netting Schemes* (Angell Report) (1989)

Bank for International Settlements, *Settlement Risk in Foreign Exchange Transactions* (1996)

Bank of England, *CREST Membership Agreements* (July 1995) p 7

Bank of England, *CREST; The Business Description* (December 1994) pp 10, 14, 17, 31 87, 93

Bank of England, *Sponsored Membership of Crest for the Private Investor* (April 1995) pp 9, 10

Bank of England, *The Gilt Repo Market* (November 1995) Bank of England Quarterly Bulletin, p 4

Benjamin, J, *Custody; an English Law Analysis* (1994) 9 JIBFL 121, 188

Benjamin, J, *Negotiability and Computerisation* (1995) 10 JIBFL 253–357

Birks, P(ed) *Laundering and Tracing* (1995) Clarendon, Oxford

Blackstone, *Commentaries* Book II

CGO Reference Manual

Chitty on Contracts (25 edn, 1989; 27 edn, 1994) Sweet & Maxwell, London

CMO Reference Manual

CREST, *Intra-day Credit and Caps in CREST* (April 1995)

Dias, RM, *Jurisprudence* (5 edn, 1985) Butterworths, London

Dicey and Morris, *The Conflict of Laws* (12 edn, 1993) Sweet & Maxwell, London

Encyclopedia of Banking Law (1994) Butterworths, London

Ewart, JS, *Negotiability and Estoppel* (1900) 14 LQR 135

Federation Internationale Des Bourses De Valvers *Improving International Settlement* (1989)

Fifoot, *The Development of the Law of Negotiable Instruments and the Law of Trusts*, Journal of the Institute of Bankers, lix, 433–456

Finn, PD, *The Fiduciary Principle, Equity, Fiduciaries and Trusts* (ed Youdan TG) (1989) Carswell, Toronto

Formoy, RR, *The Historical Foundations of Modern Company Law* (1923) Sweet & Maxwell, London

Giuliano and Lagarde Report

Glasson, J, *International Trust Laws* (1992) Chancery Law, London

Goode, RM, *Commercial Law* (2 edn, 1995) Penguin, London

Goode, RM, *Ownership and Obligation in Commercial Transactions* (1987) 103 LQR 433

Goode, RM, *The Nature and Transfer of Rights in Dematerialised and Immobilised Securities*, (1996) 11 JIBFL 162–167

Gray, K *Property in Thin Air* (1991) CLJ 252

Group of Ten, *Delivery v Payment in Securities Systems* (1992)

Group of Thirty, *Securities Clearance and Settlement* (1989)

Guynn, R, and Tahyar, *The Importance of Choice of Law and Finality* IV 2 1996 p 170

Guynn, R, *Modernising Securities Ownership Transfer and Pledging Laws* (1996) IBA, London

HM Treasury *Consultation Document on the Draft Uncertificated Securities Regulations* (January 1995) p 71

HM Treasury *Custody* (June 1996)

Halsbury's Laws of England, 16 Halsbury's Laws (4 edn) 951; 35 Halsbury's Laws (4 edn) 636

Hayton, DJ, *Underhill and Hayton Law relating to Trusts and Trustees* (15 edn 1995) Butterworths, London

Hayton, DJ, *Developing the Law of Trusts for the Twenty-First Century* (1900) 106 LQR 87

Hayton, DJ, 'International Recognition of Trusts' in J Glasson (ed), *International Trust Laws* Chancery Law, London

Hayton, DJ, 'The Irreducible Core Content of Trusteeship' in Oakley (ed), *Contemporary Trends in Trust Law* (1996) OUP, Oxford

Hayton, DJ, *The Law of Trusts* (2 edn, 1993) Sweet & Maxwell, London

Hayton, DJ, *Uncertainty of Subject-Matter of Trusts* (1994) 110 LQR 335

Holdsworth, WS, *History of English Law* Vol III (5 edn, 1942) Methuen, London

International Organisation of Securities Commissions *Report of the Technical Committee on Clearing and Settlement* (1990)

International Society of Securities Adminstrators *Report on Cross-Border Settlement and Custody* (1992)

Jowitt's Dictionary of English Law (2 edn, 1977) Sweet & Maxwell, London

Justinian's *Institutes*

Kirby, A, *One Nation No More* (Jan/Feb 1996) ICB Magazine

Law Commission, *Fiduciary Duties and Regulatory Rules* (1995) (Law Com No 236)

Law Reform Committee, (Twenty-third Report) *The Powers and Duties of Trustees* (1982) (Cmnd 8733)

London Business School, *Custodianship and the Protection of Client Property* (July 1994)

Maitland, FW, *Selected Essays, Trust and Corporation* (1936) Cambridge University Press, Cambridge

Maitland, FW, *Selected Essays, The Unincorporated Body* (1936) Cambridge University Press, Cambridge

Mann, FA, *The Legal Aspects of Money* (5 edn, 1992) OUP, Oxford

Megarry, R, and Wade, HWR, *The Law of Real Property* (5 edn, 1984) Stevens & Sons, London

Mooney, CW, *Beyond Negotiability* (1990) 12 Cardozo Law Review, 305

Morgan Guaranty Report, *Cross-Border Clearance, Settlement and Custody: Beyond the G30 Recommendations* (1993)

Moshinsky, M, *The Assignment of Debts in the Conflict of Laws* (1992) 109 LQR 591

Oditah, F, *The Future for the Global Securities Market* (1996) Clarendon, Oxford

Palmer, NE, *Bailment* SJ 75 Pal Rep 28479

Palmer, NE, *Liability of Bankers as Custodians of Client Property* (1979)

Palmer, N and McEndrick, E (eds) *Interests in Goods* (1993) Lloyds of London Press, London

Pollock, F, *An Essay on Possession in the Common Law* (1888) Clarendon Press, Oxford

Prime, T, *International Bonds and Certificates of Deposit* (1990) Butterworths, London

Quah, T, *Cross Border Collateralisation Made Easy* (1996) 11 JIBFL 117

Rogers, SJ, *Policy Perspective on the Revised UCC Article 8*, UCLA Law Rev, June 96, p 1413

Ryan, R, *Taking Security Over Investment Portfolios held in Global Custody* (1990) 10 JIBL 404

Smart, P, *Cross-Border Insolvency* (1991) Butterworths, London

Snell's Principles of Equity (28 edn, 1982) Sweet & Maxwell, London

Stroud's Judicial Dictionary of Words and Phrases (5 edn, 1986) Sweet & Maxwell, London

Tennekoon, RC, *The Law and Regulation of International Finance* (1991) Butterworths, London

Trust Law Commission, *Collective Delegation of Trustees' Powers and Duties* (October 1995)

Waters, DWM, *The Law of Trusts in Canada* (1974) Carswell, Toronto

Winfield and Jolowicz on Tort (14 edn 1994) Sweet & Maxwell, London

Wood, P, *Comparative Law of Security and Guarantees* (1995) Sweet & Maxwell, London

Wood, P, *Principles of International Insolvency* (1995) Sweet & Maxwell, London

Index